CLASS IN AUSTRALIA

Craig McGregor was born in Jamberoo, NSW, and studied arts at the University of Sydney. A writer, journalist and academic, he has written several books on Australian society, including *Profile of Australia* (1966) and *The Australian People* (1980). Previous publications include books on popular culture, two novels and a collection of short stories. He has won two Walkley Awards for Journalism.

Craig McGregor is currently Associate Professor of Visual Communication at the University of Technology, Sydney. He is married with four children and lives in Bondi Junction, Sydney.

for Rob, Kate, Sarah and Clare

Other books by the same author

fiction
Don't Talk to Me About Love
The See-through Revolver
Real Lies

essays
People, Politics and Pop
Up Against the Wall, America
Soundtrack for the 'Eighties
Pop Goes the Culture

books
Profile of Australia
The High Country
In the Making
To Sydney with Love
This Surfing Life
The History of Surfing
The Great Barrier Reef
Bob Dylan: a retrospective
Australian Built
Life in Australia
Time of Testing: the Bob Hawke victory
The Australian People
Headliners

CRAIG McGREGOR

CLASS
IN AUSTRALIA

Penguin Books

Penguin Books Australia Ltd
487 Maroondah Highway, PO Box 257
Ringwood, Victoria 3134, Australia
Penguin Books Ltd
Harmondsworth, Middlesex, England
Viking Penguin, A Division of Penguin Books USA Inc.
375 Hudson Street, New York, New York 10014, USA
Penguin Books Canada Limited
10 Alcorn Avenue, Toronto, Ontario, Canada M4V 3B2
Penguin Books (NZ) Ltd
Cnr Rosedale and Airborne Roads, Albany, Auckland, New Zealand

First published by Penguin Books Australia Ltd, 1997

1 3 5 7 9 10 8 6 4 2

Copyright © Craig McGregor, 1997

All rights reserved. Without limiting the rights under copyright reserved above, no part of this publication may be reproduced, stored in or introduced into a retrieval system, or transmitted, in any form or by any means (electronic, mechanical, photocopying, recording or otherwise), without the prior written permission of both the copyright owner and the above publisher of this book.

Typeset in 11.5/16pt FF Scala by Post Typesetters
Printed in Australia by Australian Print Group

National Library of Australia
Cataloguing-in-Publication data:

McGregor, Craig, 1933– .
Class in Australia.

Bibliography.
Includes index.
ISBN 0 14 008227 1.

1. Social classes – Australia. I. Title.

305.50994

Contents

PREFACE vii
1 CLASS COUNTS 1
2 WHAT MAKES CLASS? 20
3 CLASS JUMPERS 54
4 CLASS AND POLITICS 76
5 FEAR AND LOATHING IN THE ELECTORATE 100
6 A PERSONAL HISTORY OF CLASS 118
7 WHO IS THE MIDDLE CLASS? 134
8 CRISIS IN THE HEARTLAND 158
9 WORKING CLASS 180
10 OCKERS, ALFS, YOBBOS, HOONS AND SNOBS 214
11 UPPER CLASS 230
12 UNDERCLASS 261
13 CLASS AND CULTURE 276
14 NOT CLASSLESS BUT CLASS-LESS 305
APPENDIX: SOCIO-ECONOMIC STATUS 315
BIBLIOGRAPHY 317
INDEX 320

'It is necessary to direct one's attention violently towards the present as it is, if one wishes to transform it. Pessimism of the intelligence, optimism of the will.'

Antonio Gramsci

'All current arrangements are artificial.'

Bruce Petty

Preface

This is a book on class in Australia which, as I wrote it, developed into a general commentary on Australia as well. It is based upon both academic research and personal experience, which is as it should be. I've made use, occasionally, of material which I first published elsewhere, mainly because I didn't want those insights lost. But primarily this is an attempt to look at the class structure in contemporary Australia, how it works, how it makes an impact on particular people . . . and what might be done about it.

My thanks to a lot of people: my wife, Jane; my children Rob, Kate, Sarah and Clare; my editor, Julia Cain; and my publishers at Penguin, Bob Sessions and Bryony Cosgrove, for advice and especially for their patience during the time it took to research and write this book. I owe a lot to those who taught me about class over the years: Harry Nicolson, John Anderson, Sol Encel, Bob Connell and others. And all those who argued and discussed it with me over coffee and in the pub and over the dinner table: if you disagree with any of this, you should have shouted louder. My thanks to all those who have generously agreed to let me quote extracts from their work in the book; Janeen Baxter, Michael Emmison and John Western's *Class Analysis and Contemporary Australia* and

John Western's *Social Inequality in Australian Society* were invaluable source/reference books. My thanks also to the Literature Board of the Australia Council, whose grants over a period of time have helped keep me alive as a writer; to the University of Technology, Sydney for Professional Experience Program time for research; to my agent, Tim Curnow; and to some perceptive editors who published my initial essays on class: Susan Wyndham, Anne Summers and John Alexander.

I could have written a much longer and more academic book, but I thought the times demanded something ... well, something more like this.

CRAIG MCGREGOR
BONDI JUNCTION 1997

1
Class Counts

KYLIE V. SNOBS

It's a bit of anonymous graffiti on the bleak promenade wall at Bondi Beach, the letters all jammed together in an illiterate hand as though the writer was in a hurry or in such a fury she couldn't wait to scrawl it out proper.

I suppose that's how most Australians feel about class: class equals snobbery, and it's stupid. Especially if you're on the blunt end of it. I've always liked the way Australians tend to think of class distinction as a sort of Pommy hangover which someone else is guilty of. Class? In Australia? Isn't this place classless?

The very fact that one can even ask such questions reveals something about the nature of class in Australia. It reveals, for instance, that some people are reluctant to admit that social classes exist in Australia, or resist the idea of class distinction, or want to deny that class and class distinction (the two ideas are often confused) are important or valid. The motives of people taking this stance are often very complicated and subtle. Sometimes people stand to benefit from creating confusion about class or from downgrading its importance; it's not uncommon, for instance, for Liberal Party politicians who have benefited immensely from the class system to argue that voters should not pay too much attention to divisive concepts like 'class' and 'conflict'; it is not unknown for Labor politicians who are concerned to court the centre ground of politics, such as the former Prime Minister, Bob Hawke, to take a similar stance. On the other hand, working people sometimes resist the concept of class because it would seem to have built into it an admission that class divisions are important, or that people in other classes are 'better' than them – an offensive idea that they are right to resist – or that the sort of snobbery which may accompany the idea of class distinction is valid. And then there are some in the middle who feel themselves better off than manual labourers but worse off than professionals and company directors and rather than be typecast (or type-classed) retreat to a private lifestyle and a sort of contemporary version of the déclassé.

All this is understandable, because the cruder forms of class distinction and the assumptions of superiority (and inferiority) which accompany it are one of the most invidious ways in which a society divides itself up; but it does not minimise the crucial importance or pervasiveness of class in Australia. It is impossible to understand Australia or the lives Australians live without reference to class. It helps explain everything from lifestyles to Aussie accents, from voting patterns to real estate prices, from TV soaps to social climbers to the policies of the Labor Party, from John Howard to Ita Buttrose to Paul Hogan, from the social make-up of Australian cities to the myths and images juggled by the advertising agencies to the most profound conflicts within Australian culture. Class largely explains why some people are bosses and some people are workers. It is impossible to live in Australia without coming to realise that the different social classes have different sorts of jobs, live in different suburbs, go to different schools, get different incomes, speak in different ways, experience crucial differences in privilege and inequality, indeed *live different lives*.

To be specific and argumentative: what are a great many of the Australians who work as labourers, go to the trots and dogs, live in state high-rise blocks or the flatlands of suburbia, vote Labor, belong to unions, speak in Broad Australian accents, and call themselves 'workers', if not working class? What are ockers if not working-class stereotypes held up to middle-class ridicule? What is the former Prime Minister, Malcolm Fraser, if not a member of the Australian upper class? Isn't 'the Melbourne Establishment' a class term? What are the male characters in David Williamson's *Don's Party* if not class jumpers trying to reconcile their working-class backgrounds with their new class positions? Was Paul Keating talking nonsense when he told me, years ago, 'It's no good pretending we're working class, down at the club socking it away, out at the footie. I reckon I'm lower-middle class. I've made the move up, which a lot of Australians have. Isn't that what we're all after?' What is a yuppie? What is an Old Boy or an Old Girl? Who is in the underclass? Is class destiny . . .?

None of these questions, of course, is answerable except in terms of class. Sometimes commentators and sociologists try to avoid talking about class by using substitute or related terms such as status, prestige, elite and socio-economic group; it's as though class sticks in the throat, it's too loaded, it has too many historic associations and too much emotional force. Blander terms appeal to the bland and those with bland-ishments to sell. Then there are those who spend their lives running away from class because they feel guilty about it, or ashamed of it, or are trying to forget their class background for other more complex reasons; the Australian mass media and the Right wing of the NSW Labor Party are stuffed full of upwardly mobile operators, often Irish Catholic sons and daughters of working-class parents, who retain the sentimental rhetoric of class radicalism but who have long since moved over to the conservative side in their political ideology; they don't blink an eyelid at the idea of an elite, to which they know they belong, but class makes them uncomfortable. What, me? Class constructed? I may owe something to my class but I'm certainly not loyal to it...

Sociologically, of course, concepts such as 'status' and 'elite' have specific and valuable meanings, but they hardly make sense in contemporary society without reference to the class system which underpins them. Australia? Classless? It's a sour joke, a brittle response to the smoking-gun unequaliser which class points at nearly every Australian from the moment she or he is born. As the billionaire and millionaire entrepreneurs of post-deregulation rip slickly through the financial system, and hip techno-graduates dine stylishly beneath the grape-shrouded trellises of Carlton and Paddington, and neat little kids in white collars and slicked-back hair lock themselves into their bank-tellers' cages, and generations of westies head for the data processor and the jackhammer and the factory floor, and 2.5 million Australians rehearse death-by-drowning beneath the poverty line, it seems obscene *not* to deal with class.

The task of unravelling the nature of class in Australian society is not made any easier by the uncertainty and confusion, not to say expediency, displayed by some public figures when confronted with it. When the former Premier of NSW, Neville Wran, was launching a book on Balmain he was asked what he felt about coming from a working-class background. Wran's response was extraordinary, and is worth examining in some detail because of what it shows about the complexity of class perceptions. His first response was that he didn't really think of Balmain or the people who lived there as 'working class' – working *people*, perhaps, but not working *class*. And then, in the very next sentence, he said:

'But let me tell you, the very best thing about the working class is getting out of it!'

Now, leaving aside the fact that Wran managed to contradict himself in consecutive sentences, and that the second reply displays exactly the sort of attitude that keeps large numbers of people stuck in the working class and stuck with its characteristic underprivilege, while a few class jumpers leap out of it, his responses are typical of the ambivalence many people feel about class. In his first reply Wran seems to be at pains not to be taking a 'superior' attitude by using the term working class: after all, he is a Balmain boy made good, author of the famous 'Balmain boys don't cry' quote, back in one of Sydney's most celebrated working-class neighbourhoods to help launch a book about it, surrounded by locals, and at the time was there as a key figure in a Labor Party ostensibly dedicated to socialism and the abolition of classes of any sort. His first response, therefore, is highly political, a bit of public relations; also, perhaps Wran genuinely doesn't think in terms of classes. But in his second response Wran seems to be saying what he really thinks: yes, there is a working class, but he personally is bloody glad to get out of it – as indeed he has, being now a very wealthy property-owning man with a house in Woollahra, friends in the top business and financial echelon of Sydney, and a lifestyle almost indistinguishable from those one might call upper class.

Built into Wran's idea of 'getting out' is another familiar class concept: that of class mobility, of the possibility of climbing by sheer effort/luck/merit/education/talent into a class above the one you're in ... though little is said, publicly, about the substantial *downward* mobility of people through the class structure. Finally, it's possible that Wran's first reply is in part a recognition of the persistence of egalitarian sentiment in Australia, a sentiment which, as a Labor politician, he would not have wished to alienate;

it may even be that some vestige of Wran's own Balmain background, and some vestigial idealism, seeps out between the words. Politicians, too, are human. Class structure, class labels, mobility, egalitarianism, politics, power, media awareness – all these are raised by this single reference.

Class imagery is important in Australian public life, even if those using it intend to do nothing about the invidious effects of class itself. Advertisers know that if you want to sell utes, barbecues, pub beer or fishing tackle you use working-class blokes with working-class accents (latter-day Paul Hogans); if you want to sell housing estates, sanitary napkins, hair shampoo or retirement villages you use soft, middle-class TV actors with soft, middle-class accents. Everyone knows Rugby League is a working-class game now striving for middle-class respectability, whereas Rugby Union is largely upper-class and draws a lot of its players from private schools. The Labor Party still relies heavily on a blue-collar working-class vote, the Liberal Party on a white-collar middle- and upper-class vote, though in their pursuit of power politicians of both parties will try to appeal to cross-class voters.

In 1993 both Paul Keating and John Hewson proudly announced they came from working-class backgrounds, the first from a Catholic Labor family in Bankstown, the second from a fibro house in Carlton. Both claimed kudos for the effect it had upon them. Both claimed it helped make them fit to lead the nation. Alexander Downer, who briefly succeeded Hewson as leader of the Liberal Party, comes from a completely different background: in background, accent, education, attitude and style he is ineffably upper-class, and the obvious social distance between him and most of the Australian electorate was undoubtedly a factor in his loss of the Opposition leadership. His class position is probably better suited to his subsequent role as Minister for Foreign Affairs, where he heads a department which has traditionally recruited heavily from private-school and upper-class sources. John Howard has always made much of the fact that he is essentially middle class: small business background, grew up in lower-middle-class Earlwood, became a solicitor, moved to Wollstonecraft on Sydney's north shore, holds rigorously to mainstream middle-class values. It so happens that the majority of voters in the Australian electorate are middle class too. In 1996 John Howard became Prime Minister of Australia.

Class lives.

Class Meanings

Class has half a dozen meanings in modern usage, ranging from the trivial to the ideological; indeed, a great many contemporary debates about class revolve around differing, individual approaches to the word. Class can mean 'classy', as in the Damon Runyonesque 'that broad's got class!', where the word simply signifies approval, but even that has a more serious overtone to it; it seems to imply she's no common or garden girl but someone with a bit of breeding and style.

Class can be taken to mean mere snobbery or class distinction, the supposition that there is a snobbish or arrogant or privileged class which regards itself as superior to everyone else and expresses that superiority in its social style ... which is partly true, but of course class extends far beyond that.

Some believe class equals money and that it's only wealth which divides people up – a perception which is too simplistic but has at its core the important recognition that wealth is a typical factor in class placement. Others believe that class depends upon social status and the nature and number of possessions one accrues – a popular concept among magazine editors and advertising agencies, who tend to see the world in materialist terms.

Still others, more sophisticated, see classes as mere ranks or levels in society and multiply the number of divisions or 'classes' almost indefinitely, like the strata in a geological elevation; you could, if you wished, rule the divisions at absolutely equal intervals on some vertical wall chart and call each group a class, whether each group had any common features or not. This sort of stratification theory has been largely discredited but it does revert to an ancient meaning of the word: the Latin word *classis*, meaning a division according to property of the citizens of Rome, came into English in the sixteenth century and for some time had much the same meaning as 'group', without any social overtones.

But this changed. According to Raymond Williams, the English cultural theorist, 'development of class in its modern social sense, with relatively fixed names for particular classes (*lower class, middle class, upper class, working class* and so on) belongs essentially to the period between 1770 and 1840, which is also the period of the Industrial Revolution and its decisive reorganisation of society' (Williams, 1985). After Marx's exhaustive analysis of class structure it became common among the intelligentsia to talk of the *bourgeoisie* and the *proletariat*, which can be roughly translated as *capitalists* and *working class*, and later these terms achieved a wider currency; in popular usage, however, the other terms persisted and in Australia, throughout the twentieth century, the most common terms have been *upper class, middle class* and *working class*.

These are the terms, among others, which I propose to use: first, because they correspond to the reality of class groups in Australia; second, because there is a certain wisdom and response to lived experience built into the vernacular use of these terms which it would be stupid to ignore (it is always perilous to ignore what folklorist James Reeves calls 'the idiom of the people'); and third, because to communicate about class in Australia it is necessary to use the language which most Australians use. According to repeated surveys, at least half of Australian men and women regard themselves as middle class, about a quarter to a third regard themselves as working class, and about a tenth regard themselves as upper class or upper-middle class. This sort of terminology will not necessarily be accepted by more traditional Marxist theorists who still hold to a binary division of society into ruling class and working class, with no 'real' middle class, though many contemporary Marxists have come around to admitting the existence of a middle class. This is an important theoretical debate which will be examined in the next chapter and in Chapter 7, 'Who is the Middle Class?'; the answer depends partly upon whether one regards class as a social and economic category, which is a fairly common view, or as a historic formation and process based upon economic relationships, or as a combination of the two. The sort of class construction I have suggested does not obviate the existence of class exploitation; Chapter 13, 'Class and Culture', examines the precise way in which exploitative social control is exercised in contemporary capitalist societies. What needs to be recognised, however, is the way in which the perceptions Australians have of themselves in class terms is an important and revealing part of class relations.

To amplify: most Australians see themselves as belonging to a three-tier class structure which has the upper class at the top, the middle class in the middle, and the working class at the bottom. Earlier in the century, indeed even in the immediate post-Second World War years, it was fairly common for people, especially those who felt they were at the top of the social scale, to use the term 'lower class' instead of working class but that has, understandably, become unacceptable; some upper-class individuals may still think in terms of there being a 'lower' class but they rarely dare use the expression. This sort of change in the usage of class labels is often a valuable pointer in itself to changes which are occurring in the social structure. 'Working class', for instance, has run into some of the problems that 'lower class' ran into, as Neville Wran was obviously aware of when trying to avoid the term. To quote Raymond Williams again (Williams, 1985) – he is writing about the situation in England but the same applies in Australia:

> "Working class", for very many people, is simply a memory of poverty, bad housing, and exposure, while "middle class" is a name for money to spend, better housing, and a more furnished and controllable life. Since the styles of living of the whole society are in any case changing, this contrast very easily becomes one between past and present: "working class" is the old style that people are steadily moving away from; "middle class" is the new contemporary style ... "Working class and proud of it" may last in the older communities, and in some politically active individuals, but in most cases it is now deeply confused: on the one hand "I work for my living" (which almost everyone does); on the other hand the strong social sense of "working" = "lower" class, with inferiorities and deprivations to which nobody in his senses wants to return.
>
> In its social sense, most people only talk about class when they are anxious, and often want to get rid of the feeling that there are these kinds of distinctions between people. I think this desire should be respected, for it is an exceptionally valuable piece of social growth and maturity. But the point has been reached where the growing feeling that class is out of date and doesn't matter is being used to ratify a social system which ... is still essentially based on economic classes.

This, it seems to me, is a very clearheaded description of what has been happening in Australia as well as in England. Indeed, in Australia the process is even more confused because of the way in which the term 'worker' has sometimes been appropriated by those on the Right to describe their own initiative and entrepreneurial skills in contradistinction, apparently, to the drones who merely lean on their shovels in suburban streets; thus John Singleton, advertising agency man, media manipulator and fringe operator, can help form, some years ago, a Workers' Party of Right-wing, self-made citizens who extolled the bluff virtues of independence, hard work and the right to make a fast buck. (It disappeared.)

In the 1990s, with almost a million Australians formally out of work and perhaps another half-million of disguised unemployed, 'worker' has achieved more prestige as a term than it used to have; it distinguishes you from the out-of-work, the 'non-working working class', and the 'dole bludgers' – this last, of course, a politically motivated term which is singularly offensive in a society which has made a virtue of job-shedding and which has been using technology to deliberately throw people on the scrapheap; if there is one thing which contemporary capitalist societies have failed to do it is to find enough work for people to do, even when they want to, or to invent ways in which the existing workload is shared more evenly around different social groups: women and men, old and young, ethnic minorities and WASPS, bush and city people, Aborigines and whites, married and single, well-educated and poorly-educated, those who want to work full time and those who want to work part time. And although the Australian Labor Party was formed as a working-class party there has been an obvious desire on the part of its leaders for the past two decades to play down its working-class basis and to court the all-important middle-class vote; it is only recently that, faced with the desertion of working-class voters, the ALP has rediscovered some of its class traditions. Uneasiness about class labels even applies to the upper class. Fifteen or twenty years ago opinion polls found that many upper-class Australians were reluctant to call themselves that, perhaps out of deference to the strong egalitarian ethos of the time, and preferred to label themselves upper-middle class; nowadays that reluctance isn't so noticeable and many Australians cheerfully described themselves as upper class to the pollsters.

Class-consciousness

Class is an enormously generative and pervasive concept. Even the denial of class is illuminating. It is extraordinary that some of Australia's best-known commentators have, over the years, been reluctant to admit to the existence of class in Australia. John Pringle, author of *Australian Accent*, one of the earliest (and one of the best) of the postwar general commentaries, called Australia 'classless', which was simply wrong. Donald Horne's *The Lucky Country* makes virtually no mention of class at all. Maximilian Walsh states in *Poor Little Rich Country* that 'there are no entrenched divisions of class' in Australia, which must have been news to the steelworkers of Wollongong, the trade union movement, and the people whose names pop up every year in *Business Review Weekly*'s Rich 200. Earlier on there was columnist Alexander Macdonald's lovely send-up of Nancy Mitford's division of people into U and Non-U (*Daily Telegraph*, 12 June 1959):

> For Miss Mitford's information, Brave Little Australia has her *own* rules of social etiquette which are radically different from and basically opposed to the caste-system of Miss Mitford's mob. Australia, as Miss M. would right soon find out if she and her fellow curmudgeons ever took a Pioneer Tour around our gracious hinterland, is divided into the Youse and the Non-Youse. The Non-Youse include a sprinkling of Untouchables

who huddle together, for safety, along the North Shore Line and in the silvertail belt extending from Point Piper to Bellevue Hill. The Youse, on the other hand (so called because of their bluff, independent way of saying "Youse know what youse can do with your job", etc) are the elite of the country. They are found in the bars, on the wharves, in Government bureaus, and in the House of Representatives . . .

Earlier still, D. H. Lawrence felt when he visited Australia in the 1920s and wrote *Kangaroo* that whereas some people felt 'better off' than others, nobody felt 'better' than anyone else. This was a generous but wrongheaded account by Lawrence, because historical studies of class in Australia, such as R. W. Connell and T. H. Irving's *Class Structure in Australian History* (1980), present clear evidence of overt class awareness and class conflict at that time; indeed, there is some evidence that class formation and class conflict were stronger then, as evidenced in strikes, union militancy and employer intransigence, than at the present time.

Such blindness on the part of commentators and writers is probably due to the strength of the egalitarian tradition in our society, a tradition which has exerted great moral force throughout the twentieth century even though Australia was, and continues to be, a grossly inegalitarian society. The commentators, no less than the people they were writing about, liked to think of Australia as comparatively classless because they didn't like the idea of class. This egalitarian tradition is sometimes regarded as making Australians less class-conscious than people in parallel societies, but others have come to the absolutely reverse conclusion, namely that the very strength of the tradition makes Australians particularly conscious of class whenever it rears its ugly head, and resentful of it; part of the evidence for this is the scorn with which many 'ordinary Australians', which is usually a code word for working-class and perhaps middle-class people, regard socialites, snobs, Toorak and north shore toffs and indeed all those misguided citizens who regard themselves as 'superior' or 'upper class' (when in fact they're simply 'up themselves').

KYLIE V. SNOBS. Kylie, where are you?

The sociological evidence is contradictory, though the weight of it reinforces the view that Australians are conscious of class. Surveys repeatedly show that most Australians know what class means and readily place themselves in a particular class when asked to. They do this even if the question does not mention class as such. Thus Oeser and Hammond, in their pioneering Melbourne survey reported (Oeser & Hammond, 1954): 'The first question was phrased as follows: "A society is made up of groups of people. To what part of society do you belong?" ... There were very few responses in terms of subgroups other than social classes. The commonest responses were "middle class" or "working class".'

Similar results have been obtained in subsequent surveys. Sociologist Peter Hiller (1981) found in a detailed interview study that the majority of those questioned believed there was such a thing as social class in Australia, half introduced the term into the discussion themselves in response to quite open questions about the nature of Australian society, and another 20 per cent, it was elicited later, had been referring to class without actually using the term. Says Hiller: 'At least a hefty four-fifths of the population will freely acknowledge the existence of social classes in Australia, even to total strangers taking doorstep polls.' R. A. Wild (1978) says bluntly: 'Class awareness in Australia is extremely high. Most surveys indicate that approximately 80 per cent of people think there are classes in Australia, 13 per cent think there are not, and 7 per cent do not know. Further, about 98 per cent place themselves in a class scheme when asked ... Consequently, class awareness is present in somewhere between 93 per cent and 98 per cent of the population.' Sheer everyday evidence would seem to confirm this.

On the other hand, some Australians are very reluctant to think of themselves as belonging to a particular class. Oeser and Hammond found that a significant minority of the people interviewed, one in ten, had no idea of social classes or denied they existed. And a smaller survey by some University of NSW students unearthed several people who simply replied 'no classes, only income groups', 'everyone has equal rights', or 'only one class in Australia, the working class' (School of Sociology, unpublished manuscript). More recently, Baxter, Emmison and Western (1991), in their Comparative Project on Class Structure and Class Consciousness, which is part of a vast international project on class, found that when they asked the question 'Do You Think of Yourself as Belonging to a Particular Social Class?', just under half (46.8 per cent) were prepared to answer yes. Men and women had similar responses. There was no clear pattern as to who definitely thought of themselves as belonging to a class and who didn't, though those towards the top of the scale, and skilled workers, tended to have a more definite perception than others. Emmison points out it is quite possible for people to be class-conscious, in the sense of being aware of class differences and class mechanisms in society, and yet not attach much significance to them. The way the question was phrased may have pushed the respondents in that direction; to ask 'Do you *think of yourself*...' tends to personalise the question; it could seem to be a question about how personally aware, in an everyday sense, you are of your class rather than a question about your ultimate class position. Thus when the people who at first disclaimed that they thought of themselves as belonging to a particular social class were asked later to state a class location 'if you had to make a choice', all but 3.6 per cent were able to do so.

The results are interesting. A total of 11.1 per cent placed themselves in the upper/upper-middle class, 50.5 per cent placed themselves in the middle class, and 34.8 per cent placed themselves in the working class. These proportions are roughly parallel to previous surveys. A Morgan Gallup poll in 1976 found 60.3 per cent identified themselves as middle class. Four earlier surveys, in 1954 (Oeser & Hammond), 1961 (Gallup poll), 1965 (Australian National University) and 1967 (ANU), produced figures for the middle class of 55, 56, 49 and 50 per cent. Those identifying themselves as working class totalled 28.6 per cent in the 1976 poll; the four earlier surveys produced figures of 37, 38.5, 44 and 42 per cent.

Though all self-identification surveys have to be treated with some caution, their most remarkable feature is their consistency. The largest group, clearly, is those who think of themselves as middle class, which virtually always accounts for over half the population; this is, compared to most western countries, a high proportion and has led some commentators to call Australia the most middle-class society in the world... though recently Hugh Mackay (1993), the social researcher, has claimed that the middle class is 'shrinking'. In fact, the middle class is not shrinking, as the biggest employment growth in recent years has been in white-collar service and tertiary industries, but Mackay is right in pointing out that there has been a haemorrhaging of middle-class incomes, a point discussed in detail in Chapter 8, 'Crisis in the Heartland'. Those who think of themselves as working class consistently account for a quarter to a third of the population, which is a big fall from pre-Second World War years, when the evidence suggests the majority of Australians thought of themselves as working class. Only a tiny fraction, apparently, are willing to identify themselves as upper class, but if the 'upper class' category is conjoined with the 'upper-middle class' category, as is often done in social surveys, then approaching 10 per cent of the population see themselves in this way.

It can be argued, and sometimes is, that class is a less important divider of contemporary Australian society than such factors as gender, ethnicity, wealth, education, family background and so on. There is some force to this, but factors such as income, education, occupation and parentage are in fact components of class: they help determine people's class position, and are also deeply influenced by class. It is a complex of these inputs which crystallises your class position, and it is your class position which profoundly affects your life chances and expectations. It is no accident, for instance, that working-class Australians are typically down towards the bottom of the scale in terms of income, education, job opportunities, material possessions, home ownership, and sheer power over their own lives. Your gender and your ethnic background also inflect your class position. The days have long gone when it was assumed that a woman simply had the same class position as her husband or partner or some other male. Ethnic background is clearly likely to help determine what class you end up in (and therefore your life chances); migrants and Aborigines are overrepresented in working-class strata, and underrepresented in the top echelons. It may well be that many Australians gain their primary self-identification from their gender or their ethnicity. But class is not just about self-identity any more than it is just about snobbery; it is about *inequality*, about the utterly unjustifiable distribution of opportunity, and power, and the chance of a good life in a demonstrably unfair society. And even if you are not personally aware of class, what happens in your life can be, and usually is, radically affected by it.

Class Counts

Class counts. The fact that some people try to run away from it only confirms its importance. The evidence that the majority of

Australians, when asked, see themselves in class terms and readily place themselves in class groups confirms that there is a substantial level of class-consciousness or, if you like, awareness of class in our society. Most Australians recognise it is important.

What often isn't recognised is that class is the chief organising principle of modern capitalist societies, the mechanism by which power, privilege and inequality are distributed and institutionalised. Behind the political cant about 'equal opportunity' and the mobility of a minority of successful (and unsuccessful) individuals lies the way in which social class limits, distorts and damages the life chances of most Australians, so that those who are born into an 'inferior' class with 'inferior' opportunities and expectations usually stay in it and those born into a 'superior' class usually remain there and enjoy the power, prestige and privilege which go with it. The fact that some class jumpers managed to escape these restrictions does not diminish the crucial nature of these constraints, how they formalise brute privilege and brute underprivilege. Most working-class children stay in the working class for the rest of their lives; most upper-class children stay in the upper class; the way in which an accident of birth cruelly determines the life chances of most Australians is only one of the ways in which class works to keep people in their 'station in life' – an absurdly old-fashioned phrase, but one which points to a salient fact of social organisation. As the extremes of Australian society pull further and further apart, the sheer inequality and injustice generated by class get worse and worse; so does the social distress which accompanies them. A pointer to this is the way in which working-class Australians include a disproportionately high percentage of the unemployed, the poor, the chronically ill, and of underprivileged social groups such as Aborigines. They are also stricken by disproportionately high rates of crime, violence and suicide. The growth of a self-perpetuating underclass is part of this process of social polarisation and disenfranchisement.

Class is also an immense force for social control. It is the key to who has power over whom in Australian society, the way in which a small and extraordinarily powerful elite runs the nation, and its institutions, and the great mass of Australians, for its own benefit. This is not an overstatement; in more nakedly class-ridden societies such as Britain the way in which this occurs is only too obvious; Australians have for too long jogged along under the comfortable delusion that the same does not happen here. In the United States the overwhelming power of corporations, and those who run them, and the political/financial superstructure which dominates American society have been demonstrated from Vietnam to South America to the streets of Los Angeles. In Australia the class nature of society is disguised, and the subsequent conflicts muffled, by a comparatively high standard of living, a media-reinforced conservative hegemony, and a national ethos which seems to combine hedonism with social consensus, but the impact of class upon most Australians is equally pervasive. For most people, class is what keeps you in your place.

2
What Makes Class?

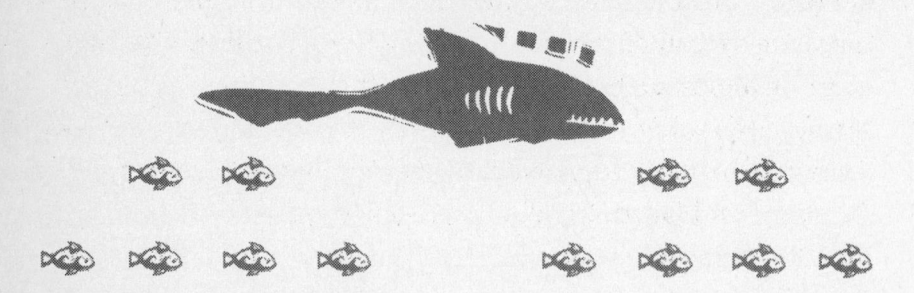

The year is 2020. Australia has expanded in a way unthought of half a century earlier. Sydney and Melbourne have become megalopolises: Sydney has 4.5 million people, Melbourne is heading for 4 million. The Olympic Games have been and gone. Both places have become 'global cities', part of the vast new planetary culture which has developed in the twenty-first century. Australia has a population of almost 20 million people. It is one of the most multicultural nations on earth, and increasingly Asian. In thousands of cities throughout the rest of the world school children study what has become known as 'the Australian experiment' and conclude . . . What? What will life in Australia be like then?

Scenario 1

Our cities, where over 80 per cent of Australians live, have finally become unmanageable. They have become too big, too polluted, torn apart by conflict and violence. Melbourne and Sydney, which between them contain almost half the population of the nation, have spilled out to the west, creating vast suburban deserts of isolation, unemployment and social distress. Acid smog chokes people for two-thirds of each year. Sydney Harbour and the Yarra have been declared no-go disease sinks. The multicultural experiment has broken down under the weight of economic rationalism and political racism. The upper and middle classes have retreated to fortress precincts while gangs of self-styled Yocker youths perfect drive-by crime, rape and block-by-block burning. The nightmare extremes of Los Angeles have finally turned Australians against each other. They are pitied, internationally, as the poor white trash of Asia. Apparently they had a chance to get it right in the 1990s and failed. Goodbye, Aussie Dream.

Scenario 2

Melbourne and Sydney have spilled outwards, but a mix of jobs and homes has created a series of urban villages where people work, play, go to school, shop and hook into the global village via their own computer workstations. Ultra-fast trains, mini-buses and bikes have relegated the car to second-choice transport. That, and brilliant homegrown technology, has reduced pollution. Sydney is a quarter Asian, Melbourne is a quarter European, there are ethnic ghettos but they have become must-sees for hordes of affluent tourists. Community services and the social wage, heightened by a nationwide Labor/Green coalition, have reduced the wealth/poverty extremes of the 1990s; the working week has been reduced to spread jobs among those who want them; expanded public services and transfer payments from the wealthy have made Australia one of the most egalitarian nations in the OECD (Organization for Economic Co-operation and Development). The latest United Nations surveys have found Melbourne and Sydney are in the top five of the world's most livable cities.

Which is the more likely scenario?

The reality

The year is 1996. The Liberal/National Party coalition, led by John Howard, has won the election and has begun instituting a more conservative program than most people expected: cutbacks to welfare, the public service, the ABC and Aboriginal funding, fiercer restrictions on payments to the unemployed, a deregulated industrial relations system, concessions for small and big business, privatisation, and a new mood of confrontation with unions, Aborigines, minority groups, protesters, 'dole cheats' and those who oppose the new regime. In the financial media, the new government is welcomed as a replacement for the 'softer' policies of the previous Labor government and as pushing Australia faster towards the globalisation of the economy, reduced protection, increased profit shares and a rapidly expanding corporate sector. Although nobody talks about it too much (it's too late anyhow), the Howard win is seen as a clear victory for the corporate sector and the 'top end of town', which is part of the Liberal Party's core constituency. It's also a victory, obviously, for those in the upper echelons of the social structure, who stand to gain most from the economic and social policies of the Liberal/National government. John Howard sees himself as a middle-class man, which he undoubtedly is; but he represents the most affluent and privileged upper stratum of that class, and as a deeply conservative man he has always supported the interests of the controlling groups in society.

The paramount phenomenon of the 1990s is the enormous impact which the new wave of global capitalism has had not just upon Australia but the rest of the world. Australians, like their counterparts elsewhere, are living through a post-industrial revolution of which the main features are only too distressingly familiar: industrial restructuring, deregulation, massive job dislocation, high unemployment, the winding back of the public sector and the substitution of a ruthless corporate culture for the civic culture which once held western societies together. This process has reached different stages of advancement in different countries; in some societies with a strong social democratic tradition it has been modified by governments which have a philosophic commitment to civic culture and social capital; in others the state has virtually surrendered to an aggrandising corporate sector. In Australia the competing ideologies are still fighting it out; nobody knows which of the scenarios described earlier will triumph. What is certain is that the people who have borne the brunt of this change, and the suffering that goes with it, are the working-class and lower-middle-class people who are most deeply affected by the process of economic and social restructuring and have the least power to resist it. Ordinary people. Suburbanites. Some highly educated, highly perceptive, but who feel themselves powerless in this Unbrave New World. Others who, because of lack of education, or opportunity, or because of sheer class underprivilege, feel they can do nothing but accept The System. Victims.

Class counts.

What determines social class? There are almost as many answers to this as there are theories about class itself; class theory is a sociological minefield of conflicting analyses, ideologies and criticisms, and the leading protagonists often give the impression of being at each other's throats. One of the problems is that many sociologists wish to retain a basically Marxist analysis of class, recognising the importance of Marx's theory of the division of labour between a small capitalist/owning class and a vast class of workers, and yet are forced to confront the way in which societies like Australia seem to have moved away from a two-class conflict situation to something much more complex and ambiguous. It is possible, as some argue, that the millions of Australians who regard themselves as middle class are in fact workers, whether they realise it or not, because basically they exist by selling their labour, no matter whether they are white-collar workers or blue-collar workers, and are simply victims of 'false consciousness' in thinking otherwise. This view has the merit of emphasising that those who sell their labour for a living (most Australians) are in fact beholden to a different group which employs them, and therefore have this unifying characteristic in common, whatever subdivisions – between manual and non-manual workers, between skilled and unskilled, between clerical and labouring – the workplace imposes upon them. On the other hand, it flies in the face of the tangible 'consciousness' of the vast majority of people who, in Australia as in most other western nations, see themselves as belonging to a class system which includes a large and identifiable middle class, many of whom feel they belong to exactly that class. Who determines that their consciousness is 'false'? What is the evidence? When does a clear change in consciousness, which has been created by real changes in the social structure, stop being regarded as 'false' and become accepted as real?

To return to the determinants of class: Marx's view that class is defined by your relationship to the means of production, and that class relations are primarily economic relations, has been followed or developed by a great many of the theoreticians who have written about class since; it is an approach which, modified in various ways, underpins a great deal of contemporary sociology. Thus R. W. Connell and T. H. Irving, in 'A Working Paper Towards a Historical Theory of Class' (in Hiller, 1981), argue:

> Socialist thought has always pointed to the system of ownership as the key ... In recent western history this has meant above all the system of private property. By "property" we mean not just ownership of land, but private ownership in general, and especially the private ownership of all those things and processes that go into the making of the goods and services that underpin our social life: ownership of "the means of production". Property, the system of employment that grows out of it, and the accumulation of capital in the hands of the owners, are the institutions and processes that form the core of the class system.

The force of this approach is demonstrated by the way in which 'occupation' figures as a key determinant in almost all contemporary class schemes, Marxist and non-Marxist. The work you do usually defines whether you are an owner who controls others, that is, whether you are a member of a small class of 'owners' of the means of production, or whether you are one of the vast majority who are controlled. There is all the difference in the world between being, on the one hand, a factory owner, or the managing director of a large corporation, or a landowning grazier, or a stockbroker, and, on the other hand, being a roadworker, or an assembly-line worker, or a bush labourer, or a checkout girl at a supermarket counter. The Canberra academics L. Broom and F. L. Jones, in their detailed surveys of occupations in Australia (Broom & Jones, 1976), discovered that working-class and middle-class people agreed in general that the work you did was the most important factor in determining what class you belonged to, followed by the amount of income you earned and what education you had. Broom and Jones argue that the most general distinction between working class and middle class was between 'the blue-collar worker "battling" from week to week on the basic wage or a little more, and the white-collar worker with a higher, regular and more secure income'. Although their work has been criticised because of its emphasis upon stratification rather than class, the attention they pay to occupation is sensible.

R. A. Wild (1978) takes a parallel approach:

> The non-manual/manual cleavage separating middle-class expertise from working-class labour power is permeable but . . . there is little mobility across the division and much more within those categories. Although there is a significant overlap in income between skilled manual workers and clerical workers, there remain crucial differences. The non-manual worker still has extra job security, often greater overall career earnings, opportunities for promotion, more fringe

benefits in such areas as pensions, sick pay, tax deductions and the availability of house and other loans, and a better work situation.

Seeing most people spend more of their wakeful time working than anything else, it is understandable that work should have such a profound impact upon class position. In the enormous Ford factory at Broadmeadows in Victoria you can see this very clearly. The great mass of employees are production-line workers, assembling Ford cars in the traditional factory situation; they are unionised, heavily ethnic, wear boiler suits and other working gear. Then there are the supervisors who walk around in white coats and give orders directly to the assembly-line workers, plus the clerks in the administrative building, and the junior management in Ford HQ: they are employees too, but they probably think of themselves as a class above the blokes on the factory floor. Then there are the Australian and American executives who run the whole operation from the squat, oblong black-glass HQ building with the big blue oval FORD sign outside; they have their own offices, faxes, telephones, intercoms, air-conditioning, strategy meetings, secretaries – and incomes to match. The managing director of Ford, David Morgan, works in a palatial office comparable to that of the Prime Minister. The white-coated supervisors are allowed to move from section to section of the factory. However, the workers on the assembly line are comparatively immobile; from their locked-in positions they can often see the advancing army of robots which, one day, may take over their jobs.

That's class in action.

Occupation

On an occupational basis, the class groups in Australia can be roughly categorised as: *upper class*, made up largely of owners, employing groups, large landholders, financiers, entrepreneurs, and some self-employed people, managers and professionals; *middle class*, largely white-collar workers, typical members being clerks, salespeople, teachers, bank tellers, affluent tradespeople; *working class*, made up largely of skilled, semi-skilled and unskilled blue-collar workers, labourers, bush workers, factory hands, and those in manual work. This sort of division has the virtue, among others, of corresponding to popular (and some academic) perceptions of class structure, and even sociologists who use more complex occupational schemes often collapse their strata into fairly parallel groupings. It is, of course, possible to subdivide these groups further. It is fairly common, for instance, to divide the middle class into an upper-middle class, which is used to describe those professionals such as high-income doctors, lawyers and so on who rank highly on the prestige scale but are not necessarily 'owners' in the traditional sense, and a lower-middle class of lower-grade clerks and service workers; similarly, the working class can be subdivided into upper-working class, which can be used to describe skilled tradespeople and artisans among others, and lower-working class, consisting typically of unskilled workers and labourers.

And still more complicated class schemes, based on occupation, are possible. J. Baxter, M. Emmison and J. Western, in *Class Analysis and Contemporary Australia* (1991) make use of two different class schemes, one a neo-Marxist formulation based upon the work of Erik Olin Wright, the other a Weberian scheme devised by John Goldthorpe and based upon the class theory developed by the German sociologist Max Weber. The two occupational maps are reproduced over the page, with permission; it is interesting, as Baxter, Emmison and Western point out, that though the two approaches come from differing theoretical standpoints they end by producing remarkably similar class breakdowns.

Distribution of Respondents into Goldthorpe Class Categories[a]

Class		%
I	Upper service, higher professional administrative and managerial, large proprietors	10.5
II	Lower service, lower professional administrators, managers etc.; higher-grade technicians, supervisors of non-manual employees	23.5
IIIa	Routine non-manual higher grade	10.3
IIIb	Routine non-manual lower grade Personal service workers	11.8
IVab	Small proprietors, own account workers, non-agricultural	8.9
IVc	Farmers, smallholders	1.6
V	Lower-grade technical, manual supervisory	7.8
VI	Skilled manual workers	11.6
VIIa	Semi-skilled and unskilled workers non-agricultural	13.3
VIIb	Agricultural workers	0.7
		100.0

[a]Distributions are of people in the paid workforce; those excluded are unemployed, housewives, retired people etc.

Distribution of Respondents into Wright's Multiple Assets Exploitation Model (Wright II)[a]

	Assets in the Means of Production			
Owners	Non-owners (Wage Labourers)			
1 Bourgeoisie 1%	4 Expert managers 6%	7 Skilled managers 10%	10 Unskilled managers 7%	+
2 Small employers 4%	5 Expert supervisors 2%	8 Skilled supervisors 6%	11 Unskilled supervisors 8%	> 0
3 Petit bourgeoisie 9%	6 Expert workers 3%	9 Skilled workers 12%	12 Proletarians 32%	−
	+	> 0	−	
	Skill/credential assets			organisation assets

[a]Distributions are of people in the paid workforce; those excluded are unemployed, housewives, retired people etc.

28 — Class in Australia

One can debate how these different occupational groupings can be collapsed together to produce a more traditional upper-class/middle-class/working-class arrangement, a process which is made more difficult by Goldthorpe's own uncertainty as to where to place iiib, which is made up largely of women, and Wright's own revisions of his class schema, but both end up by producing a significantly small group at the top which Wright calls 'owners' (bourgeoisie, small employers, petit bourgeoisie) and two much larger groups which one can justifiably call middle class and working class. In Wright's analysis, by lumping 'skilled workers' and 'proletarians' together, one gets a working class of 44 per cent and an almost equally sized middle class; in Goldthorpe, depending upon the placement of categories ii and iiib, one gets a larger middle class than working class. However, as Baxter, Emmison and Western conclude: 'Overall, the differences between the two models in the manner in which they distribute the workforce are not great.'

A three-class schema, therefore, as well as corresponding to popular conceptions of class, has significant academic weight behind it. Thus Stephen Edgell (1993, p. 53) summarises:

> Notwithstanding the differences between Marx and Weber, notably with respect to the dynamics and future of class society, the class models developed by neo-Marxist and neo-Weberian theorists look increasingly alike. Thus, there would seem to be an emerging consensus regarding the basic shape of the class system in modern societies ... There are three main sources of class power: the possession of property, qualifications, and physical labour power, which tend to give rise to a three-class structure; a dominant/upper class based on property, an intermediate/middle class based on credentials, and a working/lower class based on labour power.

'The neatness of this model is more apparent than real since the three classes may be internally divided into class fractions, the cohesiveness of which may vary in time and space. This is arguably especially true for the middle class as it includes the propertied old middle class as well as the propertyless new middle class, which in turn may be fragmented on the basis of cultural and organisational assets and by employment sector.

What else determines class? Dr Sol Encel, Emeritus Professor of Sociology at the University of NSW, argues in *Equality and Authority* (1970) that occupation, plus ownership and control, are the most important factors. Encel is influenced in his approach by Weber, who widened the criteria for class beyond Marx's original thesis and nominated status and party as important as well; Weberian theorists use these terms more broadly than the names might suggest, with status expanded to encompass prestige and social stratification and party used to encompass the formation of political and bureaucratic elites. As Stephen Edgell points out, although Marx and Weber have in the past often been regarded as taking quite different stances, more recent theoreticians have attempted a partial synthesis of the two while retaining an expanded spectrum of the determinants of class.

This book follows this approach, because it is the one which seems most suited to the reality of class in Australia. The chief determinants: occupation, power, wealth, education, family background and culture.

Power

Power, which is related to Encel's ownership and control, is one of the most important of these. Although it is difficult to define, it is often clear enough in the workplace who has power and who hasn't. Those in power give orders, those without power carry them out; the fundamental, pragmatic distinction in many Australian enterprises is simply between 'the boss' and 'the worker', which of course fits neatly into Marx's original scheme. There are constraints and restrictions on the exercise of this power relationship, and there is often a continuing struggle being waged between workers and employers over the limits of this power – by workers through awards, enterprise agreements, strikes, arbitration, court actions and tribunals to safeguard the conditions under which workers can be sacked or made redundant, and by employers through the attempt to 'free up' the labour market, avoid the award system and strip unions and workers of some of their bargaining clout. In Victoria in 1993, under the Liberal Kennett government, workers experienced a systematic attack on their rights and powers by the government with the support of many of the major corporations and businesses; much the same occurred in Western Australia under the Court government. In 1996, shortly after the Liberal/National coalition won the federal election, Kennett held a snap election and was returned with a comfortable majority. Workers in Victoria then faced a situation in which conservative parties held power both federally and in their own state – and were prepared to use that power against the interests of employees.

THE UNIONIST

John Sutton, national secretary, Construction, Forestry, Mining and Energy Union's construction division:

With minimum selfconsciousness, Sutton still uses words such as ruling class, class struggle and taking on "the hard fight" ... At 39, he is an old-style unionist with modern, some would say emphatically middle-class, credentials. But he considers himself – and the vast majority of Australian workers – as working class. "Anyone who has to get by selling their labour is, in my view, a member of the working class," he says, excluding doctors and lawyers from that category. For him, an immaculately turned-out concierge is as working class as a labourer in a hard hat.

The salaries of his members range from the low $20 000s to around $55 000. More, for miners. "Class is not just a question of the wage rate," explains Sutton. "Class is a whole lot of things. It's what wealth you have, what assets you can draw upon, it is your background, your family, it is who you mix with. It's your whole life, in a way."

Is there a class struggle in this country? "Absolutely," he replies, referring to increasing numbers of the working poor and the "immorality" of an economic system that tolerates unemployment of 8 or 9 per cent. "The class struggle is being waged and the employing class have done quite nicely in recent years. It is not just an Australian thing, it is a global thing," he says.

ROSEMARY NEILL,
in *What Does Working Class Mean Now?*,
The *Australian* Magazine, 27–28 July 1996

The position becomes complicated because many people in contemporary societies such as Australia both exert power and have power exerted upon them; in post-industrial societies the development of a hierarchy of managerial and bureaucratic functions means that the original power of the owners, for example, capitalist entrepreneurs or key corporation shareholders, is diffused downwards through a variety of executives, managers, sub-professionals, senior white-collar workers and on-the-floor superintendents. Hence the inclusion in some contemporary class schemes, including Goldthorpe's and Wright's, of such occupational categories as 'expert managers', 'expert supervisors', 'skilled managers', 'lower professional administrators', 'supervisors of non-manual employees' and so on. These people are not 'owners' in the traditional sense. Though, like most Australians, they may own their own houses, cars, and significant material possessions in the form of boats, furniture, clothes, jewellery, fridges, washing machines, TV sets, videos and other household goods, they do not own significant income-producing property and investments; they are not capitalists. However, they often work to carry out the will of the owners and pass their orders down the chain of command. The line of authority from the top to the bottom may be highly sophisticated but few people in upper-level and middle-level management, in large corporations and the public service, have any doubt as to where the real power lies. If they try working for Rupert Murdoch or Kerry Packer they soon find out. Says R. A. Wild (1978):

> The distribution of authority is a significant factor in differentiating the middle from the working class. Even lower clerical workers participate in the authority hierarchy and are often seen by manual workers to be part of the management. Levels of authority, chains of command, and therefore the opportunity to dominate others in the work situation, are the province of the middle class.

In a way nearly all Australians are beholden to this system of control and authority; they have no choice. It is one of the most invidious aspects of relationships in our society. As you move down the class hierarchy it is clear that, in general, you have less power: power in your job, power over others, power to control your own life or decide your own destiny, power to do what you want to do – even, sometimes, the power to go to the toilet when you want to (if you're a production-line worker). It is no accident that the social groups who try to wield some compensatory power outside the work situation – bikies, criminals, neo-Nazis, homeboys – are typically drawn from the working class. Nor is it surprising, though appalling, that some working-class males gain revenge upon their own powerlessness on the job by turning violently upon those few who are even less powerful than themselves: women, gays, 'wogs'. The blank, uncomprehending response of many sectors of Australian society when confronted with this knee-jerk reaction to the gross exploitation which people suffer is a bit like society's surprise that, when a million people are thrown out of work at the very time the richest are becoming richer, there should be a worrying rise in street crime, theft, violence and crimes against property. What else would they expect?

The development of a stratum of upper- and middle-level managers, who both exercise power and are subject to power, and the fact that some people in the mass media, advertising, information and computer industries seem to wield power outside the standard hierarchies, has led some commentators to speculate about the existence of a new class consisting of such people; it's a notion that has been, in the past, especially popular among the ranks of the New Right, who saw the information, education and welfare sectors of society as having been infiltrated by an upwardly mobile, Left-leaning group which had apparently taken political power out of the hands of the politicians and crystallised it within their own New Class. This came as news to many of this so-called new social grouping, which throughout the 1980s and 1990s have tended to find themselves comparatively powerless and fighting desperate rearguard actions against the tide of economic rationalism and two decades of cutting back on welfare services, social support systems and the public service. More credible is the idea of a 'managerial revolution', a shorthand phrase for describing a significant change in the pattern of corporate power in contemporary societies: namely, the move towards the separation of ownership and control due to the increased size and complexity of modern corporations, and the growing power of the managers who run these corporations as distinct from the people who own them. Parallel to this is the growth in significance of a professional group which facilitates the activities of the traditional 'owners' of industry. Theorists such as sociologist R. Dahrendorf (1959) have argued that this managerial/professional group is able to exercise power through its professional credentials and organisational clout, to the point where some of the power which in the past was exercised by the upper class has passed into its hands; in an extreme form the argument maintains that they have basically usurped and replaced the old capitalist/owning class.

There are problems with this approach. It is easy to endlessly define 'new' class groups to account for new weightings in the class structure, when what might be occurring is a marked form of the fragmentation of the middle class which is documented throughout this book but which has not necessarily reached the point where the middle class is exploded into a myriad of new class groups; subdivision and subcultural grouping have always been a feature of middle-class formation. In terms of the key characteristics of class division, the group has more in common with the middle class than any other; there is no clear and separate class focus for such a group, no history of class formation and class cohesion, and not even much commonality; as Wright's and Goldthorpe's work shows, the 'managers' cover a wide spectrum of positions at very different places on the occupational/authority scale. Nor does the change in patterns of control of corporations infer the end of the upper/owning class, which in Australia still has enormous owning power plus, often, an active role in the running of corporations. If recent Australian corporate history is any guide, from Coles Myer to the Fairfax group, the managers are still beholden to the owning group(s).

The managerial revolution, if that is what it is, has certainly affected power relations in society and made it easier for upper-middle-class Australians to pass into the class above; the media, for instance, provide examples of people who have started off as journalists, climbed into managerial positions, and have ended up as owners or part-owners of media companies (including Christopher Skase!). Managerialism is an important facet of the new post-industrial corporate culture, just as it has been significant in contemporary Australian politics. But there are effective limits to its impact and the ability of managers to challenge the power, wealth and traditional privilege of the upper class.

Ironically, the notion of a New Class originated with neo-Marxist theorists in Eastern Europe who were in part trying to explain the failure of Soviet-style revolutions to abolish the class structure, which, in theory, was one of their aims. The evolution of a vast stratum of bureaucrats to administer the centrally planned economies of the Eastern European states and the former Soviet Union itself was a significant development, and is paralleled by the bureaucratisation of much of the organisational aspect of western societies. In both clusters of nation-states, the exercise of power helps determine the class hierarchy.

Money

Occupation, power – what else? A survey by Davies and Encel (1965) found that half the Australians they interviewed thought money was the most important factor in deciding which class you belong to. Money can take the form of wealth, especially inherited wealth or income, and is typically linked with occupation; in Australia you can become a doctor or a barrister or an airline pilot and quickly amass two or three homes, a macadamia farm, a portfolio of investments, and enough money for your children so they don't have to follow the same profession that created the money in the first place.

As an index of class, money is quite a comforting one, because people tend to think they could make more money if they really wanted to (by taking two jobs, or corralling the boss, or winning the lottery), and everyone knows that money doesn't make someone *better* than anyone else, it merely makes them *better off* (shades of D. H. Lawrence). But there are problems. A very small minority (10 per cent) of the population owns most (60 per cent) of the wealth. A lot of wealth is inherited, so very rich families tend to stay very rich families, from generation to generation, long after death do them part. When a manipulative old man, Joh Bjelke-Petersen, abolished death duties in Queensland, the other states quickly followed suit in a vain attempt to stop thousands of the rich fleeing to Surfers Paradise to die; the result was that, unlike England, in Australia the wealthy can pass on everything they have without being taxed or without any attempt being made to redistribute their wealth (which is basically created by the community at large) among the rest of society. Sooner or later, however, Australian governments will have to introduce a wealth tax or similar measures to broaden the tax base; having rejected a GST, Australians will have to find other ways of remedying the fact that they are existing in one of the most lowly taxed nations in the OECD, which means that governments of all political complexions are starved of funds for civic services and infrastructure development and are under continual pressure to cut back on social and public spending. A start would be to increase tax levels on high-income earners and introduce appropriate wealth and inheritance taxes. As the then Governor of the Reserve Bank, Bernie Fraser, pointed out in March 1996, it was a pity that the Howard government had ruled out any increase in taxes, 'both because taxes are a legitimate instrument of fiscal consolidation and public saving, and because they can bear upon the fairness of the whole exercise'.

The family home is the major possession of the Australian middle class, and of course of upper-class voters as well; working-class people are less likely to own their own home but the comparatively high level of home ownership in Australia extends to some of them as well. When the house you live in is virtually your sole claim to wealth, and about the only thing of high monetary value you can pass on to your children, any threat to it is very serious indeed. This is understandable: apart from superannuation, the home is about the only thing most Australians have to buttress themselves against the system they work for and to protect themselves in old age. But the corollary is that the rich, and their political advocates, have used this fear to lock up their inherited wealth. The same tactic was used, successfully, for many years to prevent the introduction of a capital gains tax. Australians are right to discount any superiority implied by wealth, but it remains a cornerstone of the class system: wealth can keep you at the top of the class hierarchy, just as lack of it can keep you down the bottom.

Occupation, power, wealth – what else? Oeser and Hammond (1954) found in their Melbourne survey that the biggest proportion of people nominated education, followed by family background, as the main determinants of class. Both are important. Much later, Baxter, Emmison and Western (1991) found in their national survey that family upbringing and background were regarded as the main factor, followed by money/income, then job or occupation, then 'hard work/personal ability/ambition', then education, then 'inherited/born into it' (which is close to family background), with the last three factors being 'how you see yourself/your own decision', lifestyle and luck. There is a good deal of commonsense in the replies to both surveys.

Education

Education has traditionally provided a ladder for Australians to climb out of one class into another, which is one reason for the popularity of private and selective schools and the importance many parents place upon giving their kids a good education, 'so they'll have a better chance in life than I did'. In the post-Second World War years, education has been a crucial factor in the upward social mobility of, for instance, Irish Catholics from working-class backgrounds, and in the last three decades it has provided a ladder for the daughters and sons of European migrant workers as well. The equality of opportunity which the education system is meant to provide is, of course, a myth, as the very existence of the private school system shows; there are also large disparities between the various schools in the state and Catholic systems.

But worse than this is the way class background can so easily distort the expectations and educational paths of kids going to school, no matter how 'bright' or 'talented' or 'smart' they may (or may not) be. Schools in working-class suburbs, attended largely by working-class children, tend to channel their pupils into working-class jobs; the proportion of children who leave school as soon as they can is high; expectations of going to university are low; as a consequence, few working-class boys, and even fewer working-class girls, complete a university education. With upper-class children the reverse is the case: they tend to go to private schools, stay at school till the end of their formal secondary schooling, and are often expected by their parents to further their education after leaving school; as a result there is a high proportion of upper-class children at tertiary institutions.

With middle-class children the picture is more complex and more confused, but there is considerable evidence that children who go to school in middle-class suburbs have higher educational expectations than working-class pupils, and tend to aim for much the same band of occupations as their (middle-class) parents; they are well-represented at universities and colleges – so much that in 1987 the Labor government used this as an excuse to abolish the free university education introduced by former Labor Prime Minister Gough Whitlam and imposed fees on all university students. The result: working-class students have been confronted with yet another barrier, sometimes insurmountable, in any attempt to use education as an escape route from class disadvantage (see also Chapter 3, 'Class Jumpers'). Education can be a liberating factor in class construction, a way out of the class trap, but it can also lock you in to where you are.

Family

Family background is more straightforward; it is interesting that a society which sometimes prides itself on being free of the inherited class barriers of older societies such as Britain should place so much emphasis, as revealed in contemporary survey results, on family background and inherited class position. Once again, the survey respondents are merely being realistic. Despite the social mobility which does occur in Australia – a mobility which is much more limited than Australians like to imagine – family background plays a crucial part in determining social class. The upper class, here as elsewhere, typically tries to reproduce itself and pass on its privileges to its own children. Marx's bourgeoisie, or Connell's ruling class, is comprised of significant numbers of people who have simply inherited their membership of the class; they have inherited wealth, style, sometimes power, upper-class peers and usually the best education money can buy. Hence the existence of well-known family dynasties such as the Baillieus, the Falkiners, the Bonythons, the Russells, the Macarthur-Onslows; the children of these dynasties inherit the wealth generated by family investments, speculations and property; they sometimes inherit positions on the boards of family trusts and corporations; and they certainly inherit membership of the class they were born into (see Chapter 11, 'Upper Class').

Being born into a middle-class or a working-class family can have an equally pervasive effect upon the class you belong to. In fact children typically inherit their class from their parents and remain in it unless shifted out of it by the impact of the factors we have been discussing – there is an enormous immobility built into class, a weight of tradition, context and expectation which is exactly what you would expect of any cultural grouping. Nor is it right to assume that everybody wants to move out of the class location into which they were born. The upper class have no real motivation to do so, though it does spawn some idiosyncratic upper-class rebels, and many middle-class and working-class people are satisfied with the lifestyle and values of their peers; I know some working-class tradesmen who have nothing but scorn for the nouveau riche and their values and have an even greater distaste for the patrician attitudes and politics of the upper class.

This can come out in a lot of ways, from the genteel art of taking down the plutocrats of Ascot and North Adelaide to the bluff habit of stomping around the place in concrete-heavy boots, shouting and swearing, demanding space to work in, leaving intolerable mess, and generally acting like the Proles From Another Planet. As Professor Peter van Sommers, at the University of Technology, Sydney, once pointed out to me, visiting tradesmen often made a point of embarrassing the people who are supposed to be their clients simply to make it clear that they don't regard their clients as in any way 'above' them; these are working people who don't have much conventional capital but they have a great deal of unconventional cultural capital.

Culture

Cultural capital? Every class group has its own typical culture, its own rituals, values, celebrations, icons, traditions; these vary from individual to individual, and some individuals do not conform to their class typology at all, but there is enough commonality for it to make sense to talk of, for instance, a working-class culture; indeed the academic field of cultural studies originated to a large extent in the studies of British working-class culture made by the Birmingham Centre for Contemporary Cultural Studies. And so lifestyle – how you live, where you live, morals and manners, accent, what you spend your money on, who you mix with – has come to be regarded as an important, though contentious, component of class imagery. This is not the same as saying it is a determinant of class, but it is certainly a part of class identity; in popular consciousness, lifestyle is very much associated with class, and it is important to take account of the social reality which is perceived by the people who, though not sociologists, comprise the membership of the different class groups and are forced to deal with the experience of living in a class society. Class is not an abstract, objective quality; it has to do with the lived experience of people, their encounters with hostility and deference and snobbery and exploitation. People often react more strongly and directly to the images of class distinction, as expressed in, for example, a terribly affected accent, or a propensity for swearing, or an arrogant hauteur of personal style, or an ugly and boorish way of behaving (The Ugly Australian?) than they react to the solid and measurable indices of inequality between the classes. There is a world of difference between a snob and a slob, a yuppie and a yobbo. These are basically class terms.

There is also a certain magnetic or annexing power to the lifestyle of class groups which can eventually override other factors such as family background. The remittance man who came to Australia in the nineteenth century and turned himself into a swaggie may originally have been a member of the British aristocracy and 'classed' in that way, but by the time he had spent most of his life in Australia as an itinerant bush worker he may well have shifted from his own original class to membership of a very different class altogether. Those members of the middle class who deliberately involve themselves via education, sport, club membership and so on in the life of the upper class, may soon not just 'pass', but may become authentic members of the class to which they aspire, regularising their position through the acquisition and display of wealth, or power, or through marriage. We recognise members of the upper class, sometimes, by such mundane things as where they live, the way they speak and the cars they drive. Similarly a working-class lifestyle can be equally strong in pulling power, as George Orwell discovered when writing *Down and Out in London and Paris*. A parallel and powerful evocation of rural working life in Australia has been written by the swagman, bushman and folk-song writer Duke Tritton in *Time Means Tucker*, to say nothing of Albert Facey's *A Fortunate Life*. Lifestyle does not define class but it can help reinforce it.

Gender

Gender also inflects your class position; the role of women in the class structure is a problematic and sometimes hotly debated issue. In the seventies it was sometimes argued by feminist academics that women, because they constituted a clearly subordinate group in the community, comprised a class of their own. On the other hand, theoreticians such as J. H. Goldthorpe have argued that the key unit to be studied in class analysis is the family, or the household, and that the class position of the family is derived from its male 'head', in the sense that he is the family member who has the fullest commitment to the labour market.

This seems an old-fashioned view. It disregards, for a start, the fact that many households these days do not have a 'head', much less a male head; that the nuclear family is no longer even the majority family form, much less the majority household form; that one-parent families have been increasing rapidly, and in most cases the parent is a woman; and that more and more married women work outside the home, and thus have the opportunity to move into a different class to their partner – if they have one.

The right way to handle the class position of women would seem to be to regard them as individuals who are subject to the same class criteria as men and should be treated, like men, as independent members of the wider community. Many women, it is true, share the same class position as their (male) partners; this is understandable, given the tendency of most people to marry or live with people of their own class, and the easy spillover of one person's class position into another's, especially if they have been sharing their lives for a long time. Like, married, living together, lovers or just good friends. Others do not share their partner's position, or simply have no partner.

Nevertheless, there are some distinctive patterns to be discerned in women's class placement. Most women share the same class position as the partner, male or female, they are living with, though more and more women attain a position based on their own individual skills, income, career path, ownership and lifestyle, which may be different, for instance, from any men in the household. Women are also subject to more downward pressure than men in the class hierarchy because of their historic subordination in a patriarchal society and the sexism which they encounter inside and outside career occupations. The heavy bias towards part-time and casual work in women's employment reinforces this inequality. British research suggests that men have benefited to a considerably greater extent than women from the process of 'upskilling'. Women may not form a separate class, but they suffer invidious and not-so-hidden penalties of class within the general class system.

Ethnicity

Ethnicity also inflects class. The relationship between the two is complex; being a migrant, or the child of a migrant, or a member of an ethnic cultural group, doesn't automatically propel you into a particular class group; Australians with an ethnic background are subject to the same spectrum of class determinants as any other group. But ethnic Australians are more likely to be represented in the working class and the underclass than in the top class strata; the majority of migrants arrive in Australia with little money, and sometimes with few skills, and have to set about the grim task of both establishing themselves in a new land and forcing their way up the class hierarchy. A few succeed; the upper echelons of Australian corporate structure are peppered with the ethnic names of those who have 'made it'; in NSW the 'Hungarian mafia' includes some of the state's leading businessmen; in the eighties the electorate voted for its first ethnic-background premier, Nick Greiner. Recently immigration policy has been altered to favour wealthy migrants who can bring investment money into the country. But the history of Australian postwar immigration has largely been that of waves of European and, lately, Asian migrants who have moved into the labouring and unskilled/semi-skilled workforce and carried out much of the sheer hard work upon which the economy's postwar expansion has depended – in factories, on construction sites, on the roads, as outworkers, wherever labour was needed. Many were grieviously exploited; they still are. Women outworkers in the rag trade are among the most unprotected and low-paid workers in the entire system. The working class has taken in an enormous influx of ethnic workers in the last few decades. The daughters and sons of migrants may be more socially mobile than their parents; as time goes on more and more second-generation and third-generation ethnic Australians will move away from their working-class background. They will be paralleling, exactly, a movement which has been taking place among other Australians for some time. But in the 1990s ethnicity can still be synonymous with disadvantage.

Aboriginality

In the Australian class structure, most Aborigines are in an even more underprivileged position than ethnic Australians. They are the victims of racism, history and a society which not so long ago wished to either victimise or assimilate them out of existence. They are grossly overrepresented in the working class and underclass (see Chapter 12, 'Underclass'). Very few achieve a tertiary education, and so only a tiny minority ever make their way into positions of power in the white governing structure. Very few, similarly, move into the upper class; urban Aborigines, for instance, are much more likely to be found in typical working-class jobs, often unskilled, or else out of work altogether. Unemployment is dramatically higher among Aborigines than in non-Aboriginal Australia. The appalling disadvantages suffered by Aboriginal Australians is magnified by the insistent distortions of class. Once again, being Aboriginal does not necessarily determine your class, but it can be (and often is) the major factor in crystallising your place in the hierarchy.

It seems to me, therefore, that though occupation – which can be seen as shorthand for defining one's relationship to the means of production – is the primary determinant of class, your class is also affected by other factors: power, money, education, family background, and way of life. It is a cluster of factors, rather than a single overriding principle, which creates the social class of Australians. This can be seen as a neo-Weberian view; but as I have argued earlier, it is clear that power and money are commonly linked to 'what you do' and that the thread which runs through most of these determinants is where you stand in relation to the economic system in Australia. Class relations and class experience are complex; the means of dealing with them must be equally so.

BERNIE FRASER
Class Profile

On the marble wall of the austere Reserve Bank building in Sydney, emblazoned in great gold capital letters, is an extract from its charter:

> It is the duty of the board . . . to ensure that the monetary and banking policy of the bank is directed to the greatest advantage of the people of Australia . . . and will best contribute to the stability of the currency, the maintenance of full employment and the economic prosperity and welfare of the people of Australia.

Ironic – virtually nobody believes full employment is possible any longer; the currency has been deregulated; and many ordinary Australians are worse off than they have been for years. In 1996 the Liberal government forced the new Governor of the bank, Ian McFarlane, to accept low inflation as a target of equal importance as maintaining employment. The charter is mainly a matter of words.

Nevertheless the position of Governor is a crucial one in the nation's financial system and until recently it was held by one of the most extraordinary men in Australian public life, Bernie Fraser. At first glance Fraser seems to be what you'd expect of someone who headed Treasury in the eighties and the Reserve Bank in the nineties: a quiet, very softly spoken, pinstripe-suited, balding exemplar of the mandarinate, a self-confessed economic rationalist who, with former Prime Minister Paul Keating, pushed through the deregulation of the financial system. A shy, unpretentious man who can drone on for hours about the fiscal/monetary/tariff mix, he was widely admired for being both efficient and absolutely incorruptible: the very image of a Reserve-d banker.

But though Fraser bears many of the hallmarks of the financial/business/bureaucratic elite to which he belongs, he also carries with him a lot of the attitudes and values of a working-class bush boy from Junee, which is the person he used to be. Fraser is a marvellous example of the importance of class in constructing both character and social role in Australian life.

For instance, for all the conservatism of the positions he has held in public life, Fraser believes intensely that government should intervene to protect ordinary people who suffer from The System, wants better 'safety nets' for them, thinks the idea of screwing down the inflation rate at the cost of worse employment is 'crazy', and for some years was under attack from the Right for being too soft and wimpish. Just before the 1993 election he came out publicly against the GST, and John Hewson threatened to sack him when he (Hewson) became Prime Minister. As it turned out, Hewson disappeared, Fraser stayed on. For another three years. And stayed on after John Howard won in March 1996, finally stepping down when his term expired later in the year.

Fraser is a fiercely independent man who detests those who thought he was under the thumb of the former Labor government, scorns businessmen who 'got fat from doing bugger all' and politicians who 'can stuff things up pretty effectively', and believes Australia has a bright economic future as long as the 'rorts and speculators and bloody urgers', as well as the 'crazy work practices' of some unions and workers, can be shaken out of the system. The language is typical: he has a command over the Aussie vernacular which even Paul Hogan would be proud of and his conversation is littered with 'dickheads', 'fuckwits' and other (deleted) expletives. When Hewson was threatening to replace him he commented, with feeling: 'I won't go readily just to appease some dickhead minister who wants to put Attila the Hun in charge of monetary policy!'

He's no wimp. You might make that mistake when you first meet him; as he talks his body language is nervous and defensive; he holds the back of his neck with one hand, then another, wrings his fingers together, touches his own body constantly. But looking at that black Celtic face, the black-brown eyes, the immensely prominent upper lip, the jaw smashed in Rugby League, hairy black wrists and legs, a different persona emerges.

If you stand next to him, all 1.8 metres (5ft 11 in) and 82.6 kilograms (13 stone), he exudes a quite formidable physical presence. He was, he says, 'fairly big at school, which helped' – it stopped him being picked on as the poor kid in sandshoes from the house with all its windows broken, and he wasn't averse to giving school bullies 'a punch in the throat' if it came to it.

While he was still Governor, Fraser told me: 'I'm my own man. I don't feel a member of any group. I formulate what is in the interests of the public as a public servant; that means everyone, not just pressure groups. Do something to help somebody. I'm well aware that the markets don't work very well. Government intervention is absolutely essential in many areas, you can't just let the markets run rampant and let all the human debris that's flung off that operation just pile up, so you have a scrapheap of unemployed people. That's never been part of my philosophy.'

You can't understand someone like Bernie Fraser unless you understand the impact of class. In many ways Fraser has carried the stances and emotional attitudes of his working-class background right through his career, but at the same time he has adopted, intellectually, many of the beliefs and economic values of the class into which he has moved. Junee, on the south-west slopes of NSW, where he was born, he describes rightly as 'a pretty bushie town' and he grew up in real poverty; his father was an unskilled labourer, a railway worker when there were jobs around, always too proud to front up for the dole, and spent a lot of time scrounging around; his mother spent her time raising Bernie and his two younger sisters and two younger brothers; both parents were Irish, and Catholic. The weatherboard house they lived in was condemned and had no electricity; Bernie couldn't afford proper shoes even in winter. He studied for the Leaving Certificate with the help of a kerosene lamp, wrote his school essays on the kitchen table, spent a lot of his spare time chasing rabbits, getting five bob a pound for rabbit skins, driving tractors and doing odd jobs for farmers: 'there was no disguising the poverty of it'.

What also marked him, indelibly, was the way his father used to get drunk, come home, and knock Bernie and his mother around; it made Fraser acutely aware of what happens to people, especially wives and children, who get caught up in such situations and explains his commitment to safety nets and government help to those who need it.

At school's end Fraser won a scholarship, went to New England University at Armidale in NSW, studied arts and economics; his idealism got him interested in Third World countries but he ended up in the Department of National Development and then Treasury. By 1984 he was head of Treasury and with three other officials – Chris Higgins, Ted Evans and David Morgan – and the support of Paul Keating, who had become Treasurer with virtually no economic experience, Fraser and the Gang of Four, as they became known, set out to internationalise the economy, force it to become leaner and more competitive, and turned to the discipline of the market to make it work.

Deregulation, the eighties boom, the nineties recession followed. Fraser is still confident that the way he pushed economic policy is the right way to go, even though he admits 'the heart gets mixed up with the head a bit' and he still gets 'very annoyed, very angry' when he sees ordinary people suffering unnecessarily like his Mum and Dad did. And so Fraser believes in privatisation, lower income tax rates, flatter tax scales; he dislikes what he calls middle-class welfare and dole cheats; much of what he says is familiar economic rationalist rhetoric. He was, after all, a banker. How did he differ, then, from your standard merchant banker? 'Merchant bankers are bloody urgers for the most part,' he replies fiercely. 'Investment bankers, merchant bankers, some of these carpetbaggers really conned a lot of people into doing things a few years ago that they're paying pretty dearly for now.'

But Fraser, basically, does not want to change the shares which people have in society, or challenge the power of the existing financial system, or question contemporary social structures. Unlike his predecessor, Dr H. C. 'Nugget' Coombs, who was a socialist and a reformer,

Fraser is a technocrat. Asked if he is a WASP (White Anglo-Saxon Protestant), he replies: 'What's a WASP?' He doesn't seem to know much about elites, even though he's clearly a member of one. Political theory, he believes, is irrelevant to 'the real world'. Almost a rebel? Yes: but in the end he buckles under to the system which destroyed his father, and not long ago set out to destroy him as well.

These days Fraser owns a farm, and some thoroughbred horses ('from which I get fuck-all!'), and gambles a bit – 'Not in terms of putting large sums of money on horses; I put large sums of money *into* horses trying to breed a winner,' he says, laughing and laughing at the folly of it all. 'Gambling's a trait of the working-class Irish.' A colleague who worked with him in Treasury describes Fraser as 'right out there on the Right wing' and fundamentally a rural conservative rather than an agrarian socialist. A finance writer summarised him as 'a brown cardigan man amid all those gold-chain-Porsche-driving maniacs'. Says a leading academic economist: 'Make no mistake, Fraser was holding out against the barbarians at the gate,' referring to Australian economists who believe in extreme free-market theories and want the Howard government to apply them fearlessly – the New Uglies, as they're called. As for Fraser himself, he says: 'I'm an optimist. I'm an optimist about the Australian economy and have been for quite a long time. I don't know if it's because my lips turn up or whatever' – smiling – 'we've got a lot going for us, it's just a matter of stopping shooting ourselves in the head'.

The more people get to know Bernie Fraser the more they like him. He is direct, unassuming, funny and, best of all, fairly selfless. A lovely man. A great Australian? Probably. As he says himself, he has held true to the values he absorbed as a poverty-stricken kid in sandshoes running around the back streets of Junee. Sir John Kerr and Sir Garfield Barwick, both from working-class backgrounds, turned against the class that spawned them with a savagery that has traumatised the Australian political system, and the Labor Party, ever since. Bernie Fraser, despite his thirty years of brainwashing in the reactionary, air-conditioned nightmare of Treasury, has stayed loyal. In his instincts – but not his ideology. So at the centre of Fraser is a conundrum: how come a man of such idealism, of such rough and vernacular integrity, ended up as a front-row forward for an economic philosophy which emphasises capitalist efficiency at the expense of nearly everything he says he stands for?

Maybe the answer is, finally, lack of imagination. If Fraser has a Shakespearian flaw it is a narrowness, a lack of intellectual curiosity, which makes him incapable of challenging the system to which he committed his life. Because economics is a social as well as a technical science, he comes across as a goodie. It is hard to imagine the Reserve Bank could have been in saner or more compassionate hands during the turbulent eighties and early nineties. Yet, whether he wants to acknowledge it or not, Bernard William Fraser, ex-bush boy, economic rationalist, idealist, has also been a key figure in the bureaucratic/financial/political complex which wields enormous hegemonic power in Australia and which, whatever else it stands for, defends the interests of those who benefit from the current system. Even though he has now resigned from the Reserve Bank, Fraser will probably remain an active participant in The System. Hegemony has been defined as 'the rule of the governors with the consent of the governed'. Fraser's instinct is to humanise the brute power of the class into which he has moved but he's also its captive, part of a subtle system of control, governance and enforcement. *The rule of the governors with the consent of the governed.* Bernie Fraser should understand all about that: after all, he was the Governor.

3
Class Jumpers

One of the commonest arguments used to justify a class society is that of social mobility. People point to a handful of successful Australians who have risen up through the class structure – a John Laws, or Ita Buttrose, or Justice Mary Gaudron, or Bill Hayden – and argue that class can't be that important if people are able to succeed no matter what class they come from; all that is needed, apparently, is a bit of effort and initiative and the class barriers dissolve. It is the old meritocratic argument, of course: merit plus effort equals success. At first glance it can appear a seductive one, because most Australians know someone, even if it is only through the media, who has succeeded in improving their station in life, and the success merchants themselves are usually only too ready to let other people know that they have succeeded and that 'you, too, can do it if you try'.

In Australia the argument is particularly seductive because of the comparative lack of rigid class distinctions of the English sort, where the wrong accent or going to the wrong school can quickly set a limit to upward mobility; it's easy enough here to assume that the different classes are quite permeable, that is, open to intrusion by individuals from outside the class, and that there is virtually no limit to what can be achieved by someone who is determined to climb up the class ladder. The comparative lack of rigid class characteristics also makes it easier for someone to 'pass', either by passing from one class to another or by pretending he/she never belonged to any other class anyhow. It's partly a recognition of this which is behind the emphasis many Australians put upon wealth when talking about class. They know from experience that if you make enough money it is likely you will be accepted by any class you choose to move into, and the very few individuals who won't accept your credentials you can afford to ignore anyhow. The statement 'it's not class which counts, but money' is really another way of saying money can buy you class.

Mobility

What the social mobility argument ignores is that it is only a minority of people who manage to become class jumpers; and it is a very small minority indeed who manage to claw their way into the upper class. Even the case of someone like John Laws is ambiguous; he may marry a society woman and begin appearing at gala charity functions, but it's doubtful if the very upper crust of Sydney society really accepts him as one of their own; I mean, he's pretty obviously not ('The critics are the ones who failed to be a success like you and me. So they want to tear you down': John Laws to golfer Greg Norman, June 1996). More generally and more importantly, the very language which is used by people when talking about social mobility – words like 'ladder' and 'scale' and 'levels' and 'jump' and 'upwardly mobile' – implies the existence of social strata which it is necessary to climb through. Or slide down. Those who preach the ease of social mobility in

Australia often forget to mention that there is a good deal of downward mobility as well. Research by Oeser and Hammond (1954) indicated an unexpectedly high degree of downward mobility. This has been underlined recently by the phenomenon of 'de-skilling' and the downward pressure on some middle-class occupational strata. Upward or downward, mobility does not minimise the existence or importance of class.

If there is a fair amount of mobility between classes in a society then the damaging effects of class in restricting people's lives might be less than one might fear. Studies made in Australia of inter-generational change suggest that there is a certain amount of mobility in Australian society but just how much remains uncertain. Educational studies show that few working-class children ever get to universities or colleges, which draw their students disproportionately from families where the father or mother also had a tertiary education. The 1967 Martin Committee report on tertiary education in Australia said that: 'of the school leavers whose fathers were in the category unskilled or semi-skilled, and who totalled 33 per cent of the fathers of male leavers, only 1.5 per cent entered university. In contrast only 2 per cent of the fathers of male school leavers were classified as university professionals but 35.9 per cent of their sons entered university.' Later studies of school leavers by ACER (Australian Council for Educational Research) confirmed these sorts of results. By studying pupils who were leaving school in the early seventies the researchers found that only 2 per cent of the daughters and 3 per cent of the sons of unskilled and semi-skilled workers were going to university; no doubt these children had a good chance of achieving upward social mobility because of the education they were going to get, but they represented a very small fraction of the class they came from; the others were more likely to move into the sorts of unskilled and semi-skilled jobs their parents had. Comments

J. S. Western (Western, 1983, p. 62): 'Social stability, not mobility, is clearly suggested by these data.'

The abolition of university fees by the Whitlam government didn't make as much difference as had been hoped; a study made in 1975 of the social composition of students in higher education showed that they were still drawn disproportionately from families where the father had a professional or managerial occupation, and that comparatively few came from working-class backgrounds.

The holding power of class, therefore, seems to be very strong as far as education goes, and education is often the key to social mobility, as many middle-class parents realise (hence the stress they place upon 'a good education' for their children, whether in private or public schools). A study by Higley, Deacon and Smart of Australian elites – namely people with strategic decision-making power in influential organisations – emphasises this holding power. Even though their elite sample included trade union officials and leaders of ethnic and minority groups, there weren't many people from working-class homes in it; about 60 per cent of all elite Australians came from homes in which the father had been a business owner, a manager, a professional, a grazier or a farmer with a large property. 'Elite persons' fathers were heavily concentrated in the most prestigious, best-educated, most affluent and influential occupational categories', they write. You might expect this with elite groups in the business world and in the Liberal and National parties, and the study confirms this, but even Labor and trade union leaders are drawn heavily from middle-class rather than working-class backgrounds. When commentators talk about the middle classing of the Labor movement they should be referring, strictly, to the leadership of the labour movement rather than the rank and file – which, again, explains some of the conflict between Labor Party politicians and the rank and file members of Labor Party branches.

Exhaustive studies of social mobility in Australia made by the Canberra sociologists Broom and Jones have tended to emphasise the existence of occupational mobility between generations of fathers and sons. Broom and Jones (1976) examine the jobs which sons have and compare these with the jobs their fathers had; in this way they can judge how much occupational mobility there has been in a single generation. On their assessment all the ten categories of jobs, from professional occupations to farm labouring, 'display more mobility than immobility. In Australia service jobs, farm labouring, and general labouring display very high rates of out-mobility, with the largest proportions of sons entering skilled trades and to a lesser degree semi-skilled and managerial work'. Some of this job mobility, however, is due to what is termed structural mobility; for example, the marked decline in the rural workforce over the years has meant that many farm labourers, and their children, have had to look for jobs elsewhere; similarly, the expansion of the bureaucracy and of white-collar jobs has led to a considerable inflow into these sorts of occupations. In their general conclusions Broom and Jones state that 'we characterise Australia as a stratified society with relatively clear patterns of inequality in occupational position, skill and training, income, and other characteristics'; but because of the job mobility which exists they also conclude that 'Australia is not a nation in which social and economic inequalities are rigidly transmitted from one generation to the next, although as our analysis shows such transmission does occur'.

Like most sociological generalisations, this needs to be looked at carefully. For a start, Broom and Jones discovered in their analysis that most social mobility does not cross the line between manual and non-manual workers, between blue-collar and white-collar jobs; in other words, working-class and middle-class groupings have enormous holding power; if you're the son of a working-class father you're likely to have a working-class job, and if you're the son of a middle-class father you're likely to have a middle-class job; class mobility from generation to generation is strictly limited. Also, Broom and Jones use a ten-category occupational scale which obviously tends to magnify any mobility; if they had used a twenty-category scale the mobility they discovered would have been even greater; their ten-category scale is even larger than Goldthorpe's seven class groupings, and is closer to a list of occupational strata than a class analysis.

Even so, Broom and Jones (1976, p. 88ff) discovered that: 'Most mobility does not cross the nonmanual/manual line. In Australia 80 per cent of the sons of professionals remain in nonmanual jobs; in the United States the figure is slightly lower ... A small proportion, but still a majority, of sons from managerial backgrounds remain in nonmanual jobs ... Among manual workers in Australia ... a majority of craftsmen (64%) ... operatives (69%) ... and labourers (65%) remain in manual jobs ...' Those who start out their careers in jobs where access is not easy, for example, professionals, managers and proprietors, craftspeople and farm owners, display the highest rates of career immobility; 'the immobility rates in Australia are particularly high, ranging from one-half to three-quarters'. Finally, in an analysis of mobility in relation to jobs of different social standing, they conclude that 'most mobility is restricted to jobs with similar social standing'; in their sample, a third of sons remained in their father's social stratum, and a quarter moved only one occupational group up or down.

If you analyse Broom and Jones's material using the more common occupational or class groupings an even more discouraging picture emerges. Professor John S. Western, in *Social Inequality in Australian Society* (1983, p. 66) does precisely that, collapsing the ten-category scale into six groupings: professional/managerial, clerical/sales, skilled, semi-skilled/unskilled, farmers, and farm labourers and concludes: 'Upward mobility, particularly across the blue collar/white collar divide, or from working class to middle class, is clearly not great... there is... some mobility within the working class and middle class, but very little mobility indeed across class lines.' (p. 67). A similar conclusion is reached by Jean Martin in *Class and Inequality in Australia* (ed. Peter Hiller, 1981, pp. 158–62), based on surveys in Melbourne and Sydney: 'The results indicate unmistakably the tendency towards stability of class status from one generation to another... The great majority of people at all levels remain in or near to the class into which they were born.'

The reality behind the mobility smokescreen is quite different to what successful class jumpers would have us believe. In the 1990s, most Australians are still condemned to repeat, simply because of an accident of birth, the class experience of the family they grow up in. Working-class kids in the western suburbs of Sydney and Melbourne and in the southern suburbs of Brisbane, for instance, and in parallel suburbs in other cities, typically go to schools in working-class suburbs where the majority of pupils are working class, leave school early, and end up as fodder for the factory floor, the supermarket, the hospitality industry, or the dole queues. Most middle-class kids go to state or Catholic schools in middle-class suburbs with middle-class students like themselves, try to live up to their parents' expectations – which often means trying to jump up the scale – and end up as white-collar workers, or computer operators, or clerks, or salespeople, or other members of the huge non-labouring workforce upon which post-industrial society depends; the girls among them spend a lot of time as mothers and hubby-keepers, and sometimes wonder late in life what exactly went wrong. Valium, videos, glossy women's magazines proffering free advice on the menopause, and divorce offer some relief. And upper-class kids, though they inherit substantial privileges, sustain a different sort of damage; they become, usually, members of a minority social group which is heartily despised by a great many Australians, ignored by others, and suffers from a sort of social blindness which traps most of its members into a caste system they never understand. If class cripples people, which it does, the upper class is as wounded as any. (For proof, examine the repressive upbringing, personal style, career, election night breakdown and final humiliation of Malcolm Fraser.)

All this throws a harsh light upon the social *immobility* of Australians and their difficulty in escaping class constraints; although Australia may not have class barriers as rigid as Britain's the barriers are there nonetheless. There is, of course, nothing like equality of opportunity in Australia, any more than there is in comparable societies in the rest of the world. Minority groups, such as Aborigines and migrants, are characteristically disadvantaged. So are women. The chance of an Aborigine becoming Prime Minister is virtually nil; the chance of a woman or an ethnic Australian is a bit better, but it hasn't happened so far. To a certain extent Australians are beguiled by the ease of social relations in their country and the ability of a minority of individuals to move through the class structure; if *she* has made the jump, surely *I* could too – if I wanted to. Nevertheless the Comparative Project on Class Structure and Class Consciousness (Baxter, Emmison & Western, 1991) found that many people had a very clear realisation that the background you come from is a key determinant of your class position; more people (28.5 per cent) placed family upbringing and background as the most important factor than any other; another 17.9 per cent said it depended on 'inherited, [being] born into it'; this means a total of 46.4 per cent, or nearly half the sample, thought the class you come from helps decide what class you belong to. They got it right. As the studies of mobility disclose, most mobility is sideways or up and down within a class rather than from class to class. It isn't nearly as easy to shake off the disadvantages (or advantages) of class as those manipulative TV ads featuring endless upper-middle-class households, or the apologists for a class-ridden education system, would have us believe.

What happens to those who do climb up the class ladder?

One of the characteristics of the Establishment in Australia is the readiness with which it accepts and absorbs those with talent from other classes and moulds them to its own ends; it is, classically, one of the ways in which a class that exhibits a high degree of closure, and which would otherwise run the risk of etiolation and self-debilitation, reinvigorates itself. (This does not apply to classes alone, of course; many social groups have covert mechanisms to ensure replenishment even when, overtly, they are closed off from outsiders.) This process of class absorption does not occur in every case, but it happens often enough to show that the upper class exerts an immense pressure for conformity upon those who seek to join it from some 'lower' class group; it is an exceptionally strong individual who can come, for instance, from the working class, achieve the wealth and power and prestige which typifies members of the upper class, move into an upper-class suburb, spend all her/his time with upper-class friends – and still retain loyalty to the working class. Most don't, and become what Labor people used to call a 'class traitor'. It is the corrupt and tawdry side of class mobility, and is exemplified in the careers of two of the most unloved figures in fairly recent Australian history: Sir John Kerr and Sir Garfield Barwick.

Both Kerr and Barwick were working-class boys. Kerr's father was a boilermaker in Balmain, a famous Sydney working-class suburb and the very same suburb Neville Wran comes from; Barwick's grandfather was a tanner and his father a jobbing printer and typesetter. Barwick grew up in Paddington, which was then a working-class suburb, and used to walk to school past the monumental sandstone High Court building where, years later, he was to preside as Chief Justice of Australia. His family talked politics a lot because his mother was a staunch Labor supporter whereas his father, like many an artisan and member of the 'labour aristocracy', was conservative. The parents of both Kerr and Barwick emphasised education as a means of getting on, and both young men found themselves on the incredibly narrow and restricting scholarship ladder which was in those days the main instrument of social mobility; Barwick won an exhibition to Cleveland Street School and later a bursary to the highly selective, academic Fort Street High School. Kerr went there as well, under the same scholarship system, which has been widely criticised in the past as a means by which the 'best and brightest' from what were then still called the lower classes could be lifted out of the ruck and ruthlessly conditioned to accept leading roles in a society which served the interests of the upper class. Barwick, for instance, was a clever little chap, always in a class above his age group and twelve to eighteen months younger than his peers, and suffered badly from being bullied and pushed around.

Both Barwick and Kerr chose law as a career. It provided a ready ladder, then as now, into the upper class. All that was needed was ability, not money, and both had plenty of that. Barwick won a bursary to Sydney University when there were only thirty in the entire state, won the University Medal in 1926, became a King's Counsel in 1941, and quickly built up what was regarded as one of the most lucrative practices at the Bar. He became a brilliant constitutional lawyer and fought a series of crucial legal cases on behalf of private enterprise against the Labor government. In 1945 he persuaded the High Court to reject the Chifley government's attempt to set up a government monopoly of internal airlines and in 1947 he fought Dr H. V. Evatt over Labor's attempt to nationalise the banks – and won. The private banks, in gratitude, are supposed to have paid Barwick a king's ransom plus a perpetual annuity; Barwick denied it later, saying laughingly, 'I didn't get a king's ransom, but I got sufficient for the daughter of a king!'

Kerr, for his part, took a somewhat different route: that of the so-called Labor lawyer who appears in workers' compensation cases, trade union disputes, arbitration hearings and, often, uses that as a springboard to a political career. Kerr soon proved himself a strange sort of Labor man, persecuting some unions with all the force of his heavyweight rhetoric and later joining in the persecution of the philosopher, Professor Sydney Sparkes Orr, in one of the most notorious civil liberties cases of the time. Kerr became a judge and distinguished himself by jailing Clarrie O'Shea, the trade union leader, in an act which discredited the arbitration system's penal clauses once and for all and persuaded many Labor people that they should never trust Kerr – a piece of advice which Gough Whitlam, as Labor Prime Minister, ignored on the fateful day he appointed Kerr as Governor-General.

Barwick, by then, had turned to a political career. At the age of fifty-four, with the backing of the then Prime Minister, Sir Robert Menzies, he went into parliament as a Liberal member, quickly became Attorney-General, and then Minister for Foreign Affairs; for a while he was regarded as a successor to the Great Ming, but after a series of political blunders he decided, instead, to accept the Chief Justiceship of the High Court. There he played an idiosyncratic but fundamentally conservative role, much as Kerr did as a justice of the NSW Supreme Court.

When the constitutional crisis of 1975 erupted, therefore, Whitlam found himself confronted by two men in positions of immense legal and constitutional power who had virtually spent their lives proving they were no longer beholden, politically or emotionally, to the (working) class from which they had come. The parallel between the two men was extraordinary. Both were class jumpers; both provided a classic case history of the working-class scholarship boy who is force-fed through a highly competitive, elitist system, groomed for success, richly rewarded for carrying out the tasks of those who pay him, and ends, not by retaining any loyalty to his poor background, but by conforming utterly into the class into which he has moved. Sociological studies of English working-class boys who were selected at the 11-plus examination for a grammar school education, similar to Fort Street's, reveal much the same pattern. By 1975 Kerr, as Governor-General, and Barwick, as Chief Justice, were two of the most powerful upper-class figures in Australia. Both were political reactionaries. Both had long since turned against their class backgrounds. It needed one final act of repudiation, perhaps, to clinch forever their new class role.

With the inevitability of a Greek tragedy, they performed it. As the crisis of 1975 deepened, Barwick, it is alleged, early advocated that Kerr should dismiss Whitlam. Kerr's upper-class peers, especially those members of the Melbourne Establishment who were close to him, brought pressure to bear on the vulnerable, vainglorious boilermaker's son who had taken to wearing a top hat as Governor-General – as a symbol of his social eminence. Finally Kerr, formally, turned to Barwick, the Old Grey Fox, for advice. Barwick, illegally, gave it (as Chief Justice he was prohibited, constitutionally, from intervening or giving advice separate from the High Court; Barwick, the printer's son, ignored the prohibition) and advised Kerr, wrongly, that he had the power to dismiss Whitlam and appoint a caretaker prime minister. Whitlam was sacked, a motion of confidence in him ignored by Kerr, the parliament prorogued, and Malcolm Fraser – grazier, landowning millionaire, the quintessential representative of the ruling class – appointed as head of government.

Thus did two socially mobile, ex-working-class men, who had for most of their lives used their great power to deny everything their parents (and their like) had once stood for, combine to destroy the first Australian government in a quarter of a century which in any way represented the class from which they had themselves come. The symmetry of the metaphor is perfect.

Embourgeoisement

The effect of social mobility is not usually so dramatic. Kerr and Barwick climbed from near the bottom of the class scale to the very top, whereas most class jumpers tend to move, at most, one class only – up or down. In Australia there is a fair amount of movement between the upper class and the upper-middle; in many surveys and commentaries the two groups are simply collapsed together. As Encel points out, 'the line between "upper class" and the "upper middle class" is relatively faint. In the countries of Western Europe (including Britain) the "upper class" is not a simple outgrowth of the "upper-middle class" whereas in Australia the two shade into one another fairly readily' (*Equality and Authority*, 1970, p. 103). It is fairly easy for members of each group to move into the other; highly credentialled individuals such as doctors and lawyers find it possible to amass sizeable fortunes, move into positions of political and economic power, develop close relations with members of the governing elite, and eventually consolidate their positions as members of the upper class. For the upper class itself, of course, the only possible sort of class mobility is down, unless they follow the example of the Boston mandarins where, it is said, 'the Lodges talk only to the Cabots, and the Cabots talk only to God'.

A much more vexed question is that of embourgeoisement, the

term coined to describe the process by which working-class people may become absorbed into the middle class. As the proportion of Australians regarding themselves as middle class has grown, and the proportion of those thinking of themselves as working class has fallen, it has seemed a reasonable inference that many Australians who used to think of themselves as working class now think they are middle class.

I Am a Very Middle Class Person

Gary Gray, national secretary of the Australian Labor Party, grew up in the South Australian steel town of Whyalla. He got his first political job as a typist for Bob Collins, who was later federal Minister for Transport and Communications.

"Coming from Whyalla was very important because he's got that grassroots understanding of Labor politics and the Labor environment," Collins says. "I'd describe Gary Gray in the most positive way as working class. Absolutely. Real working class."

Gray himself is not so sure. At home in suburban Canberra, he sits on a tartan sofa drinking plunger coffee and says, "My parents have never owned their own house and never will. They'll always rent. The same for my sister. But here I am on $86 000 a year, with a car provided by the office, in a house with a $60 000 extension going on. It's impossible for me to say anything other than that I am a very middle class person."

JANE CADZOW,
Good Weekend, 14 August 1993

There are several explanations of this apparent swing to middle-class identification. One is the rapid growth of white-collar occupations, service industries and the bureaucracy; people in these arenas typically regard themselves as middle class. Another is the growth of affluence among working-class Australians in the post-war decades, though this process has been checked by the economic circumstances and rising unemployment of the 1980s and 1990s; workers' incomes have grown to the point where many, especially tradesmen, earn as much as white-collar workers, and sometimes more. Someone who owns his own house, a car, a TV set, a video and a weekender at the beach may still be a worker but he is less likely to think of himself as working class than he would if he had none of these things (the choice of a male worker as an example is deliberate; working women are typically disadvantaged and constrained compared to men).

Another influence is the suburbanity of much Australian life and the growth of a privatised lifestyle centred around the family and the home rather than work, and a subsequent downgrading of the work you do as the key factor in crystallising your class-consciousness. Associated with this is the development of consumerism, and the purchase of possessions (including the purchase of certain affluent sorts of leisure and lifestyle) as a way of defining your status and possible class position; you may have a working-class job, such as factory worker or plumber, but if you have enough money to buy regular overseas holidays, ski trips, the latest model Toyota Landcruiser and a houseful of Myer furniture and gadgets you may well begin to think of yourself as just as middle class as – well, as the shining white nuclear family suburbanites who promote these things on the TV shows.

But there are difficulties with the embourgeoisement thesis. The growth of white-collar occupations may well have produced an increase in the numbers of people identifying themselves as middle class but it does not necessarily mean that large numbers of people who once identified with the working class now identify with the middle class; those are two separate processes; you can get the numbers of the so-called *bourgeoisie* swelling without any process of *embourgeoisement*. A classic study of British workers by Goldthorpe (1969) found that clear differences still existed between highly paid factory workers and white-collar workers, even though the factory workers had secure jobs, lived in housing estates, and had incomes and consumption standards comparable to their white-collar counterparts. The factory workers had to work longer hours, in poorer conditions, and with less chance of promotion and escalating income, in order to achieve what seemed like an equal standard of living. They also didn't seem to be simply copying the white-collar groups in their lifestyle; clear differences persisted, and there were few social relationships between manual workers and non-manual workers living in the same housing estates. An Australian study of three groups – manual workers, white-collar workers and middle-class professionals – found significant differences in the incomes, personal networks, educational aspirations and membership of voluntary associations between the three groups and discovered little evidence of a merging of working and middle classes (R. Parsler, 1970–1, in *Sociology* vols 4 and 5). Embourgeoisement is as hard to practise as it is to pronounce.

This, again, emphasises the holding power of class and the fact that class self-identification depends upon much more than income level. It is simpler to change your income than to change your head. Mobility is often held out as a way Australians can escape their class typology and the damaging effects of class inequality, and indeed it can offer this, but the chance of moving from one class to another is much more severely limited than most people realise. Indeed, the emphasis placed upon mobility is a sign of how important class barriers and class hurdles are, and how class crucially handicaps the life chances and opportunities of most people; if the hurdles weren't so formidable, or didn't exist, there would be no need for class jumpers.

ELIZABETH EVATT
Class Profile

In a society such as Australia where many of the people who are most admired seem to be corrupt, power-hungry, wealth-centred 'heroes' it is heartening to find some people who aren't like that at all. Good people. They're usually women: 'heroines'. Elizabeth Evatt is one. She wouldn't agree, of course; the idea of heroes and heroines is pretty stupid anyway ('we don't need another hero': Barbara Kruger/Tina Turner): everyone has to be their own. But as a woman who has played out a series of major roles in public life she is probably the closest we have to that sort of person.

Elizabeth Evatt has been knocked about in her life so badly that it's possible to think of her as a tragic figure, whose humanity and stoicism have been forced upon her by fate. If the Evatt family, which is one of the great dynasties of Australian history, has had a curse laid upon it because of its brilliance and ambition the weight of it has fallen unfairly upon Elizabeth. But her friends and family say she has always been like she is: straight, dogged, unshakeably moral. No goody-goody. A bit bloody stern and puritan at times. She has about her the presence and authority of a tribal matriarch. 'She has a vision,' says a close friend. 'She's committed to it. She won't change.'

That vision is something which you can only tease out of Elizabeth Evatt bit by bit, but it has something to do with the fundamental goodness of people and the need to change society to make it 'fair and just and honest – I suppose I'm like that guy with the lamp, Diogenes, looking for an honest man!', she says, laughing in her gentle, self-deprecating way. In pursuit of her vision she helped set up the Family Court, a radical and ground-breaking initiative in the legal system, and was Chief Judge for twelve years. Then she took up the position of president of the Law Reform Commission, becoming the first woman to head it; she retired in 1993. She has been a member for years of the United Nations Human Rights Committee and in 1995 was awarded the international Human Rights Medal. She is undoubtedly one of the outstanding jurists of our time.

On most indices, Elizabeth Evatt belongs to the upper class: indeed the Evatt family is usually regarded as a particularly patrician family, one which is the closest Australia has to the great privileged families of British history like the Churchills and the Sassoons. It is an extraordinary and sometimes eccentric family which has contributed massively to the political and legal history of the nation. Dr H. V. (Bert) Evatt, Elizabeth's uncle, was leader of the ALP, president of the United Nations General Assembly, a gifted lawyer and socialist intellectual who split the Labor Party in the 1950s and ended his political career in the bitterness and controversy of the Petrov case. Her father was Clive Evatt Snr, another outstanding lawyer and a senior minister in postwar NSW Labor governments.

But the Evatts didn't always hold that class position and, as their politics demonstrates, rarely conformed to it. Elizabeth's father and his five brothers all grew up as the sons of a publican in East Maitland. 'They were all clever boys, their mother enjoined them to get well-educated, she was their inspiration,' says Elizabeth. Two were killed in France in the First World War, after surviving Gallipoli; the others came down to Sydney to try to make their fortune. Clive, who was 'an extremely charming person, oh yes, he was irresistible', married well up the class scale, to Marjorie Andreas, who came from a grand and wealthy Blue Mountains family, and Elizabeth spent a lot of her childhood in the ancestral mansion, Leuralla: stone balustrades, servants' quarters, stables, giant spruces and beeches, gilt-framed family portraits, sitting room, retiring room, grand hall, children's playroom. (Clive Jnr, Elizabeth's brother, has turned it into a remarkable museum which embalms the gracious way of life of almost a century ago.)

By now the Evatt dynasty was under way. The Clive/Marjorie branch produced three children who have all become well-known in their own right: Clive Jnr, barrister and owner of the Hogarth Gallery in Paddington, struck off as a barrister in 1967 and later re-admitted, a typical Evatt mixture of flamboyance, brilliance and eccentricity; Penelope, architect, arts patron and married to architect Harry Seidler; and Elizabeth. She is the serious one of her generation, the one who has carried on Uncle Bert's legacy of high-minded commitment to reform and social justice. Says someone who knows the family: 'She's everything her father wasn't: serious, dull, moral, heavy.'

Most of Elizabeth's growing up took place in blue-ribbon, Liberal, upper-class Wahroonga, on Sydney's north shore, where her family were virtually the only socialists. It made her feel an outsider. She spent a lot of time by herself, reading, listening to the radio, doing little woodcarvings or printing her own photos in a homemade darkroom, without, she says, ever feeling lonely. She went to Presbyterian Ladies College, Pymble, one of Sydney's leading private girls' schools, but has since written that: 'There is little of school I want to remember . . . I had a few good friends, but on the whole I was glad to leave . . . that sense of being an outsider stayed with me for a very long time.'

Her friends say she still feels that way. Indeed, in some respects Elizabeth Evatt seems to consciously reject the class her family moved into, or at least its conventions: she speaks in a broad, semi-ocker drawl (like others in the Evatt family), drives an old car, lives in an unostentatious terrace house in Paddington, and when she spends the weekend in the Blue Mountains likes to slop around in daggy old gardening clothes. Her politics are clearly left of centre. She grew up in a family which had 'a broad liberal outlook on the world; it was open to new ideas, open to inquiring about things, not accepting things that didn't seem right', and she has never turned her back on that. 'It's rather sad that the leadership of the Labor Party should put sound economic management ahead of everything else,' she says. 'I mean, no-one can criticise that but it's only part of what the goals should be.'

Elizabeth Evatt, therefore, is no class jumper herself; but the Evatt family is an interesting example of how fluid class relations can still be in Australia – from publican to the High Court in one generation – and yet how pervasive class can be in determining your life career and lifestyle. You get the feeling that Elizabeth Evatt's class is simply something which was bequeathed to her. A judge who went to the ancestral Evatt home for dinner as a young man remembers it as 'the most excruciating experience of my life': at the table Clive Snr, Elizabeth's father, was reading a brief, Elizabeth was reading a Commonwealth Law Report and Penelope was gazing at a blown-up photo of Neil Harvey, the cricket idol, while Elizabeth's mother vainly tried to borrow her own car back from her son, Clive Jnr! 'Her mother was quite a beauty but swamped by the Evatt egos,' the judge recalls. 'It was like a parody of eccentric British upper-class life.'

When she left school Elizabeth wanted to do arts at Sydney University but her father insisted she do law. Dutifully, she complied. 'I did quite well, I won the medal, I suppose . . . it has all become a bit irrelevant,' she says in her offhand way. Next came a year of postgraduate study at Harvard Law School, arranged by Professor Julius Stone; it was towards the end of the McCarthy anti-communist witch-hunt era and the beginning of the civil rights movement, and she found the experience 'mind-expanding'. Then she went to London and lived there for the next seventeen years. She married Robert Southan, a barrister, had two children, practised at the Bar, and was invited to work for the first permanent Law Reform Commission. When, in 1973, Gough Whitlam asked her to come home as deputy president of the Arbitration Commission, she accepted. Her marriage was breaking up. A year after she arrived Whitlam asked her to head the Commission on Human Relationships.

Then came the Family Court and a series of traumatic events, public and personal . . .

While she was head of the Family Court, pioneering a conciliatory no-fault concept of divorce which led the world, she experienced the gunning down of one Family Court judge, the murder of the wife of another, bomb attacks, death threats, police guards and the introduction of a security system which ran the risk of turning the court into a fortress. Then one of her two children, twenty-one-year-old Richard, committed suicide in 1985; his body was found in Sydney Harbour after he was seen falling from the Bridge. At the time Elizabeth was living as a sole parent with Richard and her daughter Anne. It was a terrible, catastrophic event.

Despite it all Elizabeth Evatt seems as gentle and forgiving as ever. She is a big, heavy-boned, slow-talking, silver-grey-haired woman with half-glasses which she wears slung around her neck on a cord; when she walks she hunches her shoulders like a burly front-row forward. At first glance, an old-fashioned, somewhat Dickensian figure. That belies, however, the woman she is; close up she has a strong, symmetrical face, long nose, sensual mouth and a rather kindly ambience which signals: friend/mother/I am honest/lover? She has a straight, slightly sardonic gaze, laughs a lot in unexpected places, and peppers her conversation with slang as she explains:

'There's a two-part legal system in Australia, a legal system for the rich and powerful and a legal system for the others . . . Parts of the system are out of touch with the community . . . Australia is very conservative on some social issues, I'm not sure why. There's this desire for some sort of uniformity . . . yeah, well, I do get heartened sometimes. I feel optimistic. There are still plenty of people who want social and economic change.' Is Uncle Bert a model for her? 'I've never thought of that. Yes, I do admire him tremendously. He was a believer . . . I suppose I've picked up the crusading side of it all by furthering the ideals I have in the legal arena, rather than in the wider political arena. No, I wouldn't have liked a political career. It's far too tough. Too many compromises. (laughing) I don't think I've got the right personality for that. And yet you have to admire people who go through political life and seem to come through relatively untarnished. Yes, Bert Evatt was like that. And Gough. I think he's held on to his vision and his ideas. God, it's not easy! You fight for what you believe in, in the ways you can . . . Yes, that's what I'm about. A striver for change.'

She sighs, and then laughs at being so corny, so heart on sleeve: 'Hopeless idealism!'

She feels guilty about coming from the advantaged background she does: she goes to the opera and theatre and gallery openings, collects Blue Mountains paintings, plays clarinet, sings in the Messiah chorus, cooks mussels, likes lunch in the sun with good wine, pâté and cheese, owns two houses (including Uncle Bert's old family home in Leura), learned Italian some years ago, takes holidays in Florence . . . but guilt, like anger, is 'rather negative and unproductive' and she tries, in a life of commitment to the public good, to counterbalance the class privilege the Evatt family has achieved.

Says a close friend: 'I appreciate her singleness. Good people get hit hard. She has had no overwhelming passion to her – except her work. She's hopeful, intelligent, an idealist.' There is a silence. 'You know, I've only just realised what a great woman she is.'

4
Class and Politics

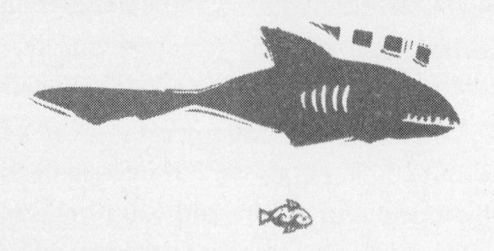

Politics in Australia is heavily influenced by class. This is partly a matter of history and partly a matter of contemporary reality; the major parties have both traditions and policies which make them appeal more to some class groups than others. The Australian Labor Party grew out of the labour movement of the late nineteenth century and for most of its existence has been regarded as 'the workers' party'; it is clearly no longer just a working-class party and must attract a substantial proportion of the middle-class vote to gain office, but in its ideology and political imagery it is still more closely identified with the working class than the Liberal/National Party coalition is. The Liberal Party is the inheritor of a long tradition of conservative parties which have basically represented business interests in Australia and it is still identified closely with the top end of the class scale, though it too must win a substantial middle-class vote to obtain power. The National Party, formerly the Country Party, has in the past represented rural interests, though it has tended to be the party of small landholders and the rural petit bourgeoisie rather than the graziers and the landed gentry; these days its constituency includes mining and other business interests. The

Democrats are less clearly identified with any particular class group, but as a 'middle' group in the political spectrum the Democrats obviously attract a good deal of middle-class support. So do the Greens. When Australians go to vote, therefore, they tend to vote partly because of their class background and because of the class character of the parties they have to choose between.

The class character of Australian politics is so apparent, and is so well understood by the parties themselves, that it would hardly seem worth restating, but in recent years there has been something of a move among commentators and academics to downplay the importance of class; this is particularly the case with such conservative critics as David Kemp (*Society and Electoral Behaviour in Australia*, 1978) and Don Aitkin (*Stability and Change in Australian Politics*, 1982). They have in fact performed a valuable function in questioning the conventional wisdom about the class base to the political parties and voting patterns by highlighting cross-class voting, the salience of factors other than class in voting behaviour, and the way the major parties have shaken off too close a dependence on class loyalties and class identification. The changes in the class structure of Australian society have created corresponding changes in the political system. The Labor Party is no longer just a working-class party; it has gone through something of the 'middle classing' that the Australian electorate itself has. It never commanded the entire working-class vote anyhow, though in the pre-war years when the majority of Australians thought of themselves as working class it was safe enough for the ALP to present heavily class-based policies and rely basically on working-class voters to win office. Now, however, that the majority of the electorate thinks of itself as middle class the ALP has had to modify its policies and its political imagery to appeal to the white collar, mortgage belt, credit card middle mass which not only contains a large percentage of the swinging voters but also forms the largest class group in the electorate.

This the Labor Party has done very successfully, in the main. Until its disastrous performance in 1996 it managed to win successive elections federally by gaining what party strategists estimate to be between one-quarter and one-half of the middle-class vote; at some elections after 1983 it won somewhat more than half. The ALP's loss in 1996 can be attributed, in part, to the loss of some of the middle-class voters whom it had managed to attract previously, though there was also a significant decline in its support from blue-collar voters. Before that, however, Labor seemed to have been able to hold on to a majority of working-class votes, because of its appeal to that traditional constituency, as well as annexing enough middle-class votes to hold on to power even when the overall political climate would seem to have shifted decisively against it – for instance in 1993, when Keating led the party to a shock victory despite economic recession, a million unemployed, a new and presentable coalition leader in the form of John Hewson, and the opposition of most of the print media (of the ten major metropolitan newspapers, nine advocated a vote for Hewson – but then virtually the entire Australian media supported conscription and the Vietnam War as well). The same process has occurred, though less coherently, at the level of state politics. Since the 1970s the state Labor parties have been led by safe, moderate, middle-class leaders such as Bob Carr, John Cain, John Bannon and Brian Burke who projected respectable images and built up close ties (sometimes too close!) with the business community; even when Cain and Bannon crashed and Burke found himself in court the party was able to find safe, respectable women such as Joan Kirner and Carmen Lawrence to follow on from them. Very few Labor members of parliament now come from a working-class or trade union background; most of them have a middle-class background, share middle-class values, and can appeal to a middle-class constituency without any trace of insincerity.

STICKING TO THE WORKING CLASS

I think our starting point is to stick to the working class like shit to a blanket. A Labor Party that doesn't adopt that starting point is perhaps no longer a Labor Party. You know, you stick to the disadvantaged, the working class, the people without, first and foremost, that's why we're here, y'know, that's the only reason we're on the political landscape.

We've got to be a party of active redistribution, that's what the Labor Party's all about, isn't it? We can't be just some technocratic economic model that just pumps out more resources for everyone equally, what we've got to be about is a transfer/redistribution system. For a lot of our working class constituents we lost the feeling that we were doing things to make society more equal.

No, I don't think we have to move closer to the centre; we're a left-of-centre party and should stay there.

MARK LATHAM
Labor MP for Werriwa, NSW

The trouble with this, of course, is that it moves the ALP away from its former radical/reformist ideology – though the party has always been a democratic socialist party rather than a truly radical one, it was committed to the socialist objective for most of its existence and as late as 1948 tried to nationalise the banks – and begins to disenfranchise the very class which it was originally formed to help. It's a double whammy: the Australian political system loses the benefit of one of its few agents for change, and working-class Australians are left behind by the very party they created. The process also has dangers for the ALP, because it begins to lose the allegiance of its base constituency.

This happened dramatically in the second half of the 1980s as the party moved closer to big business, the financial markets and 'the big end of town' (the phrase is Keating's) and Prime Minister Hawke flaunted his friendship with such luminous 'mates' as Alan Bond, Sir Peter Abeles and other entrepreneurs of the pre-crash boom. In the NSW state election of 1988 there was a massive swing against Labor, which lost seats in former industrial heartlands like Newcastle and the Hunter Valley; Labor strategists began to worry that the party, in its search for a middle-class constituency, was losing its formerly solid working-class base.

By the 1993 federal election the ALP was once again projecting itself (not necessarily cynically) as the party of compassion, collectivist social values and the traditional Australian ethos of a fair go for everyone; it was rewarded with the return of a substantial working-class vote, the consolidation of its urban working-class seats, and a national 2 per cent swing in its favour which gave it, unexpectedly, another term in office. In his speech claiming victory on election night, 13 March 1993, Prime Minister Paul Keating called it a victory for 'the true believers'. He wasn't talking about Alan Bond (who had been in jail) and Kerry Packer. But Keating, who is an extraordinarily complex character in class terms, failed to deliver to his true-blue base in the subsequent three years; emotionally Keating remains faithful to his working-class background, which can be seen in everything from his vitriolic 'gutter' language to his passionate hatred of what he calls the 'hyphenated names' of the Establishment, but politically and intellectually he has moved into the elite and has adopted most of its ideology and style, from free-market theory to Placido Domingo. The paradox did not seem to be lost on voters or, if it was, they nevertheless turned to someone who seemed to represent straight, uncomplicated, middle-class values and attitudes: John Howard.

The Liberal Party has long been regarded as the party of the bosses/the Establishment/the upper class, but this is as crude an oversimplification as regarding the Labor Party as working class. Formed in 1943 by Robert Gordon Menzies from the wreckage of the old United Australia Party, the party has always drawn upon the middle class, especially the upper-middle class, for much of its voting support; it has presented itself as the party of small business, of the self-employed, of the petit bourgeoisie, of upwardly mobile professional and business people who succeed in their personal careers through hard work and dedication and deserve the financial and prestige rewards which they achieve. In an earlier book (*Profile of Australia*, 1966) I argued that one of the reasons for the long Menzies ascendancy was the rapid growth of white-collar, middle-class occupations in Australia and the corresponding growth of a middle-class vote which tended to favour the conservative parties rather than Labor; it wasn't until 1972 that Whitlam managed to detach enough of this middle-class vote to give Labor a brief period in office. Whatever may be demonstrably wrong about the embourgeoisement thesis as applied to the Australian working class (see Chapter 3, 'Class Jumpers'), there is no doubt about the embourgeoisement of the Australian electorate. Allied to this is the perception that as you move up the social scale, or become a success, it's natural to vote Liberal. I mean, they're a class above the ruck.

The class imagery which underpins this is both subtle yet unarguable. The Labor Party was formed by workers who worked with their hands; it was originally called the Labour Party, in recognition of its connection to the labour movement, and despite the name change it is still regarded by many people as the workers' party. The Liberal Party, on the other hand, was formed by lawyers, financiers and businessmen – the 'top drawer' of society – and has always had a social cachet about it. It is no accident that the Liberal Party strongholds are the wealthier suburbs where people tend to own expensive homes, send their children to private schools, speak nicely and indulge in the multifarious rituals of the upper and upper-middle class, from cocktail parties to rugby days to charity galas to View Club functions to more mundane activities like shopping at George's or David Jones and buying a BMW. After the 1993 federal election the Liberal Party found that it had only eight of the fifty MPs from NSW in the House of Representatives, and that the only two who didn't come from Sydney's prestigious north shore were its then leader, John Hewson (who represented the equally prestigious Vaucluse area) and Don Dobie; commented the *Sydney Morning Herald*'s Mike Steketee, 'the federal Liberals have become a largely North Shore party'. In 1996 this changed; the Liberal/National coalition broadened its base of supporters dramatically, both geographically and in class terms; though exit polls are notoriously unreliable, they indicated that the Liberals picked up a substantial proportion of working-class, blue-collar voters who would normally have voted Labor. The same phenomenon occurred in the late 1980s when Nick Greiner became Premier of NSW. There is no doubt, nevertheless, that in many people's minds the Liberal Party is for those who are somewhat 'superior' in the status hierarchy. In terms of popular imagery, the Labor Party is for workers, the Liberal Party for those who are a success.

This imagery is both inaccurate and out of date, as we shall see; a substantial proportion of working-class people now vote for and even identify with the Liberal Party, and a substantial proportion of middle-class and upper-middle-class people vote for and identify with the Labor Party. There is now a great deal of cross-class voting in the electorate, and this has increased as the climate of class conflict has receded and the major parties have grown closer to each other in policies and even ideology. If you're a small business owner, there is no reason not to vote for, say, Kim Beazley and the ALP; if you're a successful tradesperson, there's no reason not to vote for John Howard and the Liberal Party. A phenomenon of voting in recent years has been the goodly number of intellectuals, academics, professionals, artists and teachers who support the Labor Party, which is sometimes formalised into public statements of support at elections (for example, Arts for Labor at the 1993 federal election) and the support which the Liberal Party regularly attracts from self-employed tradespeople and other members of the artisan working class.

One could argue, as well, that the small 'centre' parties which have risen (and sometimes fallen) in the last decades, from the Democratic Labor Party to the Australia Party to the Democrats to the Greens, act partly as a bridge by which old Labor voters can move away from their traditional class loyalties without actually voting Liberal, and old Liberal voters can move away from their party allegiance over specific issues, such as the Vietnam War or GST (Goods and Services Tax) without actually bringing themselves to vote Labor. The increasing affluence and conservatism of large sections of the old Irish Catholic working class, and their move towards a middle-class identification, made the DLP a handy bridge; similarly, the disillusionment of some Liberal supporters with the more extreme policies of their party, especially as it moved further and further along the path of economic rationalism towards a super-dry Right-wing ideology, has made the Democrats a handy outlet for disaffection.

An Open Letter from John Hewson to Liberals and All Australians

It is now clear that the momentum on the issue of Liberal leadership has built to such a point in the media that I have decided that the matter needs to be resolved as soon as possible . . .

I have worked hard, and I have played it straight, because I believe in the innate sense of Australian fair play and because I believe passionately that the Liberal Party's values are the best means of guaranteeing all Australians their freedom, the opportunity to achieve for themselves and their families, and protection and support for those in our society who need and deserve it.

I also believe in the Liberal Party, in a very personal sense, as the true party of equality of opportunity in Australia.

In making me its parliamentary leader, it showed up all the phoney Labor stereotyping of our party for what it is.

I am not from "the Establishment". I went to a state high school, not a private school. I was brought up in what Labor likes to think of as its "heartland". I got an education through my own hard work, not my parents' money. I didn't belong to the "right" clubs or play the "right" sports and even believe in the "right" religion.

If you listen to the Labor Party it would have you believe that the Liberal Party was a "closed shop" to Australians like me.

But it wasn't – and it isn't.

JOHN HEWSON,
21 May 1994, two days before losing the Liberal leadership

Nevertheless, there is a pervasive class imagery associated with the major parties which, crudely, projects the way in which they appeal to different class groups. The Labor Party is seen as the party of the trade unions, working people, the underdog, the Ordinary Aussie (whoever she or he may be). The Liberals are seen as the party of the well-educated, the well-spoken, the well-off; they represent traditional values such as the monarchy, the church and the family; they stand for good manners, good home backgrounds and even good breeding. Though Australians are supposed to hate snobs, snobbery is alive and well in the social elite which graces the society pages of the glossy magazines and in certain sections of the Liberal Party; it is, after all, the party of the toffs. It is also the party of the powerful business/financial/owning elite which controls much of the Australian economic structure, some of whom are toffs and some of whom aren't; though the party has tried to develop a more broad-based, popular base in recent years it is still very much beholden to the upper class and its key individuals and institutions. It relies upon them for policies, finance and recruits. For its mass support, however, it relies upon a different class fraction: a stratum of respectable, goodhearted, earnest, fairly conformist middle-class Australians who dutifully turn up to branch meetings, conventions and party functions, go on tours of Parliament House with their local MP, give money to worthwhile causes, hand out how-to-vote tickets at election time and *know* they are a bit above those Labor people over there in Bankstown. Many of them are women, and they form the backbone of the Liberal Party. If you doubt this, go to any standard Liberal Party branch meeting: the blue rinses and tea-party florals invariably outnumber the suits. I remember seeing John Howard 'work' a Dulwich Hill, Sydney Liberal Party election function once, and was amazed at the conformity of the crowd to what I would have thought, previously, were stereotypical notions of who the

Liberal Party faithful were: they were nearly all ageing, well-groomed, polite, carefully enthusiastic women whom one felt instinctively would have reserved their greatest scorn for anything vulgar. John Howard, apart from being a male, was almost indistinguishable from them. His connection to his own middle-class constituency seemed complete.

Voting Patterns

The popular perception of the class nature of the parties is buttressed by voting patterns. Survey after survey has confirmed that the Liberal/National Party coalition draws the bulk of its support from the upper end of the social scale and the Labor Party from the lower end – using the terms 'upper' and 'lower' purely to indicate the relative positions of the class groups on the commonplace class hierarchy, and without any acceptance whatsoever that the hierarchy is justified or that some class groups are in any way 'superior' to others, except in the sense that some have 'superior' access to power, education and so on than any other. The sense of disparagement implicit in the term 'lower class' has meant that it has almost disappeared from usage, though some of the older generation and even some students still use it, to be replaced by the more commonly accepted term 'working class'. Interestingly enough, the term 'upper class' is still commonly used and seems acceptable, presumably because not many people mind being labelled as up at the top of the social scale; but what about those at the bottom who have to put up with the assumption that there is a 'superior' or 'upper' class?

KYLIE V. SNOBS.

The Comparative Project on Class Structure and Class Consciousness asked their sample group how they would vote for the House of Representatives if the election were 'held tomorrow'. The results are shown in the following table, with the responses analysed according to the two class typologies used consistently by Baxter, Emmison and Western (1991), namely the Marxist-based schema of Erik Wright with its familiar six class fractions, and John Goldthorpe's Weberian schema with its seven class fractions:

Voting Intentions of Different Class Locations: Wright's and Goldthorpe's Class Typologies (Column Percentages)

			Wright Classes			
Vote Intention	Employers	Petit bourgeoisie	Expert managers	Managers	Experts	Workers
Australian Labor Party	20	28	39	49	48	52
Conservative coalition	78	55	51	39	33	33
Minor parties	2	18	10	12	19	14

			Goldthorpe Classes				
	I Upper service	II Lower service	IIIa Routine non-manual	IIIb Personal service	IV Own account	V Technical and supervisory	VI Skilled manual	VII Unskilled manual
Australian Labor Party	38	40	43	46	29	52	59	60
Conservative coalition	56	42	42	40	59	34	25	31
Minor parties	6	18	15	14	12	14	16	9

The results confirm what the party strategists already know: class helps determine how people vote. In the first model, 52 per cent of workers intended to vote for Labor but only 20 per cent of employers. Conversely, 78 per cent of employers intended to vote for the Liberal/National Party coalition but only 33 per cent of workers. The effect of class on voting intention was even stronger on Goldthorpe's model, with about 60 per cent of those classified as skilled and unskilled workers intending to vote Labor. (Interestingly, as the authors point out, in the group which Goldthorpe labels 'upper service', the majority of men support the coalition but the majority of women support Labor, which may be explained by discrimination against women and consequent resentment by them, which could express itself in Labor support; or it could be the result of the Labor Party's closer identification with feminist causes and the problems of working women.) Voters who 'identified' with a particular party also split up along class lines, with employers, petit bourgeoisie and expert managers more likely to identify with the conservative parties and workers more likely to identify with Labor.

Comment Baxter, Emmison and Western: 'There is clearly a systematic relationship between class position and voting intention.' Says Bob Carr, Labor Premier of NSW: 'Class is still the most accurate predictor of voting allegiance.'

Baxter, Emmison and Western's survey also found a systematic link between people's class position and their attitude to key political issues. After asking a series of questions about government intervention in the economy, free enterprise and trade unions, they found that employers were more opposed to government intervention than any other class except the petit bourgeoisie; both groups were the strongest supporters of free enterprise; both had strongly negative attitudes towards trade unions. Workers and experts, on the other hand, adopted the least conservative positions on these issues. On other issues such as sex role equality and nuclear weapons the same pattern emerged, with employers and petit bourgeoisie taking the most conservative stance and workers and experts the most liberal. The authors comment: 'It would appear that ownership of property is associated with the most conservative position on these attitudes.' (Are there echoes, in these responses, of Proudhon's *Property is theft*?)

Despite his propensity to downplay the importance of class in political behaviour, David Kemp's analysis of a series of 1979 surveys reveals a parallel link between class and party identification. Some 33.8 per cent of self-styled middle-class Australians identified with Labor, contrasted with 60.6 per cent of self-styled working-class people. A total of 44.6 per cent of these middle-class respondents identified with the Liberals, but only 21.7 per cent of the working class. A breakdown of occupations revealed that 52 per cent of semi-skilled and unskilled workers identified with the Labor Party but only 25.5 per cent of professional people; 47.1 per cent of the professionals identified with the Liberal Party, but only 18 per cent of skilled workers. And an analysis of income groups revealed that the majority of those on higher incomes identified with the Liberals, while the majority of those on lower incomes identified with Labor. After examining other features of the voting behaviour of Australians, such as age, sex, religion and place of birth, Kemp states: 'Of all these social categories the one which continues to have the strongest association with the direction of party loyalties is occupational class.' ('Political Behaviour', in Najman & Western, 1988, p. 356.)

The Politicians

Class affects more than voting behaviour and political attitudes, of course. It affects what sort of people are likely to become politicians, and for which parties. The Liberal and National parties tend to recruit their politicians from the upper end of the social scale, especially from the ranks of lawyers, businessmen (rarely businesswomen) and, in the case of the National Party, rural entrepreneurs and primary producers. The Labor Party draws heavily upon trade union officials, teachers and public servants, and much more upon those who have been tradesmen (rarely tradeswomen), artisans, clerks and secretaries than the Liberal Party does. In 1983 in the national parliament almost a third of the Liberal MPs were lawyers, proving once again that a classic track into formal Liberal politics is through the legal profession; lawyers form by far the single biggest occupational group in parliament. Some 12.5 per cent of the Liberal MPs were company directors or managers, but none of the Labor MPs had this background. Among these Labor MPs, 10.5 per cent were or had been union officials, but this had declined from 20.9 per cent some twelve years earlier. The Labor Party has clearly moved further and further away from its trade union base when it comes to recruiting its leaders; indeed very few of its federal politicians now have a working-class background and are more likely to come from such middle-class occupations as teaching, lecturing and the public service. This means that the Australian working class now relies basically for its political representation upon a party which is not only assiduously chasing the middle-class vote, and is headed by middle-class leaders, but is made up of MPs who in the main have no personal experience of working-class life.

So what? This is not a criticism of the higher political awareness of middle-class groups; a heightened political awareness by any class group can only be to the good. Historically, the working class has always relied upon middle-class intellectuals to provide it with its theoreticians and political leaders; given the burden of disadvantage which the working class suffers, this is only to be expected. But what it means is that a class group which suffers most heavily from the class structuring of society typically does not have its own class representatives to argue and act for it, but has to rely on the members of an entirely different class. This is obviously inadequate. There is an emotional and moral force to the experience of the members of any class group which cannot be reproduced or represented by members of another class group, no matter how well-meaning. You've got to be in it to understand it. (This applies as much to me as anyone else.) This is now clearly understood by other social groups, such as Aborigines or black Americans or other ethnic groups; to be empowered in the political arena these groups have to *represent themselves*. This is no longer typical of working-class Australians. It is a symptom of the damage which class does that it has produced a situation in which one of the most grievously disadvantaged groups in the community is also the one which is most distanced from the very political process which holds out the chance, however slender, of actually changing that situation. If you're down at the bottom, the system makes sure that you haven't got much chance of changing what put you there and keeps you there. Great.

This process has been going on for some time. An exhaustive study by Dr S. Encel of federal Labor MPs and cabinet ministers in the 1958–61 federal parliament revealed that only 12 per cent had come from manual worker backgrounds and those with any working-class background at all were very much in the minority. Thirty per cent had been shopkeepers or white-collar employees and 29 per cent came from professional or farm-owning backgrounds (Encel, 1970). His analysis of the occupations of the fathers of Labor ministers who held office in state and federal parliaments from 1945 to 1958 showed that more of the ministers had fathers who were in professional or semi-professional work or were farmers/graziers than had manual worker fathers. Since then, as I have outlined, it has become even less common for Labor MPs to have a working-class background, though they commonly rely on a working-class constituency to get elected. To oversimplify: the middle class supplies the politicians, the working class supplies the votes.

Getting Involved in Politics

One of the manifest shortcomings of the current political system is the way in which class affects your likelihood of being involved in the political process which affects your own life. This is seen starkly in the way politicians are drawn heavily from some class groups and not others, but it is also seen in the different levels of participation in everyday political life by different class groups.

Australian research data suggests that high levels of political participation are associated with an upper-class or upper-middle-class position, and low levels of participation are associated with a working-class position. This includes both active participation, such as attending political meetings, giving money to a political party or working for a party at election time, and passive participation, such as keeping up to date with political affairs and having opinions about political issues. In an active democracy, both forms of participation are important; to paraphrase Dylan, you don't have to be a Partyman to know which way the wind blows.

A study by Western and Wilson supports the argument that low levels of political participation are likely to be connected to low levels of knowledge about political affairs, a sense of anomie and alienation, and a lack of a sense of political efficacy – the syndrome commonly described as the famous Australian political apathy, though it might be more accurate to describe it as political disenfranchisement. The study also found that a high sense of political efficacy existed among middle-class and particularly upper-middle-class Australians, but no more than one in five working-class people felt this way. Your position in the class structure affected not only your level of participation in politics but also how powerless and alienated you felt from the political process (J. S. Western and P. R. Wilson, 1973, 'Politics: Participation and Attitudes', in H. Mayer & H. Nelson, 1976). It could be argued, no doubt, that working-class people have only themselves to blame if they do not involve themselves more in the political process, or feel powerless to affect it, but this ignores all the pressures and circumstances that go to constrain the working-class experience: typically, the drab routine of daily work, little or no power, lack of tertiary education, low access to information and organising experience, and all the inherited disadvantages and low expectations of working-class life. Class damage is in the head as well as in the social structure. Western summarises (1983; gender pronouns changed):

> The citizen's level of participation in political affairs is strongly class-determined. The class position that s/he occupies makes a difference directly to her/his level of political participation but it also affects this participation through a set of attitudes which also stem from her/his location in the class structure. If we assume that access to selected scarce and valued resources is made more likely by active involvement in the political process, then our data clearly suggests that this access is class-related and the middle class is on the winning side.

Politics should be about change; the status quo always reinforces the inferior position suffered by those who, even if they don't realise it, lead lives which are heavily disadvantaged by the power of class. Australia is not classless, it is class-ridden. You don't have to know about class to be a victim of it.

JOHN HOWARD
Class Profile

The government's just going to be . . . er, well, what you might call Average Australian. Because that's what I think I am. I think I have more empathy with people who live in the suburbs of Australia than any political leader in the last twenty years. (John Howard, 1987, before losing the election to Bob Hawke.)

I remember from my childhood . . . you had that great sense in which people were pretty much the same. Some were a little better off than others. Some didn't have cars; they all seemed to have a house and a backyard and that basic sort of sufficiency. There wasn't a big divide. You were conscious that there were some very wealthy people living in another part of the city and there were some people who were struggling, but there was a sense that you were all the same . . . Rediscovering that sense of egalitarianism is important for the cohesion of our country. It does involve not just repudiating divisions on the grounds of race and so forth, but it's also a question of repudiating some of the old language in relation to class. (John Howard, 1996, shortly before becoming Prime Minister.)

Somewhere in John Howard's head is this image of Australia as one big, indivisible middle-middle-middle family in which everyone is the same. It's an image which does credit to his heart but not to his head. It's a memory of his childhood, in which everything seemed secure, average, suburban. No extremes. No ethnic divisions. Classless. It's an Australia which has disappeared forever (if it ever existed), but which John Howard carries around in his heart as his personal Rosebud, a vision of how things used to be and how he wants them to be again. And in a society which is very aware of how much it is being torn asunder, broken up, ripped out of its old certainties, it's a vision of pre-holocaust calm which is endearing enough to help make John Howard the nation's Prime Minister.

Howard has been admirably consistent over the years. He's always had this image of himself as essentially suburban, average, middle-class, and therefore instinctively in touch with the ordinary Australian. In fact he belongs to a rather special stratum of the middle class, the upper-middle class, with a much higher-than-average income, successful and wealthy peers, and a rather smart two-storey house in Wollstonecraft on Sydney's north shore: when I went to visit him there one wintry Sunday morning, the houses standing like English picture books in the sun, unopened papers on the doorsteps, plane tree leaves scattered across the nature strip, it was so quiet, so absolutely peaceful, it seemed like nothing could ever go wrong with the world. (In Blacktown, in the outer western suburbs of Sydney, Housing Commission bungalows and spec houses stretch for kilometre after kilometre and dwindle away into empty paddocks, sagging barbed-wire fences, shacks and trailer homes; the unemployment rate is well over the national average; more than 100 000 people on welfare; a fifth of households under or on the poverty line. It was here, in a cow paddock called the Boiler Paddock between Prospect Reservoir and the F4 Freeway, that the body of young nurse Anita Cobby was found after she had been repeatedly assaulted and raped by five young western suburbs men. They murdered her so she couldn't identify them, left her naked body on the grass. For John Howard, asleep in Wollstonecraft, Blacktown might as well be on another planet.)

Nevertheless, compared to other Liberal leaders, there is a sense of plainness, a sense of gritty integrity to Howard which is the mark of a man who believes in himself, who has endured ordeals and survived. Most men would have given up after his defeat by Hawke in 1987 and his losses to his former rival, Andrew Peacock. As he remarked famously, he would have to do a Lazarus with a triple bypass to win the leadership again. Which he did. Then the 1996 election, and achievement of the position which he has been training himself for ever since he was a schoolboy and told his classmates he was going to be prime minister.

> ## Prime Minister Howard on Inequality
>
> I remember in 1979 when as Treasurer of Australia I first had the opportunity to meet Alan Greenspan, and I always remember the conversation because one of the first things he said to me was "you are from Australia, you people have the biggest middle class in the world". And I thought that was a very interesting observation coming from a man who was then the chairman of the council of the [US] President's economic advisers, I recall. And I thought it did encapsulate something about Australia which we had for a longer period of time than many other countries and that is that the gaps between the rich and the poor were not as wide in Australia and not as deep and as endemic as they were in other societies. I have to acknowledge that in the seventeen years that has gone by since that conversation we have deteriorated quite a lot in that department.
>
> Prime Minister John Howard,
> speaking to the International Monetary Conference, Sydney,
> 3 June 1996

Howard, therefore, is a man of great perseverance. Also civil, well-meaning, without pretension; watching him during election campaigns, and the immense pressure he puts himself under, I came away with considerable sympathy for him. What with his fringe of greying hair at the back of his head and dark eyebrows and balding pate he looks like a neighbourhood bank manager, stern but friendly. He is also someone who seems thoroughly integrated and undisturbed by any internal conflicts, despite that furrowed-brow worriedness which the cartoonist

Tandberg captures so well; Howard never seems to feel the need to unburden himself to anyone else, like Bob Hawke used to, because the distance between his interior and exterior is nil.

So where does it all come from, this sense of purpose that drives John Howard? Basically, it's middle-class Methodism, which is characterised by a strong sense of community responsibility and doing something worthwhile with your life. This can split two ways, into the radical/Labor Methodism of someone like Brian Howe, the Deputy Prime Minister in the Keating government and former leader of the parliamentary Left, or into the individualistic self-help Methodism of Howard's father, a Dulwich Hill garage proprietor who was a member of the Liberal Party, supported Menzies and welcomed the end of petrol rationing with a fervour young Johnnie can still remember.

Even within the Howard family the same split exists: brother Stan was a senior partner in the law firm Stephen, Jaques & Stephen, and a Liberal functionary; brother Wally is a former Burwood bookseller and Liberal; but brother Bob is a university lecturer in political science and an ALP member who opposed the Liberals (and his family) over Vietnam. He told me once: 'John's a rather serious-minded fellow, a conservative . . . he really does believe that every man is his own fortune, the free-market system works best of all . . . there's a lot of our mother's character about him. He's a very strong person, very conscientious . . . he believes in all the old values like duty, loyalty . . . he's not at all sceptical, he doesn't realise those values and symbols can be used by particular interests for their own ends.'

Throughout his career in law and politics Howard has conformed utterly to the more conventional side of his background. Joined the Sydney University Liberal Club after leaving school, president of the Young Liberals, met his wife Janette at a party for Liberal scrutineers, cultivated NSW Liberal machine man John Carrick, moved deliberately to Wollstonecraft because he knew the sitting member, Sir John Cramer, was old and likely to retire, and in 1974 won the seat. Became Malcolm

Fraser's treasurer, then leader of the Liberal Party, lost to Andrew Peacock, suffered the ignominy of watching John Hewson and Alexander Downer lead the party from disaster to disaster, and in 1996 won power in his own right.

'He's not a fanatic,' says his wife. Yet there is an ideological narrowness to Howard that makes people wary of him, an arrogant, intolerant side that comes out in the snarling, hectoring tone he uses in parliament. A national Press Gallery correspondent told me once he thought there was 'a dark side' to Howard; others detect a whiff of moral puritanism about him. He was a hawk on Vietnam, anti-abortion and less liberal than Malcolm Fraser on South Africa. He has been accused of being a racist, and certainly his record on racial issues is appalling: he was forced to recant the racist statements he made about Asian immigration in 1988, but in late 1996 he was engulfed in yet another controversy over racism because of his failure to condemn the provocations of people like Independent politician Pauline Hanson. He may have mellowed since 1987, when he advocated the most reactionary, Right-wing political program in the history of the Liberal Party, but there is still a question as to whether Howard has genuinely moved to the centre ground or has simply compromised his personal beliefs for the sake of political expediency.

And there remains that peculiar blindness of Howard's, his lack of understanding of anything outside the narrow focus of his own experience. In 1987, on the day he launched his bash-the-unemployed-and-sick economic policy, John Travers, the three Murphy brothers and Michael Murdoch, all local western suburbs men, were found guilty of murdering Anita Cobby. The next day, in Penrith, thirty-one bikies faced up to 217 murder charges relating to the massacre at Milperra, also in the western suburbs, when a girl passer-by and several bike riders were killed in a hotel yard shoot-up. The western suburbs has its own subculture, an 'underclass' syndrome of unemployment, petty crime, drugs, factory fodder aggro and sexual violence; these urban flatlands represent an Australian version of the Liverpool and Birmingham ghettos of Tory England, in which one part of the community is concreted into poverty and social repression while another revels in the easy wealth generation of the post-industrial era. When I asked Howard about this he replied: 'I am not some sort of heartless automaton who thinks if you do this and this it'll fall into place . . . I get very concerned about social deprivation . . . the decay of law and order, spread of violence, decay of parental authority, it affects working cla . . . er, less well-off people more than anyone else.'

He couldn't bring himself to say 'class'.

The task of prime ministership has a habit of bringing out the best in those who aspire to and reach it. The 1996 election proved what reserves of character Howard possesses: he kept his self-control, his sense of humour, his fierceness of purpose, his Hemingwayesque grace under pressure. But he has also kept that hard, ineradicable, Right-wing purblindness which he never seems to have had the will, or the imagination, to shrug off and which maims him intellectually. For John Howard the western suburbs, and bikie gangs, and dole kids in black T-shirts, and the underclass, and gross and desperate social inequality, are another world. Unfortunately, it's also the real world. But, for all his personal affability, he can't see it.

5
Fear and Loathing in the Electorate

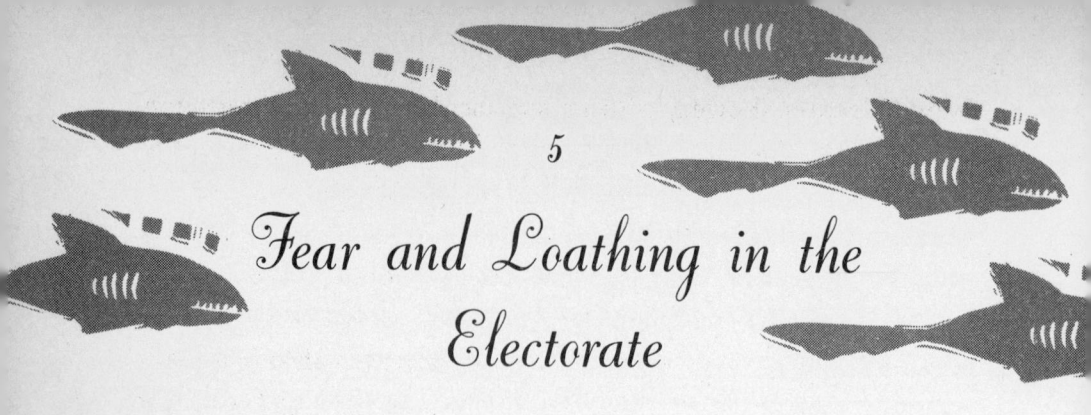

People are struggling to understand what is happening to the community and the world about them. What kind of world will their kids grow up in? And I think in their hearts they know they can't turn back the clock. They are depressed, pissed off and angry about that . . . they want solutions and the politicians don't seem to have any. The umbrella under which a successful politics will be conducted up to the year 2000 is security in the future: personal security, emotional security, job security, it's stop all this change happening. People don't like this change thing.

The speaker is Gary Gray, national secretary of the ALP, and it's as succinct a summary as one is likely to get of what has been occurring in the national political arena. Behind the overt symptoms of profound political disturbance which are manifest every day – a sour and disillusioned electorate, voter rejection of state governments of any party, cynicism about politicians, and a volatile climate of punishment of politicians and parties alike – seems to lie a search for a new politics which will somehow respond to the times Australians are living through and solve the problems which they confront in their everyday lives. As the 1996 federal election showed, with its spectacular cross-class rejection of the Labor government, there is deep fear and loathing in the electorate. Nor is it confined to the two 'battling' class groups – working class and lower-middle class – which have borne the brunt of these changes; it permeates the electorate at large.

A new politics? Is it possible? And what chance is there that a genuinely new politics will represent, or at least enfranchise, the underclass and proletarian groups which struggle along at the very bottom of the class scale?

If you look at the state of the Australian electorate in the second half of the nineties the signs are not good. Many voters are clearly disillusioned with the major parties, though when it comes to the crunch at election times they tend to cast their vote either for the Liberal/National coalition or the ALP. Others have turned to alternatives such as the Greens, the Democrats, Independents and a plethora of single-issue parties, but the institutional political process has virtually frozen these groups out of the mainstream, so that their representation in the nation's parliaments never reflects their electoral support. Perhaps former Queensland Premier Wayne Goss got it right when he said that Australians were turning against any incumbent government because governments seemed incapable of coping with the massive changes and dislocations which have occurred in their lives in the last decade; what his (defeated) administration, and others, had been faced with was 'a culture of complaint'.

The term is borrowed from Robert Hughes's book on contemporary American culture, *The Culture of Complaint*, but it trivialises the profound effects which the emergence of a new global economy and new forms of capitalist production – virtually a New World Order – have had upon those who have had to cope with and work within the new system. No wonder the search is on for a new politics; it holds out at least the possibility of solutions to the threats (of unemployment, job dislocation, redundancy, a drastic fall in standard of living) which now affect most Australians, but afflict those in the lower strata of the class scale most of all. Blue-collar and lower-middle-class workers get sacked more often than managing directors.

One result of this search which is manifesting itself is the death of managerialism as a successful recipe for political survival. In 'the good old days' when the Australian economy was booming, recessions were transient, unemployment was at least manageable and most people felt their incomes and standard of living were secure, it was possible for governments to get by through simply administering the existing system. It was, of course, a formula for conservatism, exploited by Liberal and Labor governments alike; hence John Cain's 'don't frighten the horses' when he was Premier of Victoria and Wayne Goss's 'don't scare the chooks' when he was Premier of Queensland and Nick Greiner's mantra of 'efficient, responsible government' before he was forced to resign as Premier of NSW; the idea was that states could be run like some giant corporation such as Victoria Inc. and that all the government had to do was preside over a market-driven system which eventually delivered goodies to the consumers who thronged the good-time shopping malls.

The recession of the early nineties, the restructuring of the economy, and the anger of the electorate at the failure of the politicians to manage the economy more successfully have changed all that. The quintessential case study is what happened to the Goss Labor administration in Queensland. Elected in 1989 on a reformist platform after the corruption of the Bjelke-Petersen years, Goss pushed through some vital changes and then relapsed into managerialism. During his second term in office his administration focussed on economic growth and business efficiency to the virtual exclusion of social concerns; a month before the 1995

Queensland election I was shocked at how disenchanted some of his key supporters, inside and outside the government, had become. Greens, Aborigines, welfare associations, civil libertarians and some women's groups felt they had been deliberately marginalised. The result: a nineteen-seat majority reduced to one, a blue-collar backlash in some of its once safest seats, an emergency-style post-mortem by the ALP machine, and in February 1996 the fall of the Labor government. Goss is a classic (and scary) case study in Labor conservatism. His excuse for avoiding social reforms and concentrating on the sheer business of government was that Queenslanders had to get used to the idea of a Labor administration. The result: a do-nothing government which got voted out anyhow.

In a time of turbulence and prolonged crisis such as the Australian economic/social system has been undergoing people want governments to *do something*. Being managerial is like polishing the sextant while the *Titanic* goes down. Governments might not know how to handle the distress which people are feeling so acutely, but they have to at least appear to do so. That's why the more successful governments in the nation have been activist governments such as Kennett's and Carr's. Kennett, despite the opposition to his policies, has pushed through more far-reaching changes than any state Labor administration ever had the temerity to attempt (*Victoria: on the move* say the numberplates, with typical bombast). And Carr, the NSW Labor premier, having rejected Greiner's 'remorseless focus on managerialism', has been attempting to stamp a different sort of activism on his government. 'In the past the interesting political agenda, at a state level, was being set by Kennett, with Court and Brown following in his wake,' he says. 'We're all of a sudden demonstrating it can be done differently.' CARR DECLARES WAR ON SMOG was the *Sydney Morning Herald* headline which greeted me at the airport the day I returned from Brisbane during the last days of the Queensland Labor administration. The contrast with Goss's cool and misplaced focus on sheer administration could not have been more pointed; it had been years since Goss declared war on anything.

Blue-collar Defection

In the 1996 federal election campaign both major political parties suddenly discovered the battlers: the people down towards the bottom of the class and income scales who have suffered most from the rapid increase of inequality in Australian society. This includes blue-collar and lower-middle-class workers. For the Labor Party, which has long regarded blue-collar workers as its core constituency, the haemorrhaging of its blue-collar vote has been particularly worrying.

There is no doubt that blue-collar workers became worse off during the thirteen years of the Hawke/Keating government. After a decade of accepting the government's call for wage restraint and industrial peace they were confronted in the mid-nineties with a situation in which the rich were becoming richer at their expense, work conditions were being whittled away under the enterprise bargaining regime, and a Labor government was courting the middle ground (and middle-class voters) to the point where it seemed to have lost touch with its working-class base. The result: workers began walking away from the union movement and the Labor Party. In the seven years to 1996 union membership declined from 42 per cent of the workforce to 35 per cent, leaving just 2.8 million workers as unionists. And a Morgan Gallup poll in October 1995 reported that over a quarter of the ALP's blue-collar and clerical white-collar voters had deserted it since 1983, and half of that loss had occurred since the election in 1993 which Keating had hailed as the victory of the 'true believers'. The ALP committee chaired by former federal parliamentarian Mick Young, which reported to the party on the 1995 Queensland state election, identified the loss of many traditional blue-collar supporters as a major cause of the Labor government's disastrous showing.

Some Labor politicians tend to underplay this phenomenon. Comments Bob Carr: 'I treat it with a bit of scepticism. Our blue-collar vote declined in the 1980s, rose in the 1990s when there was a more hard-edged class orientation to issues – GST, health, industrial relations. I think we are living with that volatility.' The Labor Party may be right in thinking that it can win back the blue-collar vote because of the ALP's working-class history. Carr's deliberate strategy is to highlight his government's commitment to pro-worker industrial relations and public ownership: 'I say to them, we've got a packet of industrial relations legislation that protects workers' rights, it's not unrealistic, it doesn't limit flexibility, but it runs quite contrary to what Kennett and Court are doing. It's a vivid contrast.'

However, as I have argued, Labor is no longer a working-class party. Partly because of its pursuit of the middle-class vote (which it needs to win power) and partly because of its ideological embrace of economic rationalism and the free market, it is now clearly a middle-ground party; Paul Keating's 'Ramrods' have turned MOR (middle of the road). The blue collar has turned white. Cheryl Kernot, the Australian Democrats leader, dismisses it as 'just another business party' – on most policies, especially economic ones, she says, Labor and Liberals are almost identical. It's possible that the fear of losing its blue-collar vote permanently will push the ALP back towards a more traditional stance. There is a strong strand within the party still which is committed to the idea of social capital, group cooperation and the role of the state in achieving a socially responsible community. In the United States, however, the 'hard-hat' vote has become a free-floating bloc which is easy prey for populist demagogues and the Right-wing rhetoric of Newt Gingrich. There is a possibility that in Australia confused and bitter blue-collar voters, who feel betrayed by Labor and are looking for a new 'home', could go the same way.

Lower-middle-class Battlers

Blue-collar working-class voters, however, aren't the only ones who have shown themselves to be disillusioned by the political process in Australia: 'battlers' includes a spectrum of people who are earning below $25 000–$30 000 a year and who have possibly been hit hardest by the profound restructuring of Australian society. They are mainly lower-middle-class workers, typically in white-collar clerical occupations and service industries; a lot of them are women and part-time workers; they live in the mortgage belts and outer suburbs of the major cities, raw acres of spillover from the CBDs and gentrified inner suburbs; and they represent the segment of the workforce which has been most thoroughly dislocated by the new post-industrial order. De-skilling, unemployment, redundancy, forced retraining, casual work, the forfeiture of award and union protection, and a cataclysmic loss of the security and upward mobility which were thought to be the prerogative of their middle-class identity ... this has been their lot for the past decade. It's not just that they can't make ends meet, though the daily grind of battling is hard enough; this is a group which suffered the brunt of the social impact of deregulation and globalisation (see Chapter 8, 'Crisis in the Heartland').

Gary Gray understands the politics of this and its impact on the ALP: 'These days the forces that affect families and communities are global. You can get reformed and restructured out of your job, out of your family, out of your community, out of the place you've grown up in . . . the price of the dollar means that the local widget factory closes down and widgets are now produced in South America.' He agrees the battlers are 'the angriest, most insecure and most volatile of all electoral groups'; how can Labor get them on side? 'I don't think they want to be got on side,' he says. 'They probably think, political parties can't help us, they not only can't help but they're not interested in helping. They would prefer politicians went away and just didn't exist. There's a sort of anti-view of the world: what people *don't* want is another politician. These people talk to you in anger. The anger is real.'

Social theorists such as Andre Gorz, the prominent French thinker, argue that what we are witnessing is the proletarianisation of the middle class: lower-paid, lower-echelon white-collar workers are now subject to almost exactly the same pressures, hardships and economic bludgeoning as blue-collar workers. Other commentators point to the reduction in middle-class incomes and talk about 'the disappearing middle'. This is a complex question and will be discussed in detail in Chapter 8, 'Crisis in the Heartland'; a drop in income does not necessarily lead to a shift in class position. What is clear, however, is that it is the lower-middle-class group struggling away on worsening incomes, worsening conditions and worsening job chances who have virtually given up on contemporary Australian governments, both federal and state. For them, the search for a new politics means the search for a new, stable way of life in the midst of chaos. In the United States this has led to the popularity of 'communitarianism', which involves a retreat from grand solutions and a focus on specific local issues and interventions. The same theme was taken up some time ago by Tony Blair, the leader of the British Labour Party. Communitarianism, cooperation, coexistence within capitalism – it can be seen as a utopian and hopeful direction, or as a backward and defensive fundamentalism, an admission of defeat. To use the terms of postmodern discourse, as the Master Narratives that Jean-Francois Lyotard argues held the twentieth century together (Marxism, Freudianism, the idea of Progress) dissolve and disintegrate, one of the few recourses left seems to be a sort of self-centred alienation. And nowhere is this clearer than among the young.

The Politics of Alienation

Look, we've got kids, seventeen-year-old-kids, love to buy a nice old XB Ford, six cylinder car, fill it up with leaded petrol, drive off up the highway to Gosford, drinking beer, throwing cans out the window, listening to Sheryl Crow and Crash Test Dummies, enjoying themselves, full as boots or drugged on other things, listening to Triple J or Triple M, listening to alienation. For them the bank isn't there to look after your money and provide a mortgage, the bank is there to rip you off. You just bought a can of Coke, the can of Coke is produced by a bunch of cunts who just want to rip you off, you just bought a hamburger, the hamburger is produced by Horrible McDonald's who cut down rainforests and slaughter animals just to give you a hamburger. The world is about ripping you off. They drive past Newcastle, they'll see the smokestacks, fuck BHP, polluting the atmosphere, throw another can out the window. And they'll call themselves environmentalists. The point I'm making, people will make demands of governments to take positions and do things that they in their personal lives are not prepared to do themselves. It's very easy to take a very alienated view of the world and turn it back on governments: *the government doesn't do enough* . . .

The speaker is a senior Labor man. The description is brilliant, the perception dead right, but the attitude is defensive: it's the game of blaming the electorate – as in 'we balanced the Budget, what more do they want?'

In their pursuit of economic rationalist prescriptions, microeconomic reform and fiscal discipline, Australian governments have chewed up much of the social contract upon which people have depended for a sense of security and 'cohesion' (to use former Prime Minister Keating's word) in their lives. With an appalling youth unemployment rate which in 1996 was heading towards 30 per cent, declining living standards, major cutbacks in public services, the sale of government enterprises to private owners, and the threat of continuing attacks on welfare, the question has to be asked: who is responsible for the profound sense of disillusionment with politics which seems to be prevalent in Australia in the 1990s – voters or governments?

The New Constituencies

What the Australian political system does not seem to be responding to – at least not adequately – are the multifarious separate constituencies which have grown up in the electorate: the greens, women, young people, ethnic voters, the constellation of groups and minorities which now make up a large part of contemporary Australian society. The major parties are conscious of this and the ALP in particular has made an attempt to identify and woo such groups, but they are still grossly underrepresented in national politics. The parties also seem incapable of grappling with the divisibility and fractionalising of minority groups, the way any one group speaks not with a single voice but many – and makes multifarious demands. Dr Elaine Thompson, Associate Professor in the School of Political Science at the University of NSW, says there has been a real 'movement' with women at the sub-national level (a lot of mayors are women) but not elsewhere. You could argue that the tremendous expectations held out for Carmen Lawrence (and other women) in federal politics were generated by the hope that they might bring a fresh dimension to the political arena, an approach unsullied by 'blokes' games' and the sort of antics that go on in the parliamentary bearpit. Again, the yearning for something new. The expectations heaped upon Lawrence were unrealistic, as was the apparent disillusionment when it was discovered that she too was capable of acting like 'just another politician', but the search for heroine/hero figures continues.

As an organised political party, the Greens have had a greater impact upon the Australian political system than anyone expected; they are a genuinely cross-class organisation, but most of their spokespeople and members seem to be middle class; the environment is, in Australian politics, basically a moral middle-class issue, a sort of contemporary version of the middle-class radicalism which had such a powerful effect upon the politics of the sixties and seventies. The Greens' spokesperson in Queensland, Drew Hutton, claims they affected the result in six seats in the 1995 state election and have emerged as a significant electoral force; at the national level the Greens have helped create an important balance of power for 'alternative' groups in the Senate.

But the green constituency is clearly wider than that of a single-issue party. Bob Carr, for instance, argues that young people see conservation as the biggest issue in politics; part of his strategy for survival is to push through an environmental agenda in policy areas such as old-growth forests, river regeneration and land clearing. Carr's commitment to conservation is such that he believes it has probably replaced social reform as the main push in his government. 'I'm struck by the fact that blue-collar workers and their kids are as concerned about the retreat of the natural world as others are,' he says. 'I suspect that 100 years from now people are going to be interested in these big conservation decisions in the way we're interested in how reform politicians of the nineteenth century worked on the social safety net.' A few groups have achieved what Dr Thompson describes as a 'breakout' from the mainstream electoral system. They include the Democrats, the Independents, and a plethora of single-issue groups. Dean Jaensch, Reader in Politics at Flinders University, Adelaide says there have been more hung parliaments, and parliaments where Independents hold the balance of power, in the nineties than ever before. There has been a marked though fluctuating increase in the vote for Independents and other groups, especially at state level.

The Democrats, under the leadership of Senator Kernot, have re-established themselves as a significant political force. But Kernot argues that her party and other breakout groups have been effectively marginalised by what she describes as the 'artificial polarisation' practised by the ALP and the Liberal/National coalition, whereby the two-party system is institutionalised and reinforced by everything from the electoral system to media reportage. 'The strategy of the major parties is never to allow us or anyone else to achieve the balance of power,' she says. 'The major parties have been getting closer together for the last twelve years, they're not really different, they often vote together, yet they perpetuate this artificial difference so people think, "I hate what Labor's doing, I'll have to vote Liberal".' Gary Gray admits 'there is a large institutional factor which leads to the numerical stability of the ALP and the coalition. But the fringe people out there on the margin are very small; they should not be dominating the political process'. For Kernot, this simply confirms her diagnosis. The major parties pretend to offer a choice but don't. Voters feel disenfranchised and vent their spleen against politicians in general. 'There's an incredible level of stress out there, people are slogging their guts out, so it's battler territory where the major parties are competing. It's there that the frustration level is highest, and where you're most likely to have a punishment vote,' she says.

Punishment vote: it's this that contemporary politicians fear most of all. Middle-class fear and loathing have delivered considerable electoral power to the Republican Right in the United States, so that the American system has been suffering a determined attempt to wind back the reforms and advances of the previous decades: affirmative action, the right to abortion, welfare, mass housing, all have come under sustained attack. Under the rubric of lower taxes and smaller government, the Republicans have managed to draw support from groups which once would have aligned themselves to the Democrats.

The search for a new politics in Australia may well go down a parallel path. Whatever government is in power, the electorate faces a continuation of the policies which are now only too familiar: cutbacks in public expenditure, a drive for fiscal discipline, slashed budgets, a neo-conservative agenda. Some states, as the main agencies which deliver on health and education, may attempt to resist. But the sort of massive public reaction which French workers mounted in 1996 to a similar program is unlikely in Australia, if only because the tradition of civil disobedience is much less established.

Michael Pusey, Professor of Sociology at the University of NSW, whose book *Economic Rationalism in Canberra* (1991) has become a standard text, believes that close to the core of what is happening is an attack upon the civic culture which has underpinned the Australian polity for so long: workplace awards, a stable public service, a comprehensive welfare system, and a commitment to a 'fair go' ethos. This civic culture is now fragmenting and dispersing, to be replaced by a much more competitive, aggrandising and ruthlessly individualist culture, dominated by the free market and large corporations and with a greatly diminished public sphere. It is the way in which virtually all the major political groupings have connived in this transformation, without any mandate from their voting constituencies, which has led to the malaise which afflicts the Australian political process.

Gary Gray was disheartened to find, before Labor lost the 1996 federal election, that the social wage, that is the transfer payments which the federal government relays to the sick, needy and unemployed, did not guarantee a grateful Labor vote. 'We say to them, "hang on, you get family assistance, you get rent assistance, you get this, you get that, all these transfer payments, the poor have not got poorer under Labor, you people have been looked after",' he says. 'And the people to whom we pay our transfer payments, they say to us, "what sort of Labor Party are you? You give me money but you don't care about me".'

The politics of care? But not just care – of community, of social relations, of mutuality in the 'hood. Instead of the politics of class differentiation, the politics of cooperation. Now there's a new politics worth searching for.

Kim Beazley
Class Profile

Kim Beazley is an old-fashioned sort of Australian. Maybe it's because he comes from Perth, which projects a less intensely metropolitan culture than Melbourne or Sydney. Whatever the reason, he's got a lot of the virtues that used to be regarded as typically Australian: easygoing, matey, good sense of humour, pretty conservative, a bit one-dimensional, but a good bloke. As such he's in the familiar Labor tradition – the last thing you could call him is an extremist – and when he graduated to leadership of the party in 1996, following Paul Keating's disastrous electoral loss, he was the obvious and natural choice. Right across the party. Easy does it. It says much for Beazley's strength of character, and also for his deft skill as a politician, that he is the focus of admiration across such a wide factional spectrum . . . though, sooner or later, he is going to have to come up with new ideas for the ALP or face challenges from a new generation of Labor intellectuals and activists.

Unless he does something really stupid, or falls out of the plane on the way from Perth to Canberra, Kim Beazley is set to lead Labor into the next election. He is, face to face, a very impressive man: serious, intelligent, agile (despite his 108 kilograms, or 17 stone), someone who has presence when he sits at the conference or Cabinet table. Above all he has an extraordinarily logical mind, which displays itself in an ability to marshal complex material into an ordered, well-planned sequence and then articulate it persuasively. When he answers a question it's like a short speech, everything coherent. As he says himself, 'I'm better at the pragmatic, detailed sides of politics rather than picking an ideological trend.'

That makes him a good politician but a limited thinker. Because he is so much within what his advisers call 'the mainstream' you don't expect anything particularly innovative and inspiring from him. 'I think there is a mainstream still in Australia,' he says, explaining Labor's defeat in 1996. 'Whereas in the 1980s we appeared to be addressing mainstream issues, in the 1990s these issues seemed to be settled and all we were doing was tinkering around the edges. We never made the broader vision issues sing and dance in middle Australia.' What issues? 'They were about Mum and Dad, about the opportunities for little Johnny and little Jilly . . . mainstream issues. The mainstream has changed its character but it has a common set of aspirations, there is much commonality among the people [who can be] described as middle class and working class.'

In a society as sophisticated and pluralist as Australia is today, Beazley's idea of a mainstream is open to serious objection; it is the dynamic mix of groups and minorities in our midst (ethnic, artistic, ideological, cultural) which provides the action, the impetus for change. Mainstream, after all, is a jazz term, and mainstream is where it isn't at. But at least Beazley is not afraid to talk about class: he argues that 'the lower-middle class' has been getting access to tertiary education because of the policies of the former Labor government and defends its Working Nation initiative as a 'very highly interventionist mechanism for creating opportunity and ensuring that an underclass did not develop in Australian society'.

But hasn't an underclass already developed?

'Yes it has,' Beazley agrees. 'But at least with our labour programs it enabled you to stay in touch. For Australia to be socially just, a harmonious nation . . . that will require active government, not a hands-off government. Are we going to argue for public intervention to ensure equality of opportunity, fairness, universality? Answer, yes. Absolutely.'

Like virtually all contemporary Labor leaders, Beazley comes from the Right. Over the years he has supported the nuclear industry, American bases in Australia and even the testing of MX missiles in Australian waters (he was one of the few ministers to support Bob Hawke over that, and was eventually forced to back down). He says he feels strongly about the old Aussie virtues of mateship and a fair go and sympathy for the underdog, and defends his traditionalism with his usual articulate self-perception: 'Society has to keep changing and adjust, but it can only satisfy its citizens if it changes within the framework of what they are used to,' he says. 'Why am I like that? Because I agree with that. It suits my approach to the world. I'm comfortable with Australian society and culture. The sorts of attitudes Australians have, traditionally, I don't find offensive or worth revolting against. That's not complacent, but it makes me a fairly satisfied sort of person.'

Does he feel comfortable with the direction Australia is taking?

'No!' he replies vehemently. 'In many ways I'm more interested in Clinton's America than Thatcher's England because I think that in our social structures and economic and health structures we're much more like the United States than England. I think that we were on a knife-edge between a collapse of our institutions into a society which has become very uncaring, very unequal, in which it's a real struggle to get access to a decent outcome in life, and one which allowed an optimisation of freedom without those appalling consequences. We had the society on that knife-edge, and now the knife's tipped over, and we are now headed pell-mell down the American road.'

In class terms, Beazley is pretty much the sort of politician you expect to find in parliament these days: middle-class, affluent, well-educated, from a good background, certainly no radical – what's the need? His father, Kim Beazley senior, was a long-serving Labor frontbencher who was Education Minister in the Whitlam government but was better known for his involvement in the Moral Rearmament movement; he was a deeply spiritual man, whereas his son is hedonistic (he used to be a junk food addict) and pragmatic. Beazley junior (his full name is Kim Christian Beazley) went to India for the movement but he drifted away from it as he became involved in studies at the University of Western Australia, where he concentrated on political science, marched against the Vietnam War, played Rugby Union in the 'pigs' (forwards), got his MA, went to Oxford as a Rhodes scholar, and came back to teach international politics at Murdoch University.

But it was in Australian politics that Beazley set out to make his mark. He joined the ALP, led a small Right-wing faction in what was then the predominantly Left-wing Western Australian branch of the party, and missed out on preselection to his father's safe Fremantle seat; John Dawkins, later to become treasurer, got it. Instead he was given the Liberal seat of Swan, south of the river in Perth, to contest and won it in 1980.

His electoral base has been marginal ever since, but not his career. 'Ultimately he's a career politician, and a very successful one. Has been ever since he was about four years old; in fact he can remember wandering about Parliament House at that age!' a Beazley aide told me.

'Once he sets a course he sticks to it. You've got to remember his background: state ALP secretary to Joe Chamberlain at eighteen, president of the guild at the University of Western Australia – Hawke and John Stone were predecessors . . .' Says someone else: 'He's one-dimensional. Talks and thinks politics all the time, nothing else.'

Beazley entered parliament at age thirty-seven, made a success of his portfolios, became deputy leader of the party after Brian Howe stepped down. He supported Hawke in the Hawke v. Keating battles but it's a measure of the cross-factional support he enjoys that, after Keating resigned from the leadership, the general feeling among many in the Labor caucus was 'thank God we had Kim to turn to'.

It's impossible not to like Beazley. A fine sense of humour and intelligence play over much of what he says; he laughs uproariously at his own follies; he can be self-deprecating, serious, excitable and formidable in turn. He's the opposite of pompous. He swears, carries on, worries about his weight and continually sends himself up. 'I've had ambitions satisfied, so I'm not a Cassius, either physically or intellectually,' he says, smiling, putting that down to 'the eldest child syndrome', then declares: 'I'm an Australian nationalist and social democrat', aware that that is both a boast and an admission. He's straight, and when once he described what he thought of as his constituency, he could have been describing himself: 'conservative with a small "c", generous, sees the need for change, but generally satisfied with the way things are.'

And there's the rub. Virtually everything Kim Beazley has stood for in the past reinforces the dominant culture; it remains to be seen whether, as Labor leader, he can tune in to the historic thrust of minorities, subcultures and disaffected groups for a different sort of Australia. One in which, for a start, class counted for less. His admirable 'sympathy for the underdog' becomes a subliminal excuse for not getting rid of the underdog. He's way back from the cutting edge, back with the majority. It's a good, safe place to be electorally, but it doesn't change where Australia goes from here.

6
A Personal History of Class

I can't remember exactly when I first became conscious of class. My mother and father both came from farming families, from dairy farms in different districts on the south coast of NSW – my mother's family, the Craigs, were settled around Jamberoo and the McGregors were on the hills and river flats of Brogo, just outside Bega. Now I come to think of it, I suppose both families were shifting their class position; they were being forced off their farms, slowly, by poverty and the Depression and the process by which dairy farms were split up between the children until they became so small you couldn't make a living from them. My father walked in bare feet through the frosty paddocks to go to morning lessons and left to become a bank clerk as soon as he finished school. Both my mother and my father, however, had a clear sense of pride in coming from families which had helped pioneer the Jamberoo and Bega districts, and my mother and grandmother always emphasised the need to get a good education, and speak correctly, and have polite manners.

There was one Irish family in the Jamberoo district who I got the clear impression was regarded as not one of us; they were a bit crude and uneducated and when one of them was on the local council he complained that he was always being shoved aside onto the 'shit and piss committee'! Health and Sanitation! The shit and piss committee! When I asked my Mum what was wrong with them she was a bit vague and deliberately didn't mention anything about class; she would never have liked to think of herself as snobbish; but she had very clear ideas about what was right and wrong and the correct way to behave and fussed about such symbols of gentility as not dropping your 'aitches' and polishing the brass ornaments on the mantelpiece. She and her mother always read the social pages of the *Sydney Morning Herald* and kept track of who married who among the 'good' families. Later she joined the Liberal Party and the View Club and got to know Nola Dekyvere, then one of Sydney's society leaders, but she always kept a certain independence from all that and made up her own mind how to vote at each election. Independent and moral.

When I was seven years old we moved to Gundagai and I spent the next seven years growing up on my aunt's sheep property. I think it was there I got my first whiff of the distinction between workers and owners, or workers and bosses, or workers and farmers. At Jamberoo there didn't seem to be any 'workers' as such; everyone worked, the dairy farmers and their children especially so, and the farms were too small to have employees. But in the sheep country the farms were bigger, and the families seemed to be smaller, and even the properties of just a few hundred acres had one or two stockmen working for them. The first thing I noticed was that the farm workers ate out on the verandah, not in the kitchen or breakfast room with the farming family. They treated the boss with a certain deference and sometimes they called him just that: 'boss'. 'Okay, boss, I'll git them wethers up from the flats directly.' They often lived in run-down tin shanties on the property, but well away from the main homestead; or they lived in a shanty town of poor whites and Aborigines on the outskirts of Gundagai, on the other side of the Murrumbidgee River. (One of the first short stories I ever wrote, *The Barabran Girls*, was about girls who lived there and the difference between them and the farmers' daughters; I rather liked the Barabran girls.) Only the shearers had worse places to live in; when they arrived once a year they camped in a rotting galvanised hut just outside the shearing shed which, as I remember it, had a couple of old mattresses thrown against the wall and a broken handbasin, no running water or electricity, no nothing.

The farm workers were often Irish, with names like Paddy, and good blokes, and I couldn't see much difference between them and the sheep farmers they worked for: they were all weathered, laconic men with a white brand across their foreheads where their felt hats came down, who squatted on their heels in the brown grass to talk about the crutching and when the lamb marking would start, who rode around the property on bay horses with stockwhip over arm and a couple of sheepdogs lolling along behind, and who laughed at the same things and yarned about the same things and agreed about nearly everything. But my uncle had a ute as well, and he gave the orders, and the others ate outside on the verandah.

My aunt was a kindly woman and when I questioned her about this she shrugged it off, more or less, and said they were different, because they were workers, not farmers. Not property owners, she meant.

Property.

If you owned it, you were a boss. If you didn't, you were a worker.

I didn't accept that meant people had to be treated differently. They all seemed the same to me. I didn't see why there had to be any distinction. I suppose that's where my first awareness of class distinction came from.

When I was ten I went to Cranbrook School, in Sydney, as a boarder. We were a long way from any high school and my Dad wanted me to have a good education; so did my Mum; Cranbrook was one of the leading private schools in Sydney, and later I won a scholarship which reduced the fees. I'll never forget the shock of seeing the red pebble driveway and, more intimidating still, the upstairs corridors of Rawson House with its immaculate cream-painted dormitories and polished brass door handles. The boarders were divided up into Spartans and Trojans; I became a Spartan. My co-boarders at the time included boys like Charles Lloyd Jones, Kerry Packer, Clyde Packer, James Fairfax, Miles Little, the Streets; there were sons of diplomats, squatters, company directors, businessmen, academics, the elite of the eastern suburbs. I only got in because Sir Percy Spender, a leading Liberal Party minister, had been appointed by Menzies to be Australian ambassador to the United States, and his son Peter was to go with him, leaving a gap in the hoplite ranks of the Spartans.

It says something for the ideals of the school that I was never conscious, in six years there as boarder and day-boy, of any class distinction between the pupils or felt that I was treated differently because I was a scholarship boy; displays of wealth were not only discouraged but prohibited, and it was virtually impossible to tell who was a millionaire's son and who the son of a struggling Condobolin farmer; the only outsiders were Jews and the sons of Asian diplomats. I remember, in my second last year at school, Charles Lloyd Jones, a pleasant young man, coming back from holidays with a new belt which had a watch on its buckle, which was a bit foppish but hardly superior. Once, when I was mucking around in the lower school hall, I accidentally pushed a blackboard over and smashed it and my housemaster got quite angry but said he wouldn't make my family pay for it because he knew they couldn't afford it. And when, as a senior school prefect, I argued the case for the Labor Party during an election, my companion said he could understand my taking that position because of my background – which surprised me, because I didn't feel I had a very different background to anyone else there and had been arguing for the ALP simply because I liked some of its ideas. And that was all.

The class character of the school came out in other ways. We were continually being told that we were the nation's future *leaders*, that we had to live up to our responsibilities, that we were privileged, that our nation needed us, and that the school expected us to achieve positions of distinction and influence. The Chief Justice of NSW, yet another Street, addressed us on Speech Days. The headmaster, Mr B. W. Hone, came back from a lunch with the Chairman of BHP one day and gravely asked we sixth formers to ponder why Jack, who swept the corridors outside the classroom, should have an equal vote with the Chairman, who really *knew* what the economy needed. There were whispers that one of the English masters was a Red, a socialist, or had been in his younger days, or something like that anyhow.

The school believed in God, King and Country, and Anzac Day, and the Flag, and had a Cadet Corps, and a School Captain, and Prefects who could give the cane to Juniors, and a Rowing Club, and a Motto, and badges and scrolls and uniforms and all the other paraphernalia of the sort of English Public School upon which it was modelled. Among the pupils there was a good deal of snobbery and arrogance about the 'lower classes' outside, and striking trade unionists, and Commos, and Labor ministers who spoke through their noses, and bloody engine drivers like Chifley. When the garbage truck came around some boarders would shout 'Hello, Dad' at the garbos in their striped jerseys and think it a terrific joke. Dad! A garbage man! Most of them thought that strikes should be banned, that the Reds were running the country, that Labor men like Evatt didn't even know any better than to talk to the King with his hands in his pockets, that the Communist Party should be outlawed, and that the only way to make society prosper was to give people incentives to make money. I disagreed with all this, but I regarded them as ideas rather than class attitudes.

When my family moved to Haberfield, a red-brick, inner-western suburb, and I became a day-boy instead of a boarder, and had to travel for an hour by bus and tram to school each day, class differences began to impinge upon me more forcefully. They could hardly fail to, travelling in through Leichhardt, Annandale, Glebe and Pyrmont and ending up in Double Bay and Bellevue Hill. The top deck of the bus was crammed with workers in hob-nailed boots carrying Gladstone bags, with a few white-collar workers in shiny blue serge suits thrown in; the housewives and shoppers seemed to stay downstairs. The bus drove each day through the inner-western suburbs past grimy shop awnings and shabby slum houses and down-and-outs rifling among footpath rubbish bins; in the city centre I changed to the Rose Bay tram and travelled out past tree-shrouded mansions and curving flagstone driveways and shops with silver gowns in the windows. I began to feel how unfair it all was and wondered why it was organised in that way; I didn't feel superior to anyone, or inferior, and I didn't see why anyone else should either. Our history master made us study the Communist Manifesto but it all seemed far away and in another time. What struck me was how unnecessary all the invidious distinctions around me were, why some people had cars and some not, why some houses were so much better than others.

I remember thinking that the government should give everyone a house, a car, a refrigerator, a washing machine, and all the other essentials of life when they first got married so that no-one down the bottom ever missed out. Redistribution! It was a long way from thinking in class terms, but at least by then I had learnt that there were social classes, there was an upper class, there was a 'lower' class, there were conflict and strikes between bosses and workers, and that 'class distinction' was one of the banes of our life. Like many Australians, I thought that snobbery or class *distinction* was the problem, not the existence of *classes*. I still run into people who believe there is no real class structure in Australia, only privilege – not realising that over generations and centuries of consolidation that very privilege has been institutionalised and crystallised into class. The social codes of superiority/inferiority are clear enough and often objected to, but the class system is ignored.

I had already decided to be a writer, but on leaving school I had to get a job. Journalism seemed a good way of gaining experience as a writer so I joined the *Sydney Morning Herald* as a first-year cadet; I had also decided to go to university. At my initial interview for the paper the Chief of Staff, Tony Whitelock, asked me what I was interested in; I told him, haltingly, that I was interested in the different social groups I could see around me and would like to write about them; he brushed that aside as worthless and assigned me to the Shipping Column, which meant taking a list of all the ships that went in and out of Sydney Harbour each day. (It was a few years before the *SMH* would run anything I wrote on class.)

I went to Sydney University before or after working at the newspaper each day; I wanted to study sociology but the university didn't have any such course and the one at the University of NSW had only just started, so I studied philosophy under John Anderson instead, and English, and history, and began to learn a bit about class history if not class theory. Again, like most Australians, I was never taught anything about class; I had to find it out for myself. I don't think there was a single book on class in Australia at the time, or if there was neither I nor anybody I knew was aware of it. The dominant myth was that Australia was a working-man's paradise, that there were a few insignificant snobs out there in the eastern suburbs somewhere, but basically every man (sic) was as good as the other and if you thought or acted otherwise you were a fool. C'mon have a beer, mate. It was 1951, the long Menzies era had just started, the Petrov case and the Labor split were three years away, the Cold War was burning. Menzies had almost succeeded in making it illegal to be a Communist or a Communist sympathiser. Randwick Racecourse was awash with felt hats, the Royal Sydney Golf Club still banned Jews, the government was about to introduce conscription (national service).

C'mon have a beer, mate.

I don't know how typical such a pilgrim's progress is; only, I suspect, in that most Australians are never taught about class but have to learn about it for themselves, either in their work experience or in their daily lives. Certainly they are not usually taught about it at school, any more than they learn about politics; we must be one of the few cultures in the history of the world which does not try to teach its young people, that is its future citizens, about the fundamentals of its own social and political structure. I was still a teenager; my family virtually never talked about class or had any theory of class organisation. If I'd have been asked at the time what class I belonged to I'd have had to work it out. I suppose I felt myself pitched somewhere between the upper class, the wealthy fathers and mothers of the pupils I had known at school, and the working class, who worked in factories, on buses and trams and trains, on garbage trucks, on the roads, and in the greasy printing-press depths of the *Sydney Morning Herald*.

I was, I suppose, middle class... *lower* middle class, with its typical emphasis on education as a means of getting on in the world, and white-collar work, and respect for gentility and propriety and 'nice' things like a nice speaking voice, and its geographic siting in landlocked, red-brick, mid-western suburbs, front-lawn-and-backyard bungalowland. You got born, went to school until leaving age, got a white-collar job as shop girl or insurance clerk (my father was still a clerk), went to parties, met someone, got married, settled down, saved for a car and a house, had children, and started the cycle all over again. Middle class. Humphrey McQueen and others don't believe it exists – well, he *used* to argue that. But we who have grown up through it know that the middle class, like Kings Cross, is a state of mind, And once there, like the island of Circe, you rarely leave it. If you climb upwards, and adopt the style of the class above, sooner or later some blue-rinsed lady from Toorak with an ulcerated husband and a chauffeur in the Bentley will say, 'But of course, you know he made his money from *beer*!'; if you fall downwards, and get a job as a school cleaner or doorman, your workmates are likely to taunt you about how very uppity you still are, how well-bred, how ineffably middle class. Ladders, snakes, rise and fall, levels, ranks, strata, groups, mobility up, mobility down, social climbers and phoney proletarians ... class-consciousness ... class.

Most people, I suppose, learn about it in any depth when they go to work. Class is about power, and inequality, and unfairness, about the subjugation of one person to another or one group to another, and this becomes clearest and at its most brutal in the workplace. You quickly learn there are bosses and those who get bossed about. In a newspaper office the chain of command is somewhat blurred and power relations can seem somewhat anarchic; in the *Sydney Morning Herald*, which was a tolerably civilised and old-fashioned newspaper, reporters and feature writers had a certain amount of freedom but there was a definite political limit to what you could write; you certainly couldn't go against the policy of the *owners* of the paper and it was another forty years before the *SMH* started running an Op Ed (Opposite Editorial) page for the expression of non-owners' views of the sort which the *New York Times* and other major American papers have had for a long time.

There was also a clear division between the white-collar journalists and the blue-collar printers and tradesmen. The printers, symbolically, worked a couple of floors below the white-collar journalists and clerks and administrators, were highly unionised, and were active members of the Trades and Labor Council; the journalists belonged to an association, the Australian Journalists' Association, not a union, and successive moves to affiliate it with the Australian Council of Trade Unions (ACTU) over the years were defeated by the journalists themselves. Once again, we were in the middle. If you were a leader (editorial) or feature (article) writer you could be told what to write by the editor/management/owners; at the same time you had a certain authority over the stone hands and readers and printers who set what you wrote in metal and put the paper out; you even had authority over the car drivers who took you to where the stories were happening. As a cadet reporter I committed a few blunders, and was hauled into the news editor's office for a roasting, and was threatened with demotion for not passing shorthand tests, and had to defend myself against philistine executives who thought studying for a university degree, as I was, was a waste of time.

By the time I had finished my cadetship and become a D grade reporter I had a very clear idea of power and not such a clear idea of class. Power flowed from the top down, and was wielded by people who owned things or managed things. Class meant, roughly, an upper class who owned property and companies and institutions like the newspaper, a middle class who carried out orders and sometimes gave them, and a working class who did most of the manual labour. Australia was clearly a class society; the distinctions between the different class groups were overpowering. From my knowledge of history I was able to relate the Australian situation to the European one and the history of class conflict, struggle and revolution, yet there were obvious differences – not the least of them being the way in which the people around me, most of them middle class, I suppose, seemed less oppressed by class than their counterparts in European societies. The Labor Party rhetoric of class struggle already seemed to be wearing thin, or seemed old-fashioned, not because the theory was wrong necessarily but because it seemed to have so little real relevance to the comparatively stable, affluent and middle-of-the-road society which was rapidly developing in Australia.

My own reaction to this was egalitarian. Class distinctions seemed at best stupid, at worst manipulative and deadly. I thought everybody should be equal, and class was obviously the chief source of inequality. (This is what I still think.) I believed in the old French catchcry of liberté, égalité, fraternité, and its Aussie equivalents of independence, mateship and a good time for all. I'd got some of this from my Dad, who thought he was as good as any man and a bloody sight better than most and hated the bank he worked in, the English, Scottish & Australian Bank (E.S. & A., now absorbed in the ANZ), because it was run by toffee-nosed English snobs and treated its staff abominably; he joined the Army as a private on the day the Second World War broke out, ended up a captain, and had a fierce family pride in the McGregors and bush virtues like resourcefulness, integrity and lack of social pretence. But I think I'd worked most of it out for myself; unlike many people I met later, I didn't have any inherited family sense of injustice; it just seemed bloody unfair and I felt fierce about it. I started voting Labor because it seemed to stand for some of the ideals I held. Middle-class radicalism, it came to be called. At that time the phrase hadn't even been invented.

So far, I suppose, this sociographic account of one person's developing class-consciousness has been fairly typical of numbers of Australians, which is the point of writing it; in a society in which class perceptions are often confused or repudiated it is important to work out just how people learn about class. Then I went to England for four years and found out, at first hand, what it is like to live in a society in which class formations and conflicts are much more naked than in Australia; the distance between Southwark Bridge Road cockneys and the traditional English aristocracy, and the rigour and importance of class construction, were a shock to an easygoing Australian who had tended to dismiss class as offensive and peripheral rather than perceive it as crucial to social organisation. I began to realise that class provided the basic structure of any society and that class distinction was not the foible of a few snobs but the visible effect of the way power is organised and distributed in class terms. Came back to Australia briefly, noticed the changes which affluence and the growth of the white-collar workforce had wreaked in the society I had left, read John Pringle's book *Australian Accent* (1958) and thought he was wrong in his account of the Australian class structure, and began writing *Profile of Australia* (1966). Leaving England for the second time to return home I wrote a farewell journalistic piece which some crass sub-editor headlined 'Why I Am Going Back To The Land Where Nobody Calls Me Sir'. (Shudder, shame.) As soon as my wife, who was born and grew up in England, and I stepped off the gangplank at Fremantle one of the baggage porters called me sir. Hmmmnn.

It took me three years of research and writing to complete the book, and one of the major themes was class. In the course of my research I read every book, paper, survey and piece of research which had been done in Australia on class up to that point, which was a valuable piece of self-education in itself; I became aware of the work of Encel, Davies, Congalton, Oeser and Hammond, C. Wright Mills, Weber and other sociologists, discussed concepts of class with Encel while writing for the *Sydney Morning Herald*, carried out my own analysis of occupational changes with the help of the Australian Bureau of Census and Statistics, went through every Morgan Gallup poll survey, and wrote my own account, both personal and objective, of class and class changes in Australian society. A good deal of the material on class dealt with the 'middle classing' of Australian society; this has since become conventional wisdom, but at the time it was innovative enough to draw flak from several quarters and the fact that class was emphasised at all seemed to surprise critics and readers alike. Perhaps it was because many Australians, commentators and non-commentators, still liked to delude themselves that Australia was a classless society. The old myths die hard.

There's nothing like writing about class to learn about it. In the years after *Profile of Australia* was published I did a great deal more work on class, read more, discussed it more. I wrote my first novel, *Don't Talk to Me About Love* (1971), and placed it quite consciously in Sydney's upper north shore. *People, Politics and Pop* (1968), a book of essays, dealt with class, people and popular culture. My own allegiance to 'ordinary people', of whom I was one – the people derided by Barry Humphries, and Patrick White, and the *Oz* crowd, and sometimes Left intellectuals like Ian Turner and Allan Ashbolt, and the rest of the suburbia-baiting crowd – was confirmed by my experience of the sheer power and imaginativeness of folk and popular culture, from jazz to the Border ballads to the work of cartoonists I knew like Martin Sharp and Bruce Petty. I also came across some heavy resistance to talking and writing about Australia in class terms, a resistance which was to make much greater sense later when I had become acquainted with Antonio Gramsci's theories of hegemonic consciousness, but which at the time often took the form of newspaper and magazine editors who had themselves jumped up the class ladder being sceptical of the importance or the 'holding power' of class. There's nothing like shaking yourself free of the limitations of your class background to prove to yourself that class don't count; if I can do it, why can't everyone else?

I should make one thing clear, though it shouldn't be necessary: I don't believe any class, or the people in it, is 'superior' to any other. The language of class, of course, is suffused with the imagery of higher and lower, top and bottom, ladders, scales, climbing and falling, and it is necessary to make use of this imagery in writing about it; one of the crucial facts about class-consciousness is that it is often based upon a perception, a correct perception, of the inequality which produces such imagery. Behind the use of the words 'top' and 'bottom' is the realisation that some people have more power, wealth and privilege than others. This does not make them 'superior', in the sense of 'better'; but it does mean some of them are wealthier, or better educated, or have the power to tell you what to do; sometimes, as in the case of an upper-class politician who introduces conscription for Vietnam or an upper-class businessman who induces you to work in an asbestos mine, they can kill you.

Next came two years on a Harkness Fellowship in the United States, most of it spent on the fringe of Harlem in New York. It developed my education in the nature of class because in America class exploitation, and its links with racism, sexism and imperial power, was even more naked than in England. This was not a matter of theory and ideology, it was simply a matter of living among black, brown, white, Jewish and WASP Americans during the upheavals of the seventies: Vietnam, the draft, black power, student revolts, Attica, the Newark ghetto in flames, and a machine-gun nest on the steps of the Capitol. When I came back to Australia it was like returning to cottonwool country; everything was muffled, class conflicts disguised, and some intellectuals believed that the Whitlam government signalled a completely new era in the nation's progress. The dismissal of the Labor government in 1975 shook some of that complacency, because it was so obviously an exercise in class power; and yet many Australians regarded it as merely a constitutional or, at best, a political crisis, and the readiness with which they settled down to accept the Fraser government demonstrated the strength of existing class arrangements in Australian society.

Those arrangements seem to be as strong now as ever; if anything they may have been accentuated by the economic crises of the 1980s and 1990s. During the years of affluence it was possible to imagine that class barriers and class loyalties were weakening and that therefore class wasn't as important as it had been; the middle classing of Australian society, in the sense that more and more people were in middle-level jobs and thought of themselves as middle class, meant that the majority of Australians thought themselves to be on something like the same level; the extremes at the top and bottom didn't seem to matter that much. The nineties has shattered that complacent myth. Class has as important an impact upon the making and breaking of people now as ever it did. Indeed the impact of technological change, the triumph of the market system, and the massive restructuring of work and the workforce which have accompanied the globalisation of the Australian economy, mean that the effects of class are probably more nakedly evident now than at any time since the sixties. It's hard to ignore class in a society which is becoming transparently more extreme and more unequal, and in which more and more people are becoming the victims of class power.

Class informs and shapes individual people as surely as it shapes groups and societies; that's partly why I have included in later books such as *The Australian People* (1980) and *Headliners* (1990) extended profiles of individual Australians whose lives reflect the pervasive influence of class; a certain amount of the journalism I have written revolves around the same theme. Class is something which seeps into your consciousness over a long period of time; you never really stop learning about it, and your most valuable perceptions may spring intuitively from personal experience. At the same time it helps to have some theory to codify and test that experience, just as it's necessary to use personal experience to test theory. Over the years I have been influenced, obviously, by European theorists and in particular by the social theorists of the Birmingham School, especially Stuart Hall, whom I met when I first arrived in England; in Australia by my contact with sociologists such as Sol Encel, Alan Davies, Bettina Cass and Bob Connell, historians such as Ian Turner and Manning Clark, academics such as Michael Pusey and John Docker, artists such as Bruce Petty... the list goes on and on. Almost everything helps create and modify your understanding of class, especially your everyday experience of a class society; like culture, it is inescapable. A great deal of the racism, sexism and invidious divisions in Australian society are inexplicable except in class terms; as in the United States, it is easy for minority groups to mistake oppression as purely race-based or gender-based when in fact it is the class structure of society which oppresses the vast majority of its members, black/white, female/male, Anglo-Celtic/ethnic alike. Nor is this mere ideology. I've never lost my anger at the unfairness of the class system and the way class damages so many people's lives. It's taken a lifetime to understand how class shapes the experience of all of us.

7
Who is the Middle Class?

When Australians are asked what class they belong to, more of them say 'middle class' than any other. Despite the resistance of some sociologists to the term it is in widespread use in everyday talk, in politics, in the media, and in academic class analysis. In Pitt Street, Sydney at lunchtime the pavements and shopping mall are crowded with clerks in short-sleeved white shirts and ties and young shop girls in trendy gear who would almost certainly describe themselves as middle class. In summer Governor Phillip tower and other high-rises disgorge hordes of public servants who stroll across the Domain to watch lunch-break footie; others appear in headbands and running gear and set off for a round-the-blocks constitutional; they, too, would almost certainly say they were middle class. In Canberra on a mid-autumn day the Prime Minister and his aides sit down in white shirts and sincere ties and discuss what they need to do to win more of the middle-class vote. In another part of Canberra the sociologists Broom and Jones have pronounced Australia 'the most middle-class nation in the world'. Whatever the reservations, it's clear that middle class has a definite and persistent meaning for most Australians and is used to describe a social group whose characteristics, as Wild says (1978,

p. 59), 'all combine to structure patterns of relationships that may be clearly seen as specifically middle class'.

Who are the members of this amorphous middle class? The name itself is important: middle-class Australians tend to see themselves as belonging to a middle mass which is below the upper class, because clearly they haven't got the power, wealth or sheer social clout of those at the very top of the social scale, and yet which is somewhat above the working class because they have better, safer jobs, more prestige, a higher income (most of the time) and don't work with their hands. They're not bosses and they're not labourers. They're in the middle. And they *feel* different to the working class, even if they recognise that they are themselves white-collar 'workers'. It's easy to put this down to mere snobbery, but extensive social research in Australia and in other western countries has confirmed the existence of a real distinction between the blue-collar manual worker and the white-collar clerical worker even when their incomes may be much the same.

The position of the individual in the workforce hierarchy is crucial. Manual workers often see white-collar workers, even the lower levels of clerical workers, as part of the management and as having more power than they do. If you're a worker in oil-stained overalls and you think there's something wrong with your pay packet, you often have to go up to an administrative floor in the head office building and front up to a counter behind which clean, tidy office people sit at their desks in air-conditioned splendour and it's one of these, probably one of the juniors, who finally condescends to get up, check your pay slip with the computer, and decide whether you've got the right money or not. They actually seem to *decide* these things; they may have guidelines, but they have real scope for decision-making as well – over superannuation, deductions, PAYE tax, benefits, holidays, even how much cash is in your pocket. According to D. Lockwood in *The Black-coated Worker* (quoted in Wild, 1978, p. 54):

> The converse of the working cooperation of clerks and management is the social isolation of the office worker from the manual worker. The completeness of the separation of these two groups is perhaps the most outstanding feature of industrial organisation.

The middle class is not an indivisible group, any more than any other class is. It includes, at the top end, professionals, bureaucrats and the higher grades of administrators and managers; further down are the great bulk of white-collar workers, clerks, sales assistants and other service workers who predominate in tertiary and what has been called quaternary industry (information processing, communications, education, financial services); plus small farmers, shopkeepers and other self-employed people; plus some tradespeople, foremen and supervisors who exercise executive power in their jobs. The diversity of this group is one of the reasons why sociologists have sometimes subdivided it into upper-middle, middle-middle and lower-middle; another reason is the continued fragmentation of workforce groups and the existence of a certain amount of crossover between people in the working class and the middle class. But when this mobility is analysed it becomes apparent that there is much more mobility *within* the class group, that is within the working class or the middle class, than between them (see Chapter 3, 'Class Jumpers').

Surveys and polls reveal a somewhat surprising agreement about the size of the middle class. Four separate surveys in 1949, 1961, 1965 and 1967 found that 55 per cent, 56 per cent, 49 per cent and 50 per cent of Australians regarded themselves as middle class. A later Morgan Gallup poll in 1976 gave 60.3 per cent (by combining middle class 48.8 per cent and lower-middle class 11.5 per cent). The Australian Values Study survey of 1983 produced 57.5 per cent. Baxter, Emmison and Western (1991) found that, when asked what class they would place themselves into if they had to, 50.5 per cent replied middle class. Something over half the Australian population, therefore, regards itself as middle class.

It is possible, some theorists argue, that there is no such thing as a middle class and that those who regard themselves as such are in fact workers and are simply victims of 'false consciousness'. As discussed in Chapter 2, 'What Makes Class?' there are several problems with this approach. Who and what decides when consciousness is 'false' and on what grounds? What betrays consciousness that is 'false' as opposed to 'true' consciousness? What if new classes do evolve – are they 'false'? European Marxist writers such as Althusser and Poulantzas finally came around to recognising the existence of a 'petty bourgeoisie', which sounds like a parallel to Carchedi's 'new middle class'. Academic writers such as Lockwood have argued that an approach which avoids the concept of a middle class cannot explain the real and enduring differences in class-consciousness between blue-collar and white-collar workers and that 'variations in class identification have to be related to actual variations in class situations'. (D. Lockwood, *The Blackcoated Worker*, quoted in Davies & Encel, 1965, p. 84.) Whatever the reasons for the growth of middle-class consciousness and middle-class self-identification, the fact remains that in Australia today there is an intermediate or middle group which regards itself as partially distinct from other groups in terms of jobs, power, income, education, lifestyle and so on, and that's the reality which everyone, academics and politicians and writers alike, has to deal with.

White Collar

The key reason for the growth of middle-class identification has been the enormous upsurge in white-collar workers since the Second World War. Growing up in Australia in the 1950s was like growing up in a place where myth was completely separate from reality: Australia was supposed to be 'the land of the workers', where every person was as good as the next, mateship reigned, classes didn't really exist (except for a few snobs out there in Toorak and Wahroonga), nobody called anyone sir, and equality was the clenched ethic everyone held in common – while around me the streets were full of neatly dressed clerks and shop assistants, and the pubs were full of businessmen, the trains were full of white-collar commuters travelling to and from their rows of bungalow-and-backyard homes in the suburbs, and the air was full of talk about how to get on, how to succeed, how to get a good job, what was the best school to go to . . .

I'd learnt at school that Australia was the land where everyone was equal, just about, and found when I left school that it was a land of success merchants climbing on each other's backs to keep up with the Joneses and grinding their competitors into the dirt. It seemed clear to me that Australian society was changing: it was becoming more affluent, more conservative, more *middle class*. It was while I was researching census material on occupational structure, in an attempt to find out what was really going on, that I made an interesting discovery: in 1963, for the first time in the nation's history, the number of white-collar workers had caught up with the number of blue-collar workers. The original analysis was made by Tom Fitzgerald, then financial editor of the *Sydney Morning Herald* and founder of *Nation* magazine; it was complicated, however, by the fact that the then Bureau of Census and

Statistics had changed its method of classifying occupations between censuses. With the help of bureau statisticians I managed to rationalise the census classifications and discovered that the white-collar workers, as well as being the biggest group of all, accounted for over half the increase in the workforce between 1947 and 1961 and were growing almost twice as fast as any other group.

In future the preponderance of white-collar workers can be expected to become even more marked. It is one of the paradoxes of modern technocratic societies that as industrialisation proceeds the biggest rise in employment does not occur in secondary industry, where computers and other modernisation techniques (including, of course, the deliberate move by employers to reduce their labour force and replace people with machines) reduce the rate at which the blue-collar workforce grows; the biggest growth occurs in tertiary industry. Thus in Australia in the last three decades the really rapid expansion of jobs has been in tertiary and service industries such as banking, insurance, advertising, public relations, retail trade, finance and property – the very industries where white collars predominate.

Professional and managerial occupations have seen some of the biggest jumps in numbers. This has occurred at both the upper level of the professional groups and with 'lower professionals' such as teachers and paramedicals. Comments Encel ('Capitalism, the Middle Classes and the Welfare State', in Wheelwright & Buckley, 1978): 'The expansion of the middle classes has been a major feature of the affluent society . . . This expansion is clearly linked with the growth of higher education.' What all this means is that there are now far more white-collar workers who sit behind a desk or sell things or carry out professional and technical work than there are blue-collar workers who make a living with their hands. And most white-collar workers regard themselves as middle class. Given this, the growth of the self-styled middle class is quite explicable.

There is a considerable difference between the Australian situation and overseas countries. In Britain and the United States, for instance, the biggest class group in the past has been those who call themselves working class, not middle class. Speculating on this sort of disparity, Broom and Jones have argued that the larger proportion identifying as middle class in Australia cannot be explained simply by differences in the occupational structure: 'Presumedly there are real variations in class images among these three countries, with more Australian manual workers identifying with the middle class.' Possible reasons include a high incidence of home ownership and 'relatively high social and cultural homogeneity, at least by comparison with the United States'. (Broom & Jones, in McGregor, 1980, p. 64.)

The Muddle in the Middle

When I was in high school, one of those right-on teachers with a mission to make students think tossed us a curly question: "What class do you think you belong to?"

She did not mean school class, but rather social class. We students all sat there like idiots for several minutes. I can honestly say that the issue of class had never raised itself on my mental horizons before that.

More than that, we had been told so often that Australians lived in "a classless society" that there seemed to be something traitorous about even contemplating the question. We foundered for the right answer.

Most of my classmates decided they were middle class.

> Some (myself included) were more ambitious: we thought we were upper-middle. No-one believed they were upper class. But more significantly, neither did anyone contemplate the possibility that they were working class – this despite the fact we were at a state school, and came from a mixture of blue-collar or (slightly frayed) white-collar families . . .
>
> People seem more aware (now) of their social status. I hear the words "middle class" quite a lot, and it has taken on the same meaning that it has in Britain.
>
> It seems accepted thinking now that doctors' children become doctors; lawyers' children become lawyers. And that if you come from certain suburbs, from certain backgrounds, then your chances of success are low.
>
> Maybe it's just an impression, but I sense that some of Australia's old social fluidity has trickled away.
>
> JENNY TABAKOFF,
Sydney Morning Herald, November 1995

In the 1990s unemployment has risen dramatically, accelerating during the recession of 1991–2 and reaching an unprecedented postwar level of 11 per cent in 1993 before declining somewhat to 8.8 per cent in 1996, and home ownership has faced unstable interest rates; such changes may act as a check upon middle-class identification. Nevertheless the middle class in Australia seems to have a persistent drawing power in terms of ethos, image and lifestyle. At its centre is the home, classically a bungalow with its own front garden and backyard in which the middle class lives, dreams, procreates, raises children, and enacts a ritual of work/sleep/sex/love/kids/family/death which is at the very heart of the Australian dream. It isn't a bad dream, either; in much of the world, ripped apart by poverty, war, ethnic and religious divisions and a history of civil conflicts, it can seem like paradise. The typical middle-class man, if there is such a thing, is probably a public servant with a white collar, leather shoes and a fixed salary; the typical middle-class woman is likely to be a housewife still, who either stays at home and looks after the family or works part time to help pay off the mortgage. The nuclear family, though it no longer represents the majority of family units, is still the commonest of Australian family forms, just as 'mortgage belts' still characterise most new housing developments in the capital cities. 'Two-bob snobs' was how one Mornington Peninsula housewife described some neighbours in the new cul-de-sac housing estate she lived in, relapsing into an outdated vernacular; most of her neighbours were all right, she said, good friends, but some were so mortgaged-up they could hardly afford the petrol for their flash cars.

They have been the butt of a lot of satire, middle-class Australians; David Williamson and Barry Humphries have had a lot of fun at their expense; Humphries has created some of his most successful characters, such as Edna Everage and Sandy Stone, by lampooning middle-class habits and styles – though, like Humphries himself, Edna has become more successful and is now Dame Edna, the globetrotting megastar. Humphries dismisses them as philistines, thus consigning to purgatory over half the 18 million people who live in Australia; in reality they are less bitterly reactionary than he is, and a great many of the nation's most admired women and men – artists, politicians, scientists, writers, thinkers, feminists, radicals and even satirists like Humphries – come from precisely that class background.

Middle-class people tend to be joiners, much more so than working-class people; they often belong to clubs like the Chamber of Commerce, Rotary, Apex, Lions, bowling and golf clubs, perhaps the local RSL and the Country Women's Association. They are found on local and school committees, in voluntary organisations, charities such as the Red Cross, community centres and boards of management. This gives them more power and influence, even outside their jobs, than working-class people. Middle-class suburbs, for instance, have been far more successful in combating expressways and massive redevelopment than working-class suburbs; in Sydney, the Department of Main Roads managed to push the Eastern Suburbs Expressway through the beautiful working-class terrace houses of Bondi Junction to bring shoppers to the sprawling 'Bondi Jungle' commercial centre, but a well-organised residents' campaign stopped the same thing happening to trendy Paddington. Western (1983, p. 80), in a summary of survey material on rates of political participation in Australia, comments:

> The proportion who are low participators ... increases regularly as we move from professionals and managers to other white-collar workers and to manual workers. High levels of political participation are clearly associated with an upper-middle or middle-class class position while low levels of participation are clearly associated with a working-class class position.

Suburbia

Suburbia is the heartland of the middle class. Despite the strictures of Patrick White and the current emphasis on urban consolidation, it is where most Australian life is lived. Most middle-class people own their own house or are paying it off; it is by far the single biggest item of expenditure by middle-income earners. Western states 'around 80 per cent of high-income earners are home owners, whereas only 55 per cent of the lowest income earners are' (Western, 1983, p. 72). Middle-class people are more likely than working-class people to invest in a home and less likely to pay rent; and, needless to say, they generally live in better houses in what are regarded as 'better' suburbs than working-class people.

Australians have a very well-developed awareness of the prestige of the various suburbs in which they live; Professor Athol Congalton's early research at the University of NSW revealed that people were able to rank suburbs in prestige scales which corresponded very closely to the professional perception of such suburbs by real estate agents and others. Some academics tend to talk guardedly about the 'socio-economic character' of particular localities as revealed in statistical surveys, but what they are really talking about is class. When two geographers, J. R. Davis and Peter Spearritt, set out to construct a series of computer maps of Sydney based on extremely detailed census results they found that the single most prominent factor to emerge from the statistics was socio-economic status. This served as the basis for much of the differentiation of the city as disclosed in computer maps of the workforce, education, religion, migrants, families, houses, cars, unemployment and so on (McGregor, 1980, p. 65). Class, it would seem, underlies everything else. But didn't we always know that?

Lifestyle

Middle-class people earn more than working-class people. It's common for professionals to point to what some tradesmen, such as plumbers, charge for their services and argue that tradesmen probably earn more than they do; I have even heard wealthy doctors excuse their extraordinary incomes on these grounds. The comparison is specifically invalid; doctors are among the highest income-earning groups in the nation, even after making deductions for family trusts and other tax lurks, and on average enjoy far higher incomes than plumbers. Research carried out by the Australian Bureau of Statistics and by political scientist David Kemp in his 'Society and Electoral Behaviour in Australia' (Western, 1983, p. 48) has revealed that people in middle-class, non-manual occupations have clearly higher incomes on average than those in manual, working-class occupations, which is exactly what you'd expect. The Australian Values Survey of 1983 confirmed this. Of those earning $20 000 a year or more, 43 per cent were upper-middle class and 36.4 per cent were lower-middle class; as you went further down the income groups the proportion of middle-class people generally declined, until of those earning $6000 a year only 12 per cent were upper-middle class and 28.6 per cent were lower-middle class; the majority were working class. In contemporary Australia middle-class preoccupations such as the car, the house, the club and the credit card have swamped the old working-class ones of rent, beer, the union and the races.

It is hardly any wonder, then, that many working-class people try to make the move up to the middle class, and why this can lead to middle-class identification. In terms of sheer possessions there may be little to separate such a working-class Australian from a middle-class one. Hence the phenomenon, which Encel (1970) has noted, of people regarding themselves as working class when they are on the job but as middle class when they get home, a process which can be accentuated by a heavily privatised lifestyle such as is typical in many outer suburbs – you hide behind your rail fence and native trees and watch the world through the TV screen. Hence, also, the unmistakable drawing power of certain middle-class symbols like business lunches, club membership, wine cellars, eating out, microwave ovens, freezers, dishwashers, two cars and holidays in Asia. These are not exclusively middle class, of course; as Redgum sang, 'I've been to Bali too'. Also, they are more typical of the upper-middle class than the lower-middle class, which often can't afford such things. But they are all part and parcel of a class lifestyle to which many Australians aspire and which exercises a significant influence over their ambitions, dreams and images of themselves. If a pollster knocks on the door and asks what class you belong to, answering 'working class' would seem for many people an admission of being less well-off than others, or even of failure. The middle class is where the affluence and action are.

That's Rich, Mr Hayden

It is always a delight to see a member of the rich upper class complain about middle class greed.

One of the finer examples occurred last week when Governor-General Bill Hayden used a speech to a stock exchange dinner to lambast the "strident demands" of the middle class "gimme generation".

Hayden has not done too badly himself in the "gimme" stakes over the years, spending his entire working life feeding from the public trough...

As Foreign Minister he made more than forty overseas trips. On the last trip he had only one official engagement in New York, yet ran up a hotel bill of just under $20 000 in seven days. The limo cost almost $5000 for four days, while a lunch for six cost Australian taxpayers $1335.

As Governor-General, Hayden enjoys what is almost a

> parody of an upper class lifestyle. Alternating between magnificent residences in Canberra and Sydney, he is surrounded by butlers, maids, aides-de-camp, chauffeurs, gardeners, chefs, secretaries and media minders.
>
> The bill for dining with friends and official visitors is estimated to be around $20 000 a month. He usually travels by VIP jet or stretched Mercedes limo...
>
> BRIAN TOOHEY,
Sun-Herald, 10 September 1995

Skilled workers, especially, can find it easy to switch over from working-class to middle-class identification. The switch is buttressed by the higher incomes they earn compared to semi-skilled and unskilled workers; they form, to use the common term, a 'labour aristocracy' which separates itself out from the rest of the working class somewhat by virtue of their skill and the clutch of characteristics which go with it: they are often self-employed (builders, plumbers, electricians, and other tradespeople), well-educated, protected by craft unions, and tend to come from a white Anglo or Irish background, which may stretch back some generations, rather than from the recent waves of European migration. Broom, Jones and Zubrzychi in one survey found that 'fully 39 per cent of craftsmen and foremen put themselves into the middle class' and commented: 'This figure is very much higher than those reported in recent American and British studies, and suggests that the absorption of skilled workers into the middle class may have proceeded more rapidly in Australia than in these other countries' (L. Broom, F. Lancaster Jones & J. Zubrzychi, 'Social Stratification in Australia' in J. A. Jackson's

Social Stratification, Cambridge, 1968.) This raises, again, the complex question of the 'embourgeoisement' of working-class people and the clear limits which exist to such a process; this has been discussed in detail in Chapter 3, 'Class Jumpers'.

Education

Middle-class parents like to give their children a good education. They see it, rightly, as a crucial way of getting on in society and educational qualifications as a way of climbing the class ladder. Surveys over the last two decades have shown that the pupils at government schools are disproportionately working class, though these schools also educate large numbers of middle-class students; private schools are heavily upper-class and upper-middle-class, and Catholic schools are somewhere in between. A survey of school leavers by Radford and Wilkes for the Australian Council for Educational Research (Western, 1983, p. 51) showed that pupils whose fathers had professional, managerial, clerical or sales occupations predominated in Catholic and private schools; the higher up the social scale you went the more likely the children were to go to a non-government school. This fits in, of course, with what we know from everyday experience, namely that a lot of middle-class parents save furiously and deny themselves things in order to be able to afford to send their children to fee-paying private schools.

Nevertheless, most parents simply can't afford such school fees and others have a strong and understandable aversion to the whole private school system, so the majority of middle-class children end up going to Catholic and government schools. A study of over 15 000 pupils in Melbourne schools whose parents had white-collar occupations showed that 21 per cent were in non-Catholic private schools, 15 per cent were in Catholic schools, and 64 per cent were in public schools (Western, 1983). These children often carry with them their parents' stress upon educational success with the result that middle-class children are more likely than working-class children to do well at school, stay on to the end of secondary schooling, and go on to tertiary education. A study carried out for the Commission of Enquiry into Poverty revealed that, of a sample group of eighteen-year-olds, over half of those with professional fathers had gained the Victorian higher school certificate, but only 16 per cent of those with fathers in semi-skilled or unskilled jobs had reached the same level.

Such extreme disparities have hardly anything to do with ability, though a longstanding class shibboleth is that working-class kids are 'dumber' than middle- and upper-class ones (it is, needless to say, a myth which is more common at the very top of the social scale, among those who have enjoyed the privileges of wealth, power, education and culture for generations, than among the working class itself); the disparities are in fact largely due to class background and the different educational and job expectations which kids from different classes have. Research has shown that teenagers from high-status backgrounds have higher educational and vocational aspirations and expectations than those from low-status backgrounds (Western, 1983, p. 54). Thus middle-class children are likely to aim for jobs with at least as high a social standing as their parents, if not higher, and if this means studying hard and getting the right qualifications many of them are prepared to do it. Working-class children don't generally face the same sort of pressure. So the social cleavage between blue-collar worker and white-collar worker which is such a feature of adult society is virtually perpetuated in the education system, with most working-class pupils aiming at working-class jobs and middle-class pupils aiming at middle-class jobs (see Chapter 9, 'Working Class'). In the words of Western (1983, p. 49): 'Australian education is class-bound. The school system one gets into, the length of time one stays at school, reactions to the school experience, aspirations for work or other activity on leaving school, and what the individual in fact does at the completion of schooling are all if not determined by class position, then very significantly influenced by it.'

Accent

You can pick the class of many Australians by their accent. Most middle-class people, for instance, speak in an accent which the phoneticians classify as General Australian; it is a fairly neutral accent to Australian ears, and the vowel sounds are not so broad or nasal as in Broad Australian, which is the typical working-class accent. To outsiders, it doesn't sound so blatantly Aussie. It is estimated General Australian is spoken by about 55 per cent of Australian men and women, which makes it by far the most commonly heard accent in the land and which is remarkably close to the proportion of people who identify themselves regularly in polls as middle class. It is the accent of the ordinary white-collar man in the street, the working woman in a middle-rank suburb, or something over half the children at school; phonetic surveys of school pupils show that a General Australian accent is spoken by about 55 per cent in state schools, 61 per cent in Catholic schools and 50 per cent in private schools.

Middle-class Fractions

The middle class is such a large and diverse group that attempts have been made to subdivide it in various ways. A typical division is between the upper-middle class, which can be described as those who are 'professional or managerial workers, or come from households in which the breadwinner is a professional or managerial worker', and the lower-middle class, a term which Western applies to those who 'engage in white-collar work which is, to an important extent, of a routine kind, and in which there is little job autonomy'. Encel (1970, pp. 106–7) identifies the two groups this way:

Upper-middle: professional men and women, managers and administrators (private and public), proprietors of medium-sized businesses and landholdings.

Lower-middle: the white-collar majority, small shopkeepers, teachers, small farmers, technicians and some skilled workers.

These are 'objective' assessments of class position, based upon occupation, and seem to fit fairly well with 'subjective' self-assessments of class as revealed by opinion polls. Thus in the 1983 Australian Values Study survey 25.5 per cent of people identified themselves as upper-middle class and 32 per cent as lower-middle class. One of the problems with such surveys, of course, is that most of them are 'fixed choice' polls in which the people being interviewed are given a fixed group of classes to choose between. If you change the question, you get different results. As an example, the 1976 Morgan Gallup poll added a straightforward category, 'middle class', between 'upper-middle' and 'lower-middle' and found that the biggest proportion of people put themselves in that group:

Upper-middle: 7.1 per cent
Middle-class: 48.8 per cent
Lower-middle: 11.5 per cent

This gives some force to the argument that a feature of the class system in Australia in the postwar period has been the fragmentation or fractionalising of class groups, a process by which people see themselves as belonging to subgroups or class fractions and retreat from a schema of class conflict between a ruling class and workers. The process of fragmentation is tied up with the emergence of strong subcultures and alternative movements which sometimes act as the most important means by which people identify themselves, and is also connected to the growing occupational and technological sophistication of the society at large; as jobs become more diverse and the differences between them become more marked – including the rewards, power and lifestyles which go with them – so people begin to recognise and take account of those differences. You'd have to be blind not to. There's all the difference in the (real) world between a QC earning $3000 a day in court, and getting a lot of newspaper publicity for it, and the girl at the computer who has to key in what the garrulous QC spouts. As Encel (1970, p. 103) writes:

> The growth of distinctions between the "upper-middle" and "lower-middle" classes has been a major feature of social changes since 1945. The growth of professional and managerial occupations is one reason; another and related factor is the expansion of higher education and the increased influence of education on social position. A distinctively upper-middle class style of politics has been emerging focused on "conscience" issues and taking its most active form in various protest movements and student agitation . . .

Individualism

The ethos, values and style of the middle class, because of its sheer size, have a powerful effect upon Australian life. In contemporary Australia the ethos of individualism, the hallmark of the middle class, has largely replaced the ethos of collectivism, the hallmark of the working class. The popularity of private schools which hold out the prospect of ascent up the educational and social ladder underlines this individualistic approach. My brother Adrian McGregor has argued, in an analysis of Greg Chappell and the notorious underarm bowling incident of years ago, that social changes have pushed Australians away from the 'fair go' idea which was once thought to be a dominant code in the community to a new competitive code of 'never give a sucker an even break'. It is a change from the ethos of mateship, fair shares for all, and sympathy for the underdog to middle-class concerns with success, material possessions, the rat-race, and win-at-any-cost. And it wasn't right, he argued, to expect only the cricketers to have to make a choice between these traditions. It was a choice which faced the whole society.

Of course, the middle class displays many sturdy virtues: commonsense, ambition, a clear sense of family, respect for education and culture, care for those close to you. These tend to be the virtues that middle-class Australians see in themselves, anyhow, and they may be right. There is a solid, if somewhat conservative, core of probity to the middle-class experience. The rise of middle-class radicalism in the sixties and seventies, and its subsequent incorporation into mainstream politics, is a heartening sign of future possibilities. The women's movement, the anti-Vietnam movement, the anti-nuclear movement, the sexual liberation movements, student activism, resident action, and the green/

conservation movement have been largely, though not entirely, middle-class movements; the green bans represented a significant alliance between working-class and middle-class groups. Attempts to repeat that alliance on other issues have not been so successful, but it can be argued that the hopes that Left theoreticians previously held out for the working class as agents of change have now to be transferred to the middle class or alliances based on it.

The way in which the major parties have directed their policies towards the middle ground and the middle-class vote – a phenomenon which has been described in detail in Chapter 4, 'Class and Politics' – confirms the importance of the middle class as a social group. It exerts considerable social and political power, not merely through the authority of its individual members (especially those in executive and managerial positions) but through its sheer size and electoral weight. Yet it rarely acts as a discrete, unified class; it splits every which way at elections; it lacks the sort of unifying political history described so powerfully by E. P. Thompson in *The Making of the English Working Class* (1966). And in the last decade it has been disrupted, dispersed and distressed by the enormous changes which have been taking place in the Australian economy and in the social relations of Australians. In the post-industrial, globalised world of the late 1990s, it is the lower-middle class and the working class which have borne the brunt of the transformations wrought by economic upheaval.

BONDI JUNCTION
Class Profile

Saturday morning they come pouring in through the doors of Eastgate shopping centre, Bondi Junction: T-shirts and thongs, spring prints and jeans, beginner tans and dance-club pallors, youngies and oldies, ockers and Asians, spray-perm trolley pushers and toyboy gay couples, knobbly knees and freckled elbows, thronging the walkways that lead to K Mart, Coles, Sussan, Just Jeans, Fruit World, Liquorland, Joe's Meat Market . . . Middle Australia.

By shortly after 9 a.m. the cars are queuing up outside Grace Bros, David Jones, the Plaza, Carousel, the council car parks under the expressway: Corollas, Magnas, Commodores, 4WDs, soft-tops, not many rustbuckets, a UBD on the back seat and an imitation chamois in the glovebox and a Triple M sticker on the rear window . . . Middle Australia.

They crowd in past the bloke selling Lions Club raffle tickets, the quadriplegic pencil-and-blue receipt girl, the community flea-market stall, and the salesgirl with the microphone saying, 'It's here, *unbelievable* bargains, have a squiz' . . . Middle Australia.

The Junction and the areas around it have always been my private symbol of Middle Oz. The absolute dead-spit no deviation centre, the middle of the middle. No extremes. No factories. A few offices. A lot of shops. Everything else is homes: flats, units, houses, duplexes, bungs. Suburban. In fact one of the most densely populated suburbs in the most suburban nation in the world. In the days when it was in the electorate of Phillip the district voted in every election from 1963 onwards the way the rest of the nation voted. Whoever won Phillip won government. Perhaps because it was just too much of a litmus test the seat was eventually abolished and split up between Wentworth, for whom the local member used to be John Hewson (it is now Andrew Thomson, another Liberal) and Kingsford Smith, which is represented by the former Labor Minister for Industrial Relations, Laurie Brereton. The seat may have disappeared, but not the people who made it such a classic swinger. True, the high-rises are going up – but so they are in the rest of Middle Australia. True, it is becoming noisier, zappier, trendier, edgier – like the rest of the country. And these days it is unsure whether its heart belongs to the lazy, Old Aussie, hedonistic culture of Bondi Beach or the new, materialist, angst-and-aggro culture of the Sydney metropolis; but that schizophrenia afflicts the entire nation.

In the early part of the century Bondi was basically working class, and the surf clubs the workers formed (the surf lifesaving movement began at Bondi and Bronte) were citadels of trad blue-collar masculinity. The first houses at Bondi were shacks behind the dunes. The fibro weekenders became brick permanent homes but the blokes who 'shot through like a Bondi tram' were workers and the local pubs still have a strong blue-collar clientele. But, just like the rest of Australia, many of these beachside suburbs have now climbed into the middle class. The workers' collars have turned white. As people have realised how precious it is to be close to the beach *and* the city, street after street has become 'highly desirable' – on weekend nights Campbell Parade is crammed with boulevardiers sampling the cafes, restaurants, coffee shops and late-night boutiques. Jamie Packer, Kerry Packer's son, has developed a streetcorner block so he can live there; film and theatre people have moved in. It's like Kings Cross before it turned tawdry.

Being so close to the CBD, drenched by the national media, populated by people who travel somewhere else to work, or travel there just to shop, the Junction district is seen by some as somewhat unfocussed. It's like a rainbow-cake slice of Oz: lots of layers, flavours, colours and character, but no core. Thus the paradox: at the centre, no real centre. Patrick White's 'empty heart'. You travel laboriously to the omphalos of Australia's social culture and what you find there is – space. But even this is symbolic. In this post-industrial, postmodern era 'the centre', if there ever was such a thing, has clearly fractured, subdivided, split open. Middle Australia, as I have argued, has become hundreds of Middle Australias.

Thus the famous social mix which characterises the Junction and its environs. There's a heavy Jewish presence; on Saturdays you often see Jewish families strolling along the street to their local synagogues. Suits, hats, yarmulkas. The Hakoah Club is a landmark. There are a lot of Irish, gathered around places like the Waverley Rugby Club. And Greeks. Plus

Spaniards, Hungarians, Cypriots, Czechs, Asians – you descend to the cavernous subworld of the Eastern Suburbs railway and the escalator is as cosmopolitan as one in London. At a popular coffee shop/restaurant/disco, the bouncers are Maori, the waitresses are Irish and English, the dance-floor boogiers are multicultural, and the music is standard charts Oz. It's all smart Saturday Night ethnic crossover, the girls in tight skirts and with dark Lebanese eyes, the men in high-class rackstore gear and sneakers. There is a large population of transients: New Zealanders (including a lot of Maoris), students at the University of NSW, British backpackers who cram into low-rent flats, Japanese tourists at the beach. The place is full of rented units, semi-detacheds, three-storey walkups.

The local council used to be dominated by the Uglies, the ultra-Right Liberal faction; these days it has a woman mayor, Barbara Armitage, and a Labor majority which explains its success by its commitment to grass-roots issues and the way it hooks into resident action and environmental movements.

In the midst of comparative affluence, a complex and unstable consciousness. Lots of pensioners and single parents. Homeless kids. Street threats outside Timezone in the Mall. Rotary and Lions, bikies and parking police, salespeople and surfies. Real estate prices have gone up, so have the unemployment figures. Back from the beach, some of the densest and ugliest concrete-and-red-tile suburbs in the nation. Hardly any parks or open space; the houses push right down to the promenade edge, turning nature into domestica. If this is the heartland, there's a lot of problems to work out.

8
Crisis in the Heartland

For most of the second half of this century the middle class has been stable, prosperous, secure; this was Menzies's constituency, this was the group which voted for safety and Malcolm Fraser after the turbulence of the Whitlam years, and which took a risk with Bob Hawke because he preached consensus, reconciliation and the politics of charisma. In 1996 it turned to John Howard, the quintessential suburbanite, in yet another lunge for safety. But in the last decade the middle class has found itself under fire: in a time of economic and social turmoil, in which Australian society has suffered the impact of globalisation and profound economic restructuring, the middle class has come under enormous disruptive pressure. It has become stretched, broken up, subdivided, the victim of falling incomes and falling expectations, worried about jobs, homes and kids, and many of its members don't hold out much hope for things getting better in the future. Sociologists have latterly drawn a parallel between what is happening in Australia and contemporary America, where, it is argued, the middle class has become dispersed, dispirited and disillusioned. Unemployment, de-skilling, lower living standards, a ruthless new managerial style, high stress and uncertainty are likely to afflict most

Australians as the twentieth century draws to a close. Once middle Australia used to be comfortable, optimistic, reasonably affluent and sure of its values. Not any longer. Welcome to the Brave New World of post-industrial capitalism.

We live in a time when some of the most cherished Australian dreams – a home of your own, a fair and reasonably equal society, a leisurely life – are clearly under attack. They haven't disappeared entirely. To take one crucial middle Australia ideal: home ownership is as high today (just over 67 per cent of people own their own home or are paying it off) as it ever was, and the Real Estate Institute maintains that its complex index of house prices/interest rates/average incomes shows that in the mid-1990s houses were more affordable than at any time for the previous eight years. Most of the new suburbs being built on the outskirts of the capital cities are middle class; state housing aimed at working-class tenants has been ruthlessly cut back in recent years. Proliferating housing developments, urban consolidation and long-suffering parents are helping cater for the new young middle class. But to own a home of their own this new generation has to be willing to move to the barren outer suburbs of Australia's capital cities, get two jobs, spend up to half their income on the mortgage, put off having kids or limit them to one or two, and try to make sure they don't become victims of job-shedding, downsizing, lopped incomes or the other buzz-modes of the corporate sector. They can often expect to be retrenched at fifty and have to rely on their super for their old age. Their own kids may face an even harsher, more competitive future.

The damage done to the middle class is such that some commentators, such as Hugh Mackay, the social researcher, have concluded that the middle class is shrinking. In his book *Reinventing Australia* (1993) Mackay reports that census data and estimates by IBIS Business Information Ltd show that between 1976 and 1992 the proportion of Australian households with an income of more than $72 000 (based on constant 1991–92 values) rose from 15 per cent to 30 per cent, and the proportion with an income less than $22 000 rose from 20 per cent to 30 per cent. By 1992 the top 30 per cent of households controlled 55 per cent of household income while the bottom 30 per cent controlled only 10 per cent. Comments Mackay: 'Obviously, the group in the middle has been shrinking. If we define the economic middle class being households with incomes between $22 000 and $72 000 in 1991–92 terms, then the middle class has shrunk from 65 per cent of households in 1976 to 40 per cent of households in 1992, and it controls about 35 per cent of household income ... In the early nineties, the growth of upper-income households levelled out, although the growth of lower-income households continued apace.'

Mackay's material is significant, but it doesn't at all mean that the middle class is shrinking. For a start, income by itself does not define class membership. As I have argued throughout this book, class tends to be determined by a cluster of factors; income is certainly one of these, but it is not necessarily the most important determinant. It is entirely possible to suffer what you hope is a temporary drop in income and still regard yourself as firmly middle class. Indeed, a typical strategy for middle-class households is to try to supplement the usual family income by doing extra work, through overtime, part-time work, or typically by both partners going out to work. Julian Disney, former director of the Australian Council of Social Service (ACOSS) and now Professor of Public Law at the Australian National University, says that a big change in recent years has been the growth of two-income families. During the eighties decade more than a third of employment growth went to households which already had one person working. Families with two or more members working increased by over half a million, or 30 per cent, from 1983 to 1989 (Peter Saunders, Social

Policy Research Centre at University of NSW). These strategies significantly buttress middle-class incomes and middle-class identification.

Furthermore, the changes which are occurring in the Australian work structure are leading to an *expansion* of white-collar, middle-class jobs and a *shrinking* of blue-collar, working-class jobs. The growth of tertiary and quaternary industries which is typical of post-industrial nations such as Australia is accompanied by an expansion of service industry jobs, which are typically regarded as middle class, and a fall in jobs for factory hands and unskilled workers. Thus the 1991 census revealed that between 1986 and 1991 there was a strong growth in jobs for professional, managerial, sales and other service workers; managers and administrators rose by 99 000 to 861 000, professionals rose by 121 000 to 890 000 and sales and service workers recorded the biggest increase of all, by 175 000 and 983 000. Employment for labourers, however, fell by 57 000 to 879 000 and jobs for plant and machine operators fell by 34 000 to 501 000. The biggest occupational group remained clerical workers, at 1.07 million, and sales and service workers at 983 000. Denis Farrell, the NSW Deputy Commonwealth Statistician, has pointed out that the main growth areas have been community services; financial, property and business services; recreational and personal services; and wholesale and retail trade. The sectors that have declined include manufacturing, agriculture, transport, electrical, gas and water, and mining. There has been a clear shift from traditional primary and secondary industries, which tend to be the stronghold of blue-collar workers, to tertiary industries, where white-collar workers predominate.

In occupational terms, therefore, the middle class is not shrinking, it is continuing to expand. And working-class occupations are continuing to fall. This is exactly what you would expect of a nation at Australia's stage of development. As computers, robots and hi-tech systems take over more and more manual work, and the service industries continue to explode, middle-class occupations are likely to increase still further. The phenomena of 'de-skilling' and 'multiskilling', which tend to reduce the power of the people who in the past could use their special skills to improve or support their position, are a real threat to many service industry workers; but this is not necessarily accompanied by a change in class position or a change in class self-identification. Class has enormous holding power; even if, despite the strategies outlined earlier, the family income falls, people tend to stay locked into their class position. They continue to strive for middle-class jobs, live in middle-class suburbs (the western suburbs of Brisbane, the eastern suburbs of Melbourne, the south-eastern suburbs of Sydney), drive middle-class cars, send their children to middle-class schools, and have classic middle-class aspirations (including a nice mortgage to keep you warm in winter). Above all, they still see themselves as middle class. As noted before, the recent Comparative Project on Class Structure and Class Consciousness carried out by Baxter, Emmison and Western (1991) does not indicate any shrinkage of the self-identifying middle-class group.

Nevertheless, important changes are occurring in middle Australia. Nothing seems too certain any more. For the first time middle-class Australians are being hit by the same maladies and problems which once, they assumed, afflicted only the working class: unemployment, lower living standards, fear of the sack, a week-by-week struggle to make ends meet. Losing your job is a catastrophe; once it wasn't a familiar experience for middle Australia, but now more and more middle-class people find themselves being retrenched, sacked, made to take early retirement, or forced to work under the constant threat of unemployment. Dr Bob Gregory, Professor of Economics at the ANU and a former member of the Reserve Bank board, estimated in his 1994 Copland Oration that 118 000 middle-level male full-time jobs disappeared between 1976 and 1990, which is the equivalent of a loss of 400 000 jobs if the population growth is taken into account. 'Australia is losing middle-level jobs at an astounding rate and they are being replaced primarily by jobs with weekly earnings at the bottom of the earnings distribution,' he said. 'There is no evidence that the economy has been generating demands for an increasing proportion of the population to be well-educated and available for middle-pay jobs. There must be disappointed expectations as those seeking further education are denied rewards they might have expected a generation earlier.'

Dr Gregory agrees, however, that the phenomenon he has identified does not mean that the middle class is shrinking; instead, it could be growing. His findings are confined to males, to full-time jobs, and to middle-level management only. The losses here are offset by the spectacular growth in working women and part-time jobs and the increase in jobs elsewhere in the labour force. The 'feminisation' of the workforce has been going on for some time but is now at an all-time high. So is part-time work. Between 1983 and 1991 the total number of jobs increased by over 1.5 million, but part-time jobs grew by 50 per cent compared with 20 per cent for full-time jobs. Three-quarters of the new part-time jobs went to women. The enormous growth in double-income households is largely due to women going to work.

In middle Australia, there are other survival tactics as well. The kids take part-time jobs and start paying rent to their parents. Then come budget-cutting, garage sales, trading down the family car, scanning the local suburban paper for casual work. Hence also the recent phenomenon of children staying longer at home with their parents, because that way they can be buffered against high rents and low job opportunities. Middle-class parents are having to get used to the fact that their kids may not get the same sort of jobs they have, even if their children have university degrees; graduates find themselves working as kitchen hands and sales staff and in the hospitality industry instead of in professional and management jobs. 'You get a better class of taxi-driver', says one academic. Says Dr Gregory: 'Australia has quite clearly moved into a situation where real average wages have not significantly grown for fifteen years (and) part-time employment at low weekly earnings is being substituted for full-time work.'

As the pain level grows, middle Australia holds onto its precious icons of safety – especially the home. 'Middle-class people are very good at keeping up appearances,' says a Sydney sociologist. 'But you open the front door of some houses and there's nothing inside. Virtually nothing.' Charity workers confirm that middle-level Australians will sell their furniture, their car and even their household appliances before they will give up their home. It's understandable. A house gives you security in an insecure world. It keeps you from the ugly mercy of landlords. It gives you a chance of beating The System, sort of. And it helps people keep their identity as middle class. Sometimes it's all they have left.

Yuppies and Dumpies

You don't hear much about yuppies (young upwardly mobile professionals) these days; it's almost as though they were an eighties phenomenon. But yuppies are alive and well still, though often masquerading under different names and not as evident as in the years of conspicuous consumption. Ron Horvath, the Sydney University geographer, estimates in his *Sydney – A Social Atlas* (1989) that there were just under 200 000 yuppies in Sydney in 1986, defining them as managers, professionals and para-professionals aged between twenty and thirty-four. By analysing census data Horvath concluded that yuppies were primarily single, had comparatively high incomes, and concentrated in inner-city areas. In Sydney they are to be found, statistically, in Glebe, Neutral Bay and Cremorne more than anywhere else; in Melbourne, suburbs such as South Melbourne are yuppie haunts. Assuming a similar number of yuppies in Melbourne as in Sydney, and fewer in the other cities, there must be some half a million yuppies in the nation today.

Yuppies have a much higher media profile than Dumpies (Downwardly Mobile Urban Professionals) whose numbers can be expected to increase as middle Australia continues to shed male middle-level management jobs. Class mobility in Australia is always assumed to be upwards; what the 1990s is making clearer is that there may be just as much or even more downwards mobility. Even if you don't plummet into the working class or the underclass you can find yourself right on the borderline. It's like snakes and ladders. Middle Oz is accustomed to the long slog up the class ladder; it isn't used to the swift slide down the status snake.

Stress Fractures

What's happening to middle Australia is not that it is shrinking, it is being pulled apart. Fractures are appearing in what used to be thought of as a homogeneous middle mass. It is being subdivided, dispersed, fractionalised. Sociologists have long been aware that the middle class can easily be divided into upper-middle, middle-middle and lower-middle; now middle Australians themselves are becoming aware of it and the deep divisions which exist. It's a long way from being a lower-middle-class insurance clerk or shop assistant to an upper-middle-class finance manager on three times the salary, and enjoying a different sort of house, different suburb, different car, different lifestyle.

The poles of Australian society are getting further and further apart. Phil Raskall, who has been working intensively on the Inequality Study at the University of NSW, has concluded that the gap between the rich and the poor is widening dramatically. We are becoming more and more like contemporary America: ugly extremes of wealth at one end of the scale, unbearable extremes of poverty at the other. On the Gini scale, a highly technical measurement of inequality, Australia has climbed to a coefficient of .680, which represents 'a very dramatic increase in inequality'. In his paper 'Widening Income Disparities in Australia' Raskall points out that in the fifteen years to 1991 inequality among all waged employees increased by over 25 per cent on the Gini scale. The income share of the bottom 20 per cent of all full-time and part-time employees fell from 8.2 per cent to 5.9 per cent, whereas the share of the top 20 per cent increased from 34.2 per cent to 37.3 per cent. An analysis by Lombard (1991) of tax statistics from 1982–83 to 1988–89 revealed a dramatic increase in income inequality. Writes Raskall (in Rees, 1993):

> When we extend the measure of inequality beyond wages to incorporate all forms of personal income, a similar trend emerges... When we expand the income concept to social institutions of cohabitation – families, income units and households... consistently since 1975 inequality has increased, with the lowest income families receiving progressively less and the highest income (families) increasing their shares dramatically over the 1980s.

Similarly, a paper by Dr Peter Saunders, head of the Social Policy Research Centre at the University of NSW, on 'Poverty, Inequality and Recession', found that the gap between the bottom half and the top half of Australian families had widened during the recession and had intensified a trend of worsening income inequality which emerged during the 1980s. The income share of the top 20 per cent of households had risen from 44 per cent to 47 per cent between 1981–82 and 1989–90, and the top 10 per cent had jumped from 25.7 per cent to 28.1 per cent (*Sydney Morning Herald*, 10 November 1992). In an analysis of ABS (Australian Bureau of Statistics) figures Dr Saunders found that in 1981–82 the total income of all families, or income units, was $102.5 billion, of which $4.75 billion went to the bottom 20 per cent whereas the top 20 per cent received $45.2 billion, or 9.5 times as much. By 1989–90 the disproportion between bottom and top shares had grown even greater: total family income had reached $228 billion, the share of the bottom 20 per cent was $9.8 billion, while the top 20 per cent received $106.9 billion, or eleven times as much.

There has also been growing inequality in the distribution of wealth, which includes shares, investments and houses. A separate study by Raskall found that between 1985 and 1990 the bottom half of Australian families saw their already meagre share of the nation's wealth fall from 10 per cent to under 5 per cent. But in terms of income it is middle Australia which has suffered the most; while the rich have prospered dramatically, partly because of the eighties stock market boom and the introduction of dividend imputation, and the bottom 20 per cent at least had their pensions and benefits increased by the federal Labor government, the people in the middle three deciles (tenths of the population) had their incomes cut substantially. Says Raskall: 'Middle Australia . . . let's say the families on middle incomes, with regular jobs, possibly two incomes, the man in middle supervisory positions or their equivalent . . . they lost out.'

It is worth examining some of the reasons for this growth in inequality. The extravagant years of the 1980s expanded the wealth of many Australians at the top of the income/wealth scale, some dramatically so (see Chapter 11, 'Upper Class'), especially through the long period of the share market boom. This is popularly remembered through the inglorious personal careers of Alan Bond, Christopher Skase, Laurie Connell, Robert Holmes à Court and other entrepreneurs, but the more important development was the shift in income and wealth shares towards the top of the class scale. At the other end growing unemployment, high interest rates and the overall lowering of wages (in real terms) which occurred during the years of the Hawke government certainly depressed the incomes of many working-class and lower-middle-class households; there is nothing like being out of work to push you and your family down to the poverty line, or under it, and by early 1993 over a million Australians were out of work. This was the formal unemployment figure, but it was estimated that 'hidden' unemployment – including people who had given up looking for a job, or had failed to register as unemployed, or who would have taken up work had it been offered to them – accounted for another half-million people. By 1996 unemployment had fallen from over 11 per cent of the workforce to 8.8 per cent, but over three-quarters of a million people were out of work. Youth unemployment was nearing 30 per cent, and John Howard made a promise to reduce it a key part of his victorious election campaign.

Australia's First Billionaires

In 1987 Australia achieved a somewhat dubious "first": it achieved its first billionaires. These were men whose personal fortune exceeded one thousand million dollars each. They were Kerry Packer, whose wealth was estimated at

1.3 billion dollars; and Robert Holmes à Court, at 1.4 billion dollars. According to *Business Review Weekly*, their combined wealth, if converted to dollar coins, would have filled a dozen Mallee wheat silos. Each billionaire's wealth had increased twelvefold in the previous four years. In 1987 Holmes à Court increased his personal wealth by $3205 a minute.

In the introduction to its Rich 200 list for that year, *Business Review Weekly* wrote:

"It was the age of the entrepreneur, just as surely as 1847 was the age of the squatter... You could say many of the new men were essentially traders, buying other people's assets rather than creating new ones. That was often true. But the newcomers were also creating their own aggregations of substance. Look, for instance, at the 'substance' of the Bond (private fortune $400 million) and the Christopher Skase ($40 million) aggregations after this year's acquisitions. Yet, not so long ago another Establishment saw these two as upstarts."

The names – Bond, Skase, Holmes à Court – are interesting, as are others on the Rich 200 list for that year: Laurie Connell ($80 million), Larry Adler ($300 million), George Herscu ($500 million), Bruce Judge ($250 million), Leslie Thiess ($110 million)... A few years later Holmes à Court was dead, Bond was in jail, Skase was lurking in Majorca to escape extradition to Australia to face charges, Herscu was in jail, Thiess had been found guilty of bribery, Connell was in court on serious charges of wrongdoing, and the Adler and Judge empires had fallen to the ground.

Business Review Weekly continued: "Our first billionaires come in a year so sweet for fortune-building it would have made Croesus blush... The Rich 200 carries the messages spelled out by the new men. An old financial order is being supplanted. The Anglo-Saxon ascendancy, with its roots in places like Victoria's Western District, is dying. So are concepts like the Protestant work ethic – the bit about hard work, the long haul and self-denial. The new entrepreneur does not really believe in it . . . but, if it is for sale and badly managed, he may buy it. And we can say the boast of Australia being an egalitarian society is justified. A majority of those on the Rich 200 are self-made. Many are migrants, mostly from central Europe . . ."

This was shortly before the stockmarket crash of October 1987. Most of the millionaires in the Rich 200 survived it. But as for "egalitarian society": it means, of course, a society where everyone is equal, not one (like Australia in 1987 and now) where there is opportunity for people like Bond, Packer, Skase, Connell and so on to make huge fortunes at the expense of others and dramatically intensify the *inequality* of the society they exploit.

Though no doubt it was comforting to know, as *BRW* put it, that "much of the wealth of this list has come from opportunism and daring, from financial alchemy, from asset switching and trading . . . for the millions not on the list, this is the consolation: it is still possible."

The overall consequences are unmistakable: heightened inequality, a growing recognition that the society is becoming more and more unfair, and a palpable sense of the stretching of the class structure between two extremes which are growing further and further apart. This explosive pressure, the separating out of groups from each other and the growing distance between the extremes at either end, has produced severe splits in the middle group or 'middle mass', as well as making it more obvious that there are very significant social strata which don't fit into the middle group at all; behind the apparent 'middleness' of Australian society a quite complicated process of differentiation and separating-out is going on. Hugh Mackay (1993), to his credit, recognises this; he comments:

> As Australia moves through the 1990s, that almost universal expectation of comfortable prosperity is breaking down into sharply contrasting alternative expectations. At the top end, prosperity is greater than could have been imagined twenty years ago; at the bottom end, the prospect of poverty is descending like a chill on those Australians who are living through the long night of unemployment . . . Increasingly, it is necessary to acknowledge that there are many different "ways of life" and that the increasingly unequal distribution of household income in Australia is opening up big cracks in the rosy picture of a comfortable, middle-class society.

The large middle group clustered around the national median income of $30 000 to $35 000 a year isn't the most vulnerable group in the nation: that unenviable distinction belongs to those without jobs and on welfare, followed by the working poor. But it *feels* vulnerable. And rightly so. As well as suffering falling incomes, these people have been forced to confront the increase in inequality between themselves and those at the very top of the class scale, and of the growing inequality *within* their own class. It has become much more obvious to individuals whether they are languishing down at the bottom of the old middle group (lower-middle class), or still managing to hold to the centre (middle-middle class), or reaping some of the benefits of the growing polarisation of privilege, income and power (upper-middle class). This last group is so clearly identifiable that some sociologists have argued for the construction of a separate professional/managerial class to account for it (See Chapter 2, 'What Makes Class?', and Mark C. and John S. Western, in Najman & Western, 1988). Whether this is theoretically justifiable or not, and there are serious objections to the construction of yet another 'New Class' on such grounds, it underlines the way splits and fissures have opened in what used to be regarded as the old 'middle mass'. The middle class is not shrinking, it is being strained and stretched. It is on the rack.

In the Heartland

Despite this stress and divisiveness, not everything at the centre is gloomy. Middle-class Australia shows surprising resilience; it's as though there is some solid core to middle-class life which can withstand a high degree of strain and social pressure. Research shows that the nuclear family, despite the criticism of it and the growth of alternative family modes, is still the most common household type among middle Australians. There has been an increase in single-parent households and group households (often young people living together), but there has been an equally significant increase in families with adult family members (the grown-kids-still-living-at-home syndrome). It's as though the extended family is beginning to re-create itself. Middle Australians, like the rest of society, are better educated than they used to be; most university students come from middle-class or upper-class families ('the preferred postcode set', as one University of Technology, Sydney lecturer calls them). They still average two children per family, despite the overall fall in the birthrate. They shift house about every seven years, and shift husbands (or wives) not quite so often. They are typically equipped with a car, a TV, a video, a fridge, a washing machine, a bank account, credit cards, membership of a club, and some disposable income which is spent on shopping for clothes, the house, alcohol, entertainment, gifts and holidays.

Roy Morgan Research Centre, in Melbourne, has constructed a fascinating profile of the middle quintiles (fifths) of the Australian population, using the advertising codes of AB for the top socio-economic segment, FG for the bottom, and C, D and E for the middle three. The results, briefly: 75 per cent of middle Australians have a credit card; 41 per cent have a loan; 88 per cent live in a freestanding house; 57 per cent are married, 28 per cent single, the rest separated, divorced, in de facto relationships and so on; 36 per cent intend to buy a car in the next four years, but most of them are going to buy a secondhand one; 41 per cent work full time, 15 per cent work part time and 13 per cent are 'home duties'. In the four weeks to the 1995 Morgan survey 67 per cent had been to a fast food place. In the previous year 73 per cent had worked in the garden, 60 per cent had redecorated or refurbished the home in some way, 60 per cent had been to a licensed restaurant, 34 per cent had been to a club with the pokies, about the same had worked on their car or motorbike and 21 per cent had been to an art gallery or museum. A quarter had gone on holidays interstate, and 7 per cent had holidayed overseas. About half had incomes in the $20 000 to $35 000 a year range (this refers to the main breadwinner); household incomes were significantly higher.

Morgan Research, in conjunction with Colin Benjamin of the Horizon Network, has also developed ten 'value segments' to characterise the life attitudes of the people they survey. Among middle Australians, only 7 per cent think they get 'a raw deal out of life'; 17 per cent are young people seeking 'an exciting, prosperous life'; 12 per cent fall into the category of 'people who are well-educated, confident, ambitious, and tend to be in secure full-time employment'; only 7 per cent are in the 'real conservatism' segment. The biggest group by far, 32 per cent, are in the straight/traditional categories of people 'whose values are centred around the events in their personal and family lives'.

It's almost what you'd expect: middle level, middlebrow, middle style.

Yet middle Australians are not quite as conservative as commentators and politicians would have us believe. Survey material over the years has shown that they consistently support human rights, equality for women, abortion, and Aboriginal land rights. When it comes to politics just about as many vote Labor as vote Liberal. The Comparative Project on Class Structure and Class Consciousness (Baxter, Emmison & Western, 1991), in which people were asked how they would vote if there were a House of Representatives election, found that a clear majority of workers voted Labor and a clear majority of employers and self-employed voted Liberal/National Party. But the middle groups split both ways: 'lower service' workers were pretty evenly balanced, 'routine non-manual' and 'personal service' workers had slight majorities for Labor. In some ways the Australian middle class may even be a pointer to the way the rest of the world is going to go: suburban, materialist, stressed out, insular, a shopping trolley chained to both hands. Also sensible, home-centred, leisure-loving. Also good with kids. It suffers vicissitudes, problems, panics, severe emotional and ethical problems; sometimes it's hard to find a parking spot in Myer. It provides the nation with most of its politicians, administrators, artists, brides, corner shops and of course its dominant social ethos. Its ideals and ambitions, if not its standard of living, remain intact.

In some areas of their lives therefore, middle Australia seems to be coping. However, Michael Pusey, Professor of Sociology at the

University of NSW and author of *Economic Rationalism in Canberra* (1991), worries whether middle Australians can go on coping indefinitely or whether they are using up a slack which must eventually be exhausted – like the people themselves. 'It means gobbling up more and more of your leisure time, spending more and more of your income on your house, making people work under more and more stress ... all this in a context where people no longer have churches or the family to fall back on, where the public culture has been degraded ... it's asking for trouble,' he says.

> You've got a situation where people are working under constant supervision, less autonomy, with aggressive management, no tenure, increased stress ... plus the trauma of socially devalued education, so you get kids who are graduates moving into the hospitality industry or selling life insurance, or taking up do-it-or-the-boss-will-shoot-you jobs. How do you put the genie back in the bottle? You obviously can't. I think economic rationalism has done irreparable damage to our social relations. The idea that you can drive a nation on an economic philosophy, and there's no need to think of the social outcomes, is madness.

Others are not so pessimistic. Phil Raskall believes that despite 'the real feeling of uncertainty' among middle Australians, their fear of losing their jobs, there has been a significant shift of opinion against the extremes of the eighties and its emblematic heroes (yuppies/Skase/Bond/Connell) and a move towards more traditional social values. More and more women are finding work. Australia has not suffered the nineties American backlash against abortion. The minorities, tribes and subcultures of the fragmenting middle offer escape from the Great Australian Blight of conformity. To many young Australians the mainstream is a one-way street to job loss, freedom loss, self-loss: dead end. For others, the middle ground still offers stability and (hopefully) security. Politically the signals are mixed. At the 1993 election Middle Australia was given the opportunity by John Hewson of following Middle America and Middle England down the Thatcher/Reagan path of economic rationalism and social cleavage: it didn't. In the 1996 election, however, John Howard offered much the same direction, albeit disguised – and won. No matter who is in power in Canberra, however, Middle Australia faces a new order: continuing high unemployment, downsizing, redundancies, retraining programs, heavy competition for jobs, restructuring, labour market deregulation, a ruthless new managerial style. The New Brutalism.

Will the middle hold?

The Nuclear Family
Class Profile

In some ways they seem to be classic middle Australians. Husband and wife, middle income, middle class, upwardly mobile, own their home, three blond kids under eight years old, and the typical list of possessions: station wagon, fridge, dryer, washing machine, dishwasher, TV, video, stereo, two credit cards. They're ambitious for themselves and their children, work hard, spend half their income on the mortgage on a second house, go skiing and regard themselves as 'comfortable'. Says the wife, Gail: 'There's people better off, there's people worse off. I don't envy others. Most of my friends are like us – they're leading good lives. Hard-working, but good.'

They're very conscious of their class position. Politically, for instance, Gail (not her real name) takes a very class-conscious view. 'I think we're being sucked dry,' she says adamantly. 'The poorer people get it too easy. The tax system is totally unfair . . . if we were on the dole we'd be just as well off! It's a very socialist society – we're not supposed to be, but we appear to be. The government is propping up the poor; how are they going to get off their handout situation if they're given too much?' Socialist? An Australian government? Hardly; but Gail is typical of many middle-class people who argue that the taxes they pay go to help people who don't work as hard as they do. As voters she and her husband have, she says, a 'green tinge'; most of the locals, she believes, vote Independent or vote Labor. 'If the Liberals want our vote, they have to start looking after middle-class Australia. How? Reduce taxes!'

In other ways, however, the family doesn't conform to any familiar middle Australia stereotype; if anything they chart the change from suburban WASP to inner-city ethnic, from two-car to two-house, from blue-rinse Liberal to green-rinse Labor, from one-dimensional nuclear to multidimensional cultural crossover. The husband, who works as a senior technical officer, is the son of middle European migrant workers. His wife comes from a working-class Sydney suburb: 'the hardworking poor, my parents were never homeowners.' They live in a dilapidated terrace house in in an inner-city area which is being rapidly gentrified, after an initial spell in a three-bedroom, brick-veneer bungalow in exurbia: 'very suburban, very boring, a typical dream home, backs onto the park; it's lovely, just don't want to live there,' says Gail. Goodbye classic Oz suburbia. They bought the house, nevertheless, and now rent it out. Many of the neighbours where they now live – the homeowners, at least – send their kids to school in a trendy nearby suburb, 'because of the snobbery, they don't want them mixing with the "inferior" kids from the Housing Commission estates'. Gail, however, doesn't believe in that sort of class distinction. They deliberately send their daughter to the local state school, which is '50 per cent Chinese, 10 per cent Bangladeshi, plus Greeks, Turks, Yugoslavs, a few Australians, a few black children, Fijian Islanders, we're European Australians – I think it's great to have that mix'.

A lot of wives in the neighbourhood go out to work to help pay the bills. Part time. One works two days a week as a secretary. Another works at home as a book editor. Another is going to university to re-educate herself. Gail herself left school at fifteen because her parents didn't believe in higher education, 'girls were just supposed to get married and have kids', but later she went back to studying, did her HSC and graduated in the public service from secretary to clerk. She met her husband on a blind date. She's an activist, spends time at the pre-school, was secretary of the local neighbourhood centre. They have hardly any money to spend after the mortgage repayments on their second house (it's an investment) and live a day-to-day life of what most people would consider near penury. When they pay off the second house, their standard of living may go up. Or they may try to set themselves up in a small business. Gail describes her husband as 'very capitalistic'. Or they may invest in another house.

Indeed, at the centre of their lives, and many of their peers, is the effort to own their own homes. The key distinction seems to be not between haves and have-nots, but homeowners and non-homeowners. 'This is such a mixed area because housing prices are so different,' says Gail. 'Owning a house is crucial. A lot of my friends are homeowners, and those that aren't want to be. We're all aware of everyone else's position. Everyone tries to portray a certain standard of living. The renters tend to be working class. Blue-collar jobs, Housing Commission. Whereas with people like us it's common to buy a terrace house, do it up, and sell. One I know has moved to Epping, another to Kiama, another to the Blue Mountains. They're making a killing on their real estate.'

To do this, middle Australians are prepared to make enormous sacrifices. The family wears hand-me-downs, cast-offs, gifts from friends. Their furniture is secondhand and battered. They don't drink or smoke, hardly ever go out, watch TV instead. They budget extremely 'close to the bone'. Gail avoids packaged food, expensive items like fruit yoghurt, makes her own muesli, virtually never shops for herself. The wagon is an '83 Sigma which fortunately never breaks down. The stereo and video don't work. They can't afford a CD player, are wary of microwave ovens. The cot, high chair and bassinet were given to them. The living room walls are half scraped back. 'We're doing it up – you wouldn't believe it, but we are!' The feeling is one of poverty, as though the house is still as it was when the area was a working-class slum.

But they own it.

The family operates on a monthly budget; in the month that there happen to be three pay days they are able to save enough for a holiday. Like, take the kids to Seaworld and Warners Movie World at Surfers Paradise. Lurking over much of their network of friends is the fear of unemployment. Some are scared to take any of the leave that is due to them in case they're found to be dispensable. The pressure is increasing, the workload is heavier, they work longer and longer hours – but don't get paid for it. No overtime. The corporations and institutions they work for have cost-cutting targets. The family knows one man with two children who got sacked, another who was made redundant after thirty years; 'How can they do it?' Gail talks sympathetically about an ESL (English-as-a-Second Language) teacher who starts work at 7 a.m., finishes at 6 p.m., is forced to take on extra programs, spends his spare time looking through magazines for other job ideas. Men 'worry about it all the time; nothing would be worse than being fifty and out of a job'.

Why do they live as they do? Her answer is beautifully symbolic. 'To provide for our old age,' she says. 'And to provide for our children. We're ambitious to increase our equity, so if we ever do retire we'll be comfortable. The plan is: suffer quickly . . .' She gives a wry smile. 'We enjoy our lives,' she says. 'I can't understand why people aren't more ambitious, if they were they wouldn't be where they are. Australia's a strange society.'

9
Working Class

Up on the north coast of NSW is a youngish bloke, a short story writer, who works as a labourer. A brickie's labourer. He's worked as that all his life – when there's work around. When there isn't he and his wife and kid try to exist on the dole. His wife works shift work at the local hospital as a nurses' aid. They live in an old weatherboard house in the flood-prone river bank area of Lismore. Lloyd grew up around there; his father was a worker; all his mates are labourers or brickies or tradesmen or work with their hands one way or another. They drink in the local after work each day, go home to their wives and kids, bet on the horses at the TAB and go to the local races, barrack for Aussie on the TV, spend weekends at the footie or the Workers Club or, sometimes, pighunting with high-velocity rifles and pig dogs. The women don't go on the pig hunts, but they go to the club to drink beer and play the pokies and keep their men company.

Lloyd's proud of his background and the people he spends his time with, their no-bullshit approach, their arrogance towards the boss, the fact they do an honest day's hard work and don't complain about it even when they're working on some doctor's two-storey colonial-brick ABBA-style (All Bloody Balustrades and

Arches) mansion whose wife's a shit and only worries about the tradesmen walking builder's sand onto the slate tiles in the kitchen. He writes about them brilliantly, with affection; yet he's also aware of the limitations of the life and wants to write his way out of it. He doesn't want to be a brickie's labourer for the rest of his life... getting old, unable to take the physical stress (he's strong, and when he's had to he's thrown a wheelbarrow of cement up onto the next floor), getting pushed around by the young blokes. Next, no job. He's part of that section of the workforce which regards a job on the council as utopia. His short stories are all about working people and their lives. Why?

'I'm working class,' he explains. 'I write about workers – I s'pose you could call it working-class culture. I don't know nothin' else.'

It used to be common to talk about 'the disappearing worker'. Despite the glibness of the phrase, there seems at first glance some sound sociological reasons for the apparent erosion of the traditional working class in Australia: the growth of secondary and tertiary industries and the development of computer-based new technology which throws workers out of a job and replaces them with machines. There may also have been a real decline in working-class 'consciousness' as measured by the proportion of Australians who identify themselves as working class. But these processes need to be looked at more closely to decide exactly what they mean... and whether there are changes occurring in the class structure which lies behind the labels.

In Australia, in common speech, working class usually refers to unskilled, semi-skilled and skilled workers – the 'blue-collar' workers who are tradespeople and artisans or work in factories, the labourers who work on building sites and on the roads, manual workers who have jobs on farms. Truck drivers, railway workers, fitters and turners, storemen and packers, production-line workers, women outworkers, road labourers and wharfies are typical in the city; farm labourers (women and men), shearers, canecutters, drovers, building workers and stockmen are typical in the country. Occupation, then, typically defines the working class – or the lack of it, because unemployment is higher among this group than any other class (except the underclass) and economic recession usually hits it harder. The working class also includes large numbers of Aborigines and migrants; indeed most urban Aborigines, which means the great majority, work at unskilled and semi-skilled jobs or exist on the dole. A 1961 Gallup poll found that of those who called themselves working class, three-quarters were skilled, semi-skilled or unskilled workers or were farm employees; the rest were spread thinly through other occupations. A later 1983 survey found that 47 per cent of skilled workers regarded themselves as working class, as did 59 per cent of semi-skilled workers and 55 per cent of unskilled workers; only 4 per cent of professional people chose to call themselves working class. Broom and Jones (1976) came to the conclusion that the most general distinction between working class and middle class was between 'the blue-collar worker "battling" from week to week on the basic wage or a little more, and the white-collar worker with a higher, regular and more secure income'.

In surveys, over a third of Australians consistently regard themselves as working class. Four different surveys in 1949, 1961, 1965 and 1967 found that 37 per cent, 38.5 per cent, 44 per cent and 42 per cent respectively identified themselves in this way (1949: Oeser & Hammond; 1961: Gallup poll; 1965: Australian National University survey; 1967: Australian National University survey). A Morgan Gallup poll in 1976 produced 28.6 per cent, a significant fall from the 1961 figure of 38.5 per cent. However, the later Comparative Project on Class Structure and Class Consciousness (Baxter, Emmison and Western, 1991) found that 34.8 per cent chose working class when asked to choose a class location. The discrepancy in these results is to be expected, given the different forms of survey and the differences in the precise nature of the questions asked. While one wouldn't want to place too much faith in such surveys, it's interesting that academic surveys carried out by sociologists and general public opinion surveys carried out by polling organisations should come up with somewhat similar results; consistently, somewhat over a third of Australians regard themselves as belonging to the working class. Despite the rapid growth of white-collar workers, the possible swing to middle-class self-identification, and the development of new technology, a clear Australian working class exists. It doesn't look like disappearing.

When you leave the surveys behind, the existence of this class and its social and symbolic significance become even clearer. These are the people who carry out most of the hard work in Australia, the heavy manual labour which most people avoid like the plague: on the roads, in the mines, in the steelworks, on farms, in warehouses and on the wharves and building sites. They also form the bulk of mass production workers in factories; they are often women and often working in gloomy, unsafe, barn-like structures where the work is repetitive, boring and endless. In the film *Modern Times* Charlie Chaplin had to put up his hand before he could leave the production line and go to the toilet; unbelievably, more than half a century later in Australia, this is still sometimes the case. The pressure can be immense; my younger brother once worked at the end of a production line in one of the nation's biggest glass manufacturers and had to scoop the glasses off the line before they reached the end; if he got too far behind the glasses simply smashed onto the floor. Some production workers go slowly mad, others become depressed, bitter and cynical, some last only a few weeks, resign, try to find work elsewhere. The alternative communities are full of young people who have dropped out of the workforce, who recognise the factory system for what it is – a charnel house – and are trying to find an alternative to a system which they know will destroy them.

Some manage to get into TAFE or university. 'I'm never goin' to work in a factory again,' one student told me, 'I'd rather starve on the dole.' These are desperate escape routes; they aren't available to most working-class men – or women. In the last decade or so many married women have moved into the workforce and have got jobs at the bottom of the scale: as checkout girls, office cleaners, sandwich makers, rag trade seamstresses, chicken packers and so on. Before the Second World War about 5 per cent of married women held jobs, in 1996 about 40 per cent do. Some working-class wives have entered the workforce as a means of independence and fulfilment, but others have been driven to get a job to bring the family income up to a bearable level; often, when they finish their away-from-home work, they have to turn around and do the cooking and housework as well, especially as this is still regarded as 'women's work' in many traditional working-class households. This is, of course, a fruitful source of tension in such homes; some husbands agree to help out, others refuse. Still others feel their patriarchy is being challenged, especially if their wives get more highly regarded or more highly paid jobs than themselves. It also threatens their relations with their children. As Kessler, Ashenden, Connell and Dowsett point out in *Ockers and Discomaniacs* (1982): 'The issues here are very complex, but we can be clear about one point, that the masculinity of working class men is often under threat, or at least under pressure, because of their work situations; and that has important consequences for the kids.'

It also has important consequences for the relationships of working-class men and women. There is an argument that many young working-class males, having been raised in a highly masculine environment in which they are made to feel they are powerful and dominant, suddenly find when they get jobs that their class has condemned them to a demeaningly inferior role; almost as a reflex action they try to reassert their 'powerfulness' in their sexual relations with women. Hence, in part, the familiar syndrome of working-class men harassing and intimidating women, strangers and partners alike – and the levels of domestic violence in working-class neighbourhoods. Whether the argument is correct or not, it is statistically the case that working-class people suffer from higher levels of violence than middle- and upper-class groups; they also have higher levels of ill-health and unemployment; and die younger (Ann Daniel, 1988). Class, therefore, not only colours the life you live; it can even affect whether you live at all – a fact which young working-class blacks in American cities, and working-class Aborigines in Australia, have been familiar with for generations.

Working-class Australians generally live in different suburbs, speak in different accents, work different hours, vote for different parties, and belong to a different culture to middle- and upper-class Australians. In the big cities they typically live in the dilapidated terrace houses which were built as workers' homes in the nineteenth century, often in inner-city suburbs such as Brunswick and Fitzroy and Darlinghurst and Redfern; or else they have been shunted out to the outer western suburbs, to Blacktown and Mt Druitt in Sydney or Altona and Broadmeadows in Melbourne. Some of these inner suburbs have been gentrified in recent years, as artists and young professionals and upwardly mobile middle-class families have moved into them because of their period charm and closeness to the centre of the city; Paddington, in Sydney, is the most famous example of this; but other inner suburbs, especially the poorer ones which have industry and wharves mixed up with them, remain basically working class. In the outer suburbs, where land is much cheaper, working people often live in state government housing, the equivalent of Britain's council houses; some are shoved into high-rise blocks but these gravestones of failed social planning are more typical of earlier, inner-city slum clearance schemes such as took place in Carlton and Waterloo. The outer suburban ghettos are sometimes, in their own way, just as bad. They are terribly isolated from the main part of the city and all it has to offer, and lack the feeling of belonging to a community; they often involve long trips to work; they lack back-up structures such as community centres, parks, hospitals and play centres, and they often display a high incidence of social distress in the form of violence, crime, suicide and sickness. Housewives in these areas can be the most vulnerable and isolated of all.

Being in the working class is a synonym for underprivilege. Working-class people in general earn less than other groups, own less, have a poorer education, have less access to the goods of the society they live in, and have less opportunity for a good life: equal opportunity simply does not exist in Australia. Equality of rewards is even more of a chimera. Understandably, working-class people tend to have lower expectations than middle- and upper-class people, which in itself can act as a barrier to achievement – especially among working-class kids who simply may not believe a university education and a professional career are a real possibility for them. Scraping by on low wages, struggling to make ends meet, and gambling to boost your income are characteristic working-class preoccupations. Typically they rent homes rather than own them, having been disqualified by lower incomes (and sometimes by cultural tradition) from entering into the middle-class own-your-own-home mortgage race; this sometimes gives them marginally more disposable income than equivalent groups who do not rent, but it puts them at the mercy of landlords and of a social system which doesn't look after pensioners well, so that at the end of a lifetime of work they are left without a home to live in and are thrown upon the mercy of a less-than-benevolent state. Unlike England, old people do not get the pension as a *right* because they have contributed specifically to it. All this makes people vulnerable to sickness and misfortune and old age, and to the country's political vicissitudes; after all, who would like to depend upon the quality of mercy of a John Howard or a Bronwyn Bishop?

Working-class outer suburbs have a clear tone of their own. In Sydney those who live in the outer western suburbs are often labelled 'westies', especially the younger men and women who, at night and weekends, may hang around the space-age entertainment centres playing video games and pinball machines, or go to the movies to see action films and space epics, or maybe work on their motorbikes – bikes are common in the west, partly because they are cheaper than cars and because of the distance you have to travel to get anywhere; the 'bikie cult' has always been a primarily working-class phenomenon.

As the Sydney megalopolis has sprawled westwards the population centre has moved steadily with it until it is now located closer to Parramatta than the city centre; Parramatta now has its fair share of clubs, pokies, dance venues, beer gardens, video hire centres and middle-of-the-road entertainers for the oldies and wrinklies, but it's still no rival to the CBD. At weekends lots of working-class kids try to break out of their landlocked isolation and head for the coast; it means a long train trip, but each Saturday and Sunday hordes of these kids pour off the train at Cronulla or off the Manly ferry and head for the surf. Kathy Lette and Gabrielle Carey, authors of *Puberty Blues*, have given a lovely description of the reception they get:

> There were three main sections of Cronulla Beach – South Cronulla, North Cronulla and Greenhills. Everyone was trying to make it to Greenhills. That's where the top surfie gang hung out – the prettiest

girls from school and the best surfies on the beach. The bad surfboard riders on their "L" plates, the Italian family groups and the "uncool" kids from Bankstown (Bankies), swarmed to South Cronulla – Dickheadland . . .

Cronulla surfies wage an endless war against the kids who come from the Western Suburbs. They're called Bankies, Towners or Billies. Cronulla being at the end of the train line, all sorts of tattooed, greasy, bad-surfing undesirables slide off . . .

To pass the time we kept an eyeball peeled for our dreaded enemies – the Bankies, from the greasy western suburbs. They were easy to spot with their yellow T-shirts, Amco jeans, terry-towelling hats, one-piece swimming costumes, worn-out Coolite surfboards and white Zinc plastered from ear to ear.

"Oh, I'd wear Amcos for sure."

"Spot on. Huh! Like ya Coolite!"

"Bankstowner . . . Er . . . Pew."

We gave them heaps.

This is class hostility in action: the Cronulla surfies in *Puberty Blues* nearly all came from affluent middle-class homes with parents who went to Europe on holiday. One of the surfer girl/authors lived in 'a three-storey red brick house with three bathrooms and a pool', whereas her boyfriend, Bruce, was the son of a brickie's labourer and lived in a small fibro house. 'It was very embarrassing when I first brought him home. "Jeez! This is a fuckin' mansion!" Bruce said.'

The hostility between Cronulla surfies and westies hasn't changed much since then. Cronulla has climbed even further up the real estate scale, but the westies remain . . . well, at the other end of the train line.

Schooling

Working-class children usually go to state schools, because their parents obviously can't afford anything else. Sometimes they go to Catholic schools; they virtually never go to private schools, though occasionally an Italian greengrocer who has made good or a dairy farmer who has been saving all his life may send their sons off to a private school as a boarder or day-boy to 'get a good education'. The education of working-class children is typically much poorer than that of any other social group (except Aborigines, who are generally members of the working class or 'underclass' anyhow). Many leave school as soon as they can, either to go straight into the workforce or to go on the dole while they look around for a job. Children from upper-class backgrounds are much more likely to stay on to the end of Year 12 at school than those from working-class backgrounds. Western (1983, p. 57), after surveying several educational studies, concludes:

> Early school-leavers come overwhelmingly from working class backgrounds. They are typically over-represented in lower status jobs, and find it difficult to enter work that offers security and advancement prospects. In general, those from lower down the socio-economic scale are less likely to get jobs, and when they get jobs, more likely to get jobs which reproduce the socio-economic position from which they come.

The effect of class on education is even clearer at the tertiary level. Comparatively few working-class students ever get to university; the reintroduction of university fees (HECS) by the Labor government in 1989 has added another hurdle to be faced by would-be students from working-class backgrounds.

A poor education, of course, is a major factor in ensuring that those who are born into the working class stay there. As society has become increasingly technocratic those with the education to suit them to skilled jobs have a great advantage over those without skills. The 1983 Australian Values Study found that of those with a primary education only, 70 per cent were working class; of those with a university-level education, half were upper class or upper-middle class and only 12 per cent were working class. The holding power of a working-class background, and of a working-class education, is immense. The 1976 report on Poverty and Education in Australia (quoted by Western, 1983, p. 61) described the effects of the schooling system as 'disturbing' and concluded:

> For those who stay on to complete the final year of secondary schooling and proceed to tertiary studies, the . . . rewards are obvious. They will occupy jobs attracting a high income which in turn tends to give access to a range of opportunities for personal growth and development, as well as increased satisfaction. At the same time they are likely to enjoy relatively more freedom in choosing a lifestyle which suits their personal needs and tastes. For the unskilled and unqualified, society holds out quite different expectations. They must contend with the instability of the unskilled job market and with increasing unemployment. The jobs they can get are mostly repetitive, uninteresting, physically exhausting and often dangerous. They are jobs which rarely provide opportunities for acquiring skills, for promotion or for responsibility. They encourage mobility, but not to achieve better things. Mobility for these people is lateral, from one dead-end job to another. Their jobs will be lowly paid, reflecting the worth society places on unskilled labour. They will lack their fair share of money, status and influence. In our hierarchical society they will be its least powerful members.

The same applies today. A teacher at a comprehensive high school in a new working-class suburb was appalled at the pupils' hostility when she first went there. Given what awaits them, who can wonder?

Accent

Working-class people are divided off from other Australians in ways subtle and unsubtle, important and trivial. There is, for instance, a very clear working-class accent. It is basically what the phoneticians A. G. Mitchell and A. Delbridge (1965) have labelled a 'Broad Australian' accent: the vowel sounds tend to be very broad and are spoken with a slow, marked glide; it is often a nasal accent; and people who use it often speak slowly and run their words and syllables together, or even leave sounds out entirely. It's often regarded as an uneducated or 'ocker' accent; when he was Prime Minister Bob Hawke used it whenever he spoke to workers, John Singleton uses it self-consciously, and about 34 per cent of Australians use it quite unself-consciously. When people talk about someone having a very *Aussie* accent, that's the accent they mean. It is very easy to parody, of course, and everyone from Nino Culotta to Barry Humphries to Paul Hogan has had a go. It was once regarded as too extreme to be allowed on radio except in interviews with footballers and boxers, and it positively disqualified you from becoming an announcer or disc jockey – especially for the ABC, which went in for half-arsed imitation English accents. The popularity of the 'ocker' ads of the 1970s changed that, and for a while it was impossible to turn on the radio or the TV without being confronted with yet another working-class accent extolling cheap groceries, secondhand cars and bargain carpet remnants. The master of them all was Tex Morton, the famous hillbilly singer and showman, who stunned his listeners with a rapidfire list of tongue-twisting bargains, ending with the catch-call: *'that's* where you git it!' The ocker ads have receded somewhat and John Singleton, who produced many of them, has turned to racehorses, advertising campaigns and capital gains, but the phenomenon did have the effect of freeing up the airwaves somewhat and making a working-class accent at least acceptable . . . some of the time.

The class basis of this accent is clear from the analysis phoneticians have made of the differences between people who speak in the three major Australian accent types, namely Broad, Cultivated and General. Those who speak in Broad Australian typically have parents who are farmers, labourers or semi-skilled workers whereas most people who speak in a Cultivated accent come from homes where the father is a professional or in a higher administrative occupation. State schools are the stronghold of the Broad Australian accent, private schools of the Cultivated accent (Mitchell and Delbridge, *The Pronunciation of English in Australia*). Needless to say, any accent can be found in any group; prime ministers can speak in a working-class accent, especially if they are Labor leaders, and some workers speak in the most educated of voices; but the general class pattern remains. Of course, the author John O'Grady understood all this years ago. In his book *They're a Weird Mob* (1957) he uses an Italian migrant, Nino Culotta, to poke fun at Broad Australian speech and its typical phrases; the Aussies that Nino learnt how to speak proper from were building workers:

> He was holding out his hand. I took it, and said, "You are Mr Joe?"
> "Cut the mister, matey. 'Ow yer goin' mate, orright?"
> This last word I did not know. I said, "I am delighted to know you."
> He said, "Okay. Let's get crackin'. The truck's over 'ere."
> A thin, dark young man, wearing old boots, was rolling a cigarette.

He did not get up when we approached. He just said, in a very flat slow voice. "Where yer been?"

Joe said, "Had to pick up yer new mate, mate. 'Ow yer goin' mate, orright?"

"Yeah, mate. 'Ow yer goin', orright?"

"Orright, mate. Nino, this is Pat. Pat – Nino."

Pat extended a hand and said, "Pleased to meet yer."

I shook hands with him and said, "How do you do?"

... Pat said, "Wot a bastard you turned out ter be."

Joe said, "Give 'im a go, mate. 'E 'asn't done any before, but 'e'll be orright. Give 'im a go."

Money

Working-class people are down the bottom of the income scale. You would expect this, given the typical low-paid jobs which working-class people have. In the 1983 Australian Values Study, none of those who earned under $6000 a year were upper class but 55 per cent were working class. Of those who earned $20 000 a year or over, only 16 per cent were people who called themselves working class. An Australian Bureau of Statistics analysis of incomes in 1973–74 showed that on average professional and technical occupations drew incomes which were half as much again as tradespeople, production process workers and labourers. It doesn't require much knowledge of the real world to be aware of the fact that doctors, male and female, on $200 000 a year and barristers on $3000 a day earn more than garbage collectors, nurses and teachers. Baxter, Emmison and Western (1991) found that class was a key determinant of people's incomes, and summarised the mean annual incomes of different groups (as formularised by Goldthorpe) thus:

	$ Women	$ Men
Upper service	29 469	37 505
Lower service	20 382	28 737
Routine clerical workers	15 634	20 451
Personal service workers	13 943	16 306
Petit bourgeoisie	15 176	25 766
Supervisors, lower technicians	15 638	23 011
Skilled manual workers	14 680	19 707
Semi- & unskilled manual workers	10 907	17 753

As can be seen, women on average earn substantially less than men. On the other hand, after a somewhat different statistical analysis based on Erik Wright's class scheme, they conclude that 'disparities between exploiters and the exploited are clearly greater among men than women, with the differences between the incomes of proletarians and asset exploiters being larger for men than women in seven of ten class locations. In other words, there is considerable evidence that men receive greater absolute returns for their ownership of productive property, skills or organisation by comparison with proletarians than women do' (Baxter, Emmison & Western, 1991, p. 122). Nevertheless, whether you are a man or a woman, if you are working class you are likely to be at the bottom of the income list. The gross inequality of income which exists is accentuated by the fact that the rich can use family trusts, income splitting and other tax avoidance devices to both escape tax and to make their incomes appear much lower than they actually are. Working-class people don't normally have access to such ploys. The Henderson report on poverty in Australia estimated that 10 per cent of people were existing below the 'poverty line'. Many of these were almost certainly working-class families on low incomes or without jobs; in times of economic recession it is the working class which bears the brunt of high unemployment.

In terms of wealth, as opposed to income, working-class Australians are even worse off. Wealth can take many forms, from ownership of possessions, land, property and companies to investments, shares and accumulated money. The inequality of the distribution of wealth in Australia is startling, and makes nonsense of claims that there is no need for a radical redistribution of wealth, income and services. An analysis in 1978 revealed that the top 5 per cent of Australians owned more than the bottom 90 per cent put together (Raskall, in Western, 1983, p. 46). Just 1 per cent of the population owns 22 per cent of personal wealth; the top 5 per cent of people own 46 per cent of wealth; the top 10 per cent own almost 60 per cent of the wealth. Half of all Australians own less than 8 per cent of the wealth. Many working-class people don't own a house or any other major material possession except maybe a car and a TV set. The high rate of home ownership in Australia – in 1996 approximately 67 per cent of homes were occupied by their owners or by people paying them off – has sometimes fostered the delusion that wealth is comparatively evenly distributed, but the fact that some workers manage to pay off their houses after a lifetime of mortgage repayments doesn't much affect the grossly uneven distribution of wealth in the country. And what of the one-third of Australians who do not own a house? M. J. Berry, in his study of inequality in *Australian Society* (ed. Davies, Encel and Berry), points out that:

> Although the current buying power of the skilled blue-collar worker may be approaching that of the white-collar worker, the latter are, through generous investment in their houses, ensuring a vastly expanded future power. Houses continue appreciating long after the cars, boats and colour televisions of the workers have depreciated away to nothing.

It's worth looking closely at working-class housing. In Britain about one-third of housing is 'public', for example council houses, which is provided primarily for working-class families at subsidised rents; this is one way in which the nation's wealth is redistributed, slightly, to help families at the bottom end of the income scale. In Australia only about 11 per cent of housing is public. Working-class Australians, whether they live in private homes or in public housing estates, often have to live in outer suburban areas where allotments are small and public services and facilities are meagre. Owning a house, even when it is possible, in this sort of situation is not that marvellous. As Western comments (1983, p. 73):

> In many of the new outer suburbs public transport is woefully inadequate, schools are overcrowded and health and welfare services are often not adequate. When home ownership is available to the working class, then, the infrastructure in the area in which the home is located is frequently not able to meet the demands placed upon it.

Power

The Australian worker's main access to power is through the trade unions. One might have thought that the Labor Party, which began as a working-class party and still obtains the majority of working-class votes, would provide the most direct access to power, but there is a clear lessening of working-class influence upon the party's leaders, its ministers and its policies (see Chapter 4, 'Class and Politics'). The change in the nature of the ALP should have made the union movement even more important, but this has occurred at the very time that Australian trade unions are suffering a major decline in union membership and have come under sustained attack from the advocates of labour market deregulation – including the Howard government, which in 1996 set out on a path of sidestepping or, if necessary, destroying the power of the union movement.

During the seven years to 1995 union membership as a percentage of the workforce declined from 42 per cent to 35 per cent, and is likely to decline still further, despite nationwide drives for union membership; by 1996 only 2.8 million workers were unionists and the unions were being deliberately frozen out of the wage bargaining process. They have, in fact, been under more sustained attack than at any time in the last half-century. The increasing unionisation of white-collar workers, about a third of whom now belong to one union or another, has helped the union movement generally and has strengthened the ACTU, but it hasn't increased working-class power. Indeed, as Bob Connell writes in *Ruling Class, Ruling Culture* (1977, p. 209): 'Union membership as a percentage of the workforce, an important long-term index of working-class organisational strength, stopped growing in the middle 1950s, and indeed went into a slight decline.' The militancy of these unions is hard to measure. Australia has a reputation for strikes, but of course the mass media deliberately highlight what strikes do occur, especially those by comparatively militant unions. The truth is the thirteen years following the advent of the 1983 Labor government were characterised by the lowest level of industrial unrest since the Second World War, partly because of the way in which the unions were locked into the Accord; this, despite the fact that workers suffered a decline in real wages under the various Accord agreements.

Kiss My Arse

Half a dozen drinks later Hawke starts to leave. Throughout it all it's become obvious just how popular, how widely admired, Hawke is; he is the focus of a great deal of affection right across the spectrum: men, women, workers, sportsmen, businessmen. It buoys him up, even exhilarates him, but he remains easygoing, serious, arguing or defending himself when necessary.

Just as he reaches the door, however, Hawke runs into George Polites, director of the Employers' Secretariat, an old adversary and good friend. George grabs Hawke's arm and drags him protesting back to the bar. George wants to have a sing-song; Hawke suggests "Keep the Red Flag Flying"; they compromise with an old parody of the "International":

"THE WORKING CLASS
CAN KISS MY ARSE
I'VE GOT THE FOREMAN'S
JOB AT LAST...!"

From *The Australian People*, by Craig McGregor

Although the media tend to present all strikes as unnecessary, strike action is commonly an expression of real class conflict which has been channelled into the comparatively narrow area of wages and conditions. Some workers see the class structure in conflict terms, some do not. Broom and Jones looked at several surveys and concluded that 'a minority of Australians – but a significant number – hold class interest views in which classes are seen as having opposed interests, as being inevitably in conflict over those interests, and as expressing conflict partly through the political system' (Broom & Jones, p. 75, in Western, 1983, p. 61). Working-class people are more likely than any other group, except those at the very top, to take this conflict view (Wild, 1978, p. 61). This is understandable, as it is often working-class people who are the victims or losers in class conflict; this also explains, in part, the fierce loyalty many workers display to their unions. The sentiment is clearly not as strong as it was in Henry Lawson's day when, as short stories such as *The Union Buries Its Dead* show, the union could be the focus of a working-man's life, but among working-class Australians 'scabs' are still loathed and picket lines hard to break. On the other hand, the long years of the Accord and of comparative industrial peace may have lessened working-class militancy and induced most working people to simply accept the status quo – which means, of course, a situation in which working-class Australians stay where they are, at the bottom of the heap.

The class background of contemporary union leaders may also help explain this. You would expect them to come from a working-class background, and many do, but a 1979 study of Australian elites found that of fifty of the nation's top union leaders, a quarter came from homes in which the father had been a professional, a business owner, a manager, a grazier or a large farmer and about 20 per cent came from homes where the father had been an employer or self-employed. Comments Western (1983, p. 85): 'The conclusion is inescapable that even in the union movement itself, the working class is underrepresented in positions of power, influence and authority.' This is compounded, of course, by the even grosser underrepresentation of the working class among Labor leaders.

A look at the career of Bob Hawke illustrates these sorts of statistics. Hawke came from a comfortable background, went to an elite school and then Oxford University, became a legal advocate for the ACTU, and eventually became president; his career, in other words, was that of a lawyer. When he moved to parliament and became prime minister he quickly established himself on the Right of the party. The most powerful unionist in the land, and later the most powerful Labor leader, was a man without any working-class background at all. Working-class Australians are also less likely to join organisations, clubs and societies, and less likely to achieve power within them, than middle-class people (Western, 1983, p. 86). The picture that emerges is one of a class with only limited access to power of any sort led by people from a different class altogether.

This understates the day-to-day reality of union rank-and-file activity, the shop floor agitation, the endless round of meetings, elections, deputations and, occasionally, strike action, in which a knowledgeable and sometimes militant working class acts for itself. Some of Australia's most famous union leaders, from Lance Sharkey through to John Ducker and Bill Kelty have come from the working class and their rhetoric often shows it. (So do their accents.) What these leaders come up against, however, is the institutionalisation of the union movement in general. The arbitration system, which before the advent of enterprise bargaining has traditionally siphoned off direct conflict into legal and imposed solutions, is partly responsible for this. Historically, Australian workers have been more concerned with better wages and material conditions, that is, a form of labourism and economism, than with political theory or with radical change to the existing system; they have been more concerned to bend capitalism to their own short-term advantage than to confront it, and have relied more on the social ethic of egalitarianism and mateship than on a European-style revolutionary consciousness. The idea has not been to cripple the bourgeoisie but to become more like them.

This approach has undeniably helped working-class people to obtain a higher standard of living and has protected them against the worst forms of exploitation, but it hasn't changed their position in the class structure. There isn't much of a push towards worker control, or worker participation, although in the past there have been token appointments of a few union leaders to enterprises like Qantas. Throughout Australia the boss remains the boss, the worker remains the worker. Workers think that by being able to call the boss 'mate' they have gained something, but it only emphasises their failure to gain more. Despite the arbitration system, union action, and a labour movement which commands the loyalty of a great many working-class men and women, the system remains one in which the powerful dominate the comparatively powerless – with their consent.

Iconography

Despite all this, the working class plays a major role in the myths and iconography of the Australian nation. Historians such as Russel Ward have argued that it was the bush worker, 'the semi-nomadic drovers, shepherds, shearers, bullock-drivers, stockmen, boundary riders, station-hands and others', who first gave Australians an image of themselves and created a national stereotype which was to be reinforced by the Diggers – again, nearly all working-class soldiers – of the First World War. Later critics have modified or rejected this thesis, partly because of its emphasis upon men rather than women; others have maintained that the image of the 'typical Australian' is really derived from the urban proletariat which, shortly after the start of this century, had already become the largest social group in the nation. Whatever the precise origin, it's clear that in the past this image has been drawn from the working class rather than any other. As I wrote in *Profile of Australia* (p. 21), back in the sixties:

Even more powerful than the bush myth . . . is that of Australia as the land of the worker. Ask most people to describe an Australian and they will probably reply in terms of a bloke with a sports shirt under his coat, a glass of beer in his hand and an accent a yard wide who is against the boss (he is never thought of as *being* the boss), gambles heavily, calls his wife "the missus", was a digger in one war or another and is satisfied to be an ordinary bloody Australian. His is the tough, gnarled Albert Tucker face which looms from the cover of Donald Horne's *The Lucky Country*. ("The image of Australia is of a man in an open-necked shirt solemnly enjoying an icecream," writes Horne.) The dinkum Aussie everyone talks about, almost always with a certain unreal sentimentality, is clearly a worker.

This myth, which was out of date then, is even more so today; working-class Australians have been overtaken and overshadowed by a white-collar stratum which regards itself as middle class and which has such social and political clout that it is now the target of all the major political parties. Yet it says much for the richness and strength of working-class culture that for most of this century it has provided Australia with an image of itself. That richness persists today; as Richard Hoggart pointed out years ago in *The Uses of Literacy* (1958), working-class life has its own classic rituals and institutions. Mateship is regarded as a general characteristic of Australians (among men, at least) but it evolved basically among Australian workers. Institutions such as the trade union movement, the surf lifesaving movement, the RSL and workers' clubs and the adult education movement are primarily working-class creations, despite the changes which have occurred among them in recent years. Rugby League has been a working-class sport for most of its history (more of this in Chapter 13, 'Class and Culture'), just as Rugby Union has been a middle-class/upper-class one.

The Labor Party has been captured by the middle class but it was created by the working class and still retains the bulk of the working-class vote and some working-class ideology. Many of the radical movements of the last decades, such as the anti-nuclear and anti-uranium movements and even the conservation movement, have relied upon the involvement of a solid segment of working-class activists even when appealing to a largely middle-class constituency. The trots, the dogs, the ponies, the pokies – a great deal of Australian popular culture is fundamentally working class in tone and origin. Working people remain enormously important in the iconography of contemporary Australian culture, and working-class styles and stances have had a permanent effect upon the national ethos.

The details of this style are constantly changing. Working blokes these days often desert their trad flannies and workboots for T-shirts, stubbies and thongs, so much so that the outfit is often banned by pubs and clubs striving for a bit of 'class' – a different class. In the pubs of the steel cities and frontier towns like Darwin and Cairns, however, the uniform remains. The women are more diverse; maybe jeans instead of shorts, a T-shirt with a slogan across the front (NOT A PROBLEM), a hairdo culled from *Woman's Day*, *New Idea* or *Dolly*. Few punks. In the mining towns of the Hunter Valley and the NSW south coast and in industrial cities like Newcastle and Wollongong greyhound racing is still popular; you even see the occasional whippet, a real hangover from the mining villages of Wales and the north country. (Early dawn, Centennial Park, Sydney: owner-trainers with a clutch of muzzled greyhounds loom out of the mist, stumble across the expressway, head for kennels in terrace house backyards.) Workers tend to drink in the public bar of the local pub after they knock off work in the afternoon – the worker's day is often from 8 a.m. to 4 p.m., the middle-class man's or woman's from 9 to 5 – buy tickets in meat platter raffles and maybe take home a bag of prawns or a pizza for the family. At weekends there might be a night out at the RSL club, or a Sunday drive in the country, or Saturday arvo at the footie, especially in Victoria, where the AFL matches draw big crowds of supporters who barrack for teams based on working-class suburbs like Collingwood, though the players may come from anywhere. At holiday time the caravan parks and campgrounds of the coast fill up with families who can't afford a motel but acquire old boats, trailers, fishing gear and surfboards instead. The atmosphere in the camps is much like it was thirty or forty years ago: friendly, boisterous, no bullshit, a sense of who-gives-a-bugger camaraderie. Only the emblems, the portable TV, the gas barbecue, the home-repaired fibreglass canoe, have changed.

SURFIES

To all you surfie mothers,

We are sick to death of hearing all this shit about us westies. You gutless wimps think you own the beach in your half-filled sluggoes and white thongs!

I doubt all you skegs with your prunehead girlfriends have ever been further west than the Caringbah Inn, so what do you know about westies? And as for the dickhead who thinks that west girls are "bushpigs" we'd like to say "get fucked", and have a look at your own surfie chicks with their floppy brown tits trotting along behind you waxheads like drooling puppies.

So up yours.

MICHELE AND LISA,
Mt Druitt, NSW, from *Tracks* surf magazine

The typical qualities of Australian workers don't seem to have altered much either; they still tend to be independent, crude, against the boss but authoritarian with their kids (the fathers more than the mothers), blessed with a sardonic sense of humour and a contempt of pretence, cursed with a narrowness of imagination which can make them philistines, serious about their politics and the union, and sure they're the salt of the earth. The men are good blokes to their mates, the women perhaps closer to their children than to other women. The lives of the kids focus on bikes, sport, cars, sex, rock, computer games, apprenticeships – and, of course, the TV. If there is pervasive fault it is the overt, chauvinistic masculinity of working-class life. There tends to be an ever-present possibility of violence: by parents to their children, by men to women, among peer groups of young men; you have to be prepared to use your fists to stand up for yourself. There's a fair bit of racism, especially against Asian migrants who might take scarce working-class jobs in a time of high unemployment. Intolerance – of minorities, of queers, of nonconformists, of outsiders – runs like a dark thread through working-class life; it is the obverse of the matey egalitarianism which is reserved for those *inside* the group.

So powerful is this working-class style, which I have been trying to describe in an impressionistic way, that it has considerable holding power even over people and groups who don't really belong to the class. As some working people have moved up into the lower-middle class, and the distinction between the two has become more and more blurred, so they have taken their style and attitudes with them; a lot of Australian men, especially, adopt the style in public in bars, RSL and Leagues clubs and when they are travelling overseas because it seems to be an 'authentic' Aussie style and because, certainly, it makes it easier to get on with your mates. A classic satire of this is David Williamson's play *Don's*

Party. Some of this working-class ethos has been diffused (and diluted) throughout Australian society. A considerable amount of TV advertising uses working-class accents and language and comes across as a deliberate celebration of working-class idioms. Discount furniture stores and used car saleyards feature their owners talking stiltedly but without bullshit direct to camera. Beer ads have often combined sporting heroes (footballers, cricketers) with close-ups of blokes in shorts drinking beer straight from the can, slapping each other, carrying on in a rough and rowdy way.

Mates.

How the Dogs Stole the Final

While Federal sports minister John Faulkner, the NSW Governor Peter Sinclair, and Opposition Leader John Howard were circumspect about the Bulldogs' victory, Prime Minister Paul Keating was overjoyed. "A victory for class," he said in the Bulldogs dressing room, and he wasn't referring to class as in skill, athletic ability, sophistication in attack and defence.

Pointing through the double-brick walls of the Sydney Football Stadium tunnel to the Manly dressing room, he said: "It's the other side and this side, and this side won."

Following the tartan-tied Keating was Canterbury chief executive, Peter "Bullfrog" Moore, who wryly observed: "There are more Fibros in the world than Silvertails."

Roy Masters,
in the *Sydney Morning Herald*, 25 September 1995, after the Sydney Bulldogs (the "Fibros") beat the Manly Sea Eagles ("the Silvertails") in the Rugby League Grand Final

The marketers and merchandisers, however, realise that class changes are under way and are changing the nature of the audiences they are trying to reach. Aussie Rules football and Rugby League both began as working-class games, but some years ago the promoters of Australian Football decided to crack down on violence and make the game more socially acceptable to a wider audience; now Rugby League is doing the same, by shedding its working-class image and aiming its TV commercials quite deliberately at middle-class audiences. Terry Connaghan, a principal of the advertising agency Connaghan & May, explained disarmingly about one of these ads: 'The commercial is pitched at Sydney's great middle ground, the middle class. We wanted to show that you don't have to come from the inner city or the far west of Sydney to follow League. After all, the statistics show that the blue-collar segment of the population has been shrinking for many years.'

The move met with some resistance from those who want the game to keep its working-class character. Graham Lovett, a director of the NSW Rugby League, commented that 'the game has strong roots in the working class and it would be a falsity to try to change its image.' Roy Masters, when he was a coach of Western Suburbs, encouraged the idea that Wests was a tough 'fibro set' team and huge crowds of supporters used to hold up pieces of fibro in V-for-Victory shapes at Wests' games; he's still sceptical of the moves to change the game's class image, which is emphasised by the closeness of the teams to local Leagues Clubs and the consciously 'lowbrow' presentation of the sport through the media in footie commentaries, ads, prizes and so on. But the organisers and TV promoters know which way the wind is blowing, and as time goes on Rugby League, like Australian Football before it, will become less and less a working-class game.

The working class doesn't have the social and mythic power it once had, not the old, traditional, proletarian class anyhow; and nowhere is this more clearly demonstrated than in the phenomenon of that classic working-class stereotype, the ocker. Like yobbo, Alf, hoon and snob, ocker is a class term. KYLIE v. SNOBS. On the graffiti walls, the vernacular of class hostility.

Jimmy Barnes
Class Profile

'JIM-MEE!' Clap clap clap. 'JIM-MEE!' Clap clap clap. 'JIM-MEE!' Clap clap clap. The voices rip and roar around the hall, spiralling to a crescendo as a short, aggro figure powers on to the stage, grabs the mike, clenches his eyes, opens a great square mouth like a bawling kid and that familiar raspy rock'n'roll scream emotes through the massed banks of Marshall speakers:

> 'Always easy to please
> Never get off your knees
> Give and you will receive
> Just like a kick in the teeth
> How long can you just turn the other cheek
>
> STAND UP . . .'

Jimmy Barnes. The wild one of Cold Chisel, hell-man idol of a generation of westies, rock'n'roll superstar, Working Class Hero – or as much of a one as it's possible to be when you've come from Scotland, made a fortune in Australia, half-lost it, gone off to France to live, and then had to claw your way back into the local scene again. Not the least complicated thing about Jimmy Barnes is how he has managed to remain a major Australian figure through it all . . .

But even more complicated is his class position. It's as apparently paradoxical as that of the former Prime Minister, Paul Keating. Like Keating, he's a working-class man made good. Like Keating, he's held on to the loyalties and values he grew up with. But whereas Keating relishes the style and sophistication which his success has given him access to, Barnes is uneasy with his. He's channelled all his aggression and energy into music instead of politics and he doesn't seem to have changed that much: he is still a pure Scottish bovver boy, a rough-as-guts Glasgow refugee with a thick Scots accent, a square-jawed square-toothed big-eared Scots face, a fiery, joyful and extroverted ex-slum passionate man who is just about as funny and fast on his feet as Billy Connolly and who understands class because it's made him what he is.

He was born in working-class Glasgow, inner city, near the Gorbals, which used to be notorious as the worst slum in Europe. His father was a champion featherweight boxer and taught him how to fight, which was probably just as well; the district was buzzing with street gangs and if you went into the wrong area you were in trouble. While he was still living in Cowcaddens he and a young friend strayed into the wrong street and, Barnes recalls: 'The local gang next door caught us, and what they did was put us in this little garden shed, started throwing rocks at us and said "We'll give you five seconds to run", so I got the hell out of there but my mate panicked, froze, and they hit him with rocks and split his head open. He had to be taken to hospital, and they set fire to the shed. It was a really rugged place. It moulded part of my character, like, it was almost natural to me.'

At the age of five he and his family migrated to Australia; he grew up in migrant hostels in working-class Elizabeth in South Australia, surrounded by Scots and Poms and Irish. He wanted to be a soccer player but spent a lot of his time drinking and brawling. 'Where I grew up,' he says, 'if you didn't fight, you were a victim. When I was sixteen, seventeen we used to go out and fight for fun, y'know, stupid . . . Friday, Saturday night, have a few beers, think you were the king of the world, and start trouble. I was lucky I didn't get locked away. A lot of my friends from that period are either in jail or dead. There were so many working-class people there, not a lot of money, obviously you get major marital problems, there was that much pressure on them, and the kids were just running riot, thieving, fighting . . .'

Barnes's parents were among the casualties; they broke up, and then his mother married Reg Barnes, so James Dixon Swan became Jimmy Barnes. He sort of drifted into music; he's not a natural, it's something that developed: 'all my mates were better musicians than me.' Still, his dad and mum used to sing and he and his five sisters and brothers would join in at the local church, youth clubs, Friday night stuff, a bit like another Scottish migrant, Vince Jones. In part it's a working-class tradition, transposed from Britain to Australia; he even learned to play cornet in the Salvation Army for a year but it was his elder brother John Swan, nicknamed Swanee (he later called his band that), who was heavily into music. Barnes remembers: 'We used to stand on the porch at Elizabeth, pretend we were the Beatles, cut-out guitars, bits of wood nailed together, wigs, all that sort of stuff, miming Beatles songs.'

Barnes left high school in third year and went to work in a foundry with the South Australian railways, pouring molten metal at 1700 degrees Celsius. Things were closing in. He seemed destined for the life of a working-class man. For a while he thought he might be a boxer. 'I think I had one real fight,' he says. 'I was reasonably fit, playing soccer, and they put me up against this young guy and said "Take it easy on him, he's only been fighting two weeks", and this guy beat the shit out of me and like a few weeks later he becomes the state champion!' End of career. But there's a lot of aggro about Barnes which can explode suddenly and which makes people wary of him. He's a brown belt in karate, never takes off the bushido cross his instructor, Noel Watson, gave him. 'I reckon I coulda been a warrior,' he says. His mates remember him trashing hotels in the old days when he was lead singer of Cold Chisel, punching out doors, hitting the booze and drugs (favourite drug? wadderyergot?), brawling in corridors with drummer Steve Prestwich. Though he's calmed down he still drinks a lot.

'Like, a few years ago, I had nothing to live for and, literally, didn't give a damn . . . I was a rebel when I was sixteen, I was a rebel when I was twenty-five, I still don't agree with everything that goes on in the world, if I can help it I'll do it, but I'm not going to fucking die for any bastard. I think y' just change.'

Jimmy Barnes's grey-green eyes glitter. He's wearing a puke-yellow T-shirt, the karate cross on a chain around his neck, day-old stubble; his wife, Jane, is Thai-born; they have four children. Was he always aggro? 'Nah, not me,' he says. 'Perfectly balanced. A chip on both shoulders!' And he laughs, yelling and falling around.

What changed him was getting married to Jane – and music. One night, when he wasn't long out of school, he went to a local youth club where a garage band, Tarkus, was playing; the singer didn't turn up so Barnes, as in classic showbiz mythology, was invited to take his place: 'That was the first band I joined, sang the whole night with my back to the crowd, I couldn't look at anybody.' By this time his elder brother John had formed a band called Soul Union (though they misspelt it Soul Onion on the drum kit) and Jimmy was listening to black soul singers, Jimi Hendrix, Deep Purple and trying to sound like Paul Rodgers of Free. Then in 1973 a band called Orange got itself together and asked John Swan to be lead singer; when he said no, the band's roadie said, 'Well, he's got a little brother, let's give him a go.' Jimmy auditioned, got the job and at the age of sixteen began rehearsing in the Women's Liberation Centre in Adelaide. Their manager got bored one day and began doodling the words 'dyke bitches' on the notepad next to the phone. The band got thrown out. But shortly after that it changed its name to Cold Chisel and Barnes went on to front one of the great bands in Australian rock'n'roll history.

Jimmy Barnes retains a lot of that working-class ambience; his core Australian audience is still basically young workers, who buy his records and go to his concerts when he tours the local Leagues and RSL clubs. During his Cold Chisel days, with songs like 'Star Hotel' and 'Khe Sanh' and his wild antics like leaping off the stage into the arms of his audience, Barnes created a rebel persona that has never left him. He justifies himself now by saying, look, he's trying to give his kids the good start in life he never had, he hasn't turned Right wing, he hasn't found God, he hasn't changed that much except now he can see the stage when he climbs onto it. Sometimes.

'I still identify with that working-class background, I fought to get out of it, I remember not being able to go to school, y'know, because I didn't have shoes . . . I think the only difference between me and a lot of kids that were there is a lot of luck and a bit of determination. I'm just living out what every one of those kids would do if they had the same opportunity,' he says.

Yeah, but what's he doing for them?

Nothing.

'I'm not involved in politics, I know I should be, but it bores me shitless,' he says. 'I've got the attention span of a small soapdish.' He's full of contradictions: kicked his way out of 'the shit', but has no idea of how to make the system different. Yet his background has given him some clear insights into what's wrong and he relates it instinctively to class.

'I've got a theory,' he says. 'I think the government deludes people into thinking they have to stay where they are. I think that's the way politics is structured. It works back to the class system, the old English thing about keep the masses down otherwise who's going to serve dinner, y'know? Or man the factories? Like I was a top student, top of my year at high school, but I wasn't encouraged to think I could go to university; I was told to go out and get a job, or at best an apprenticeship. In that working area, you don't have any goals, you take things day to day, you're fatalistic. It wasn't until I got away from it, and particularly when I met Jane, that I became more ambitious. I feel very close to kids working in the west. I bump into 'em in the street and they say "Hey Barnesy, how ya going?", like we're old mates, and I like that.'

A sociologist could hardly put it better: low expectations, low motivation, a bright kid thrown into the steelworks as soon as he left school, not much chance of escape except through fluke or raw talent. Unlike most of his mates, Barnes forced his way out of his background and has turned himself into . . . well, a sort of icon, a culture hero, a powerhouse rocker and now international star who injects a lot of that original anger and desperation into his music. Like other Working Class Heroes, he's not sure how to help others along the same trajectory (or change the set-up so that it is no longer important to do so), but he has at least created his own unique cultural mix: black music, white life, Scottish soul, Aussie head, Thai wife, Jewish manager, American producer, Buddhist spirituality, brown kids, working-class audience. It could be the right mix for the global suburb.

10

Ockers, Alfs, Yobbos, Hoons and Snobs

Class stereotypes multiply almost as quickly as racial stereotypes – and are often equally invalid. But they do indicate something about class relations and what attitudes people in different class groups may have to each other. The stereotypes are also almost always out of date; by the time an image has fixed itself in the popular imagination the social group to which it applies has moved on, leaving an empty shell which even the social group itself feels safe to lampoon (hence the prevalence of anti-Jewish jokes among Jews, anti-Irish jokes among Irishmen and so on). When I was growing up there were lots of standard jokes among my school peers about 'Paddy' and 'Mick', and it wasn't until years later that I realised they were Irish names; the satirising of all Irishmen as dumb working-class oafs was completely lost on me, because no Irish person I knew was remotely like the stereotype.

The class nature of some stereotypes is obvious if you look at a term like 'snob'. This usually refers to someone who regards himself or herself as your social superior and sets out to make you aware of it; and it usually refers to someone in the upper class, though middle-class people can sometimes indulge in snobbish behaviour ... especially if they are trying to climb up the social hierarchy and establish some distance between themselves and what they used to be. Snobs are, of course, ludicrous and snobbery is always unwarranted; it's such an old-fashioned term you like to think the behaviour it refers to is dying out, but if it is regarded as shorthand for a particular sort of class hostility (which it is) then it is unlikely to disappear completely until class distinction itself disappears.

'Yahoo' and 'yobbo' are usually labels for working-class stereotypes, especially young, beer-swilling, loud-mouthed working-class men, chundering on pub pavements, throwing tinnies at the footie, harassing women who walk past... there doesn't seem to be a female equivalent, which is significant in itself. Those key characters in Barry Humpries's satires, Edna Everage and Sandy Stone, are quintessentially middle-class characters, though Dame Edna seems to have taken off on a fame trip of her own these days; before she became Humphries's jetsetting alter ego she was a parody of the suburban housewife of that era, with her blue rinse hairdo and rhinestone spectacles and worries about spilling curried eggs on the burgundy axminster carpet, just as Sandy Stone, pathetically searching for his own car in the RSL parking lot, was the ageing middle-class husband. The men die first, of course; you can tell because the women on the tour buses are always wearing their hubbies' wristwatches. Humphries is a marvellous satirist and it's no accident that he has chosen the middle class as his prime target: that's where most Australians are, that's where the action is... though, as time has gone on, both Edna and Sandy seem strangely out of date; Humphries these days lives in Europe and doesn't seem to be as instinctively in touch with Australian social mores as he used to be; for contemporary satire you have to go to people like Max Gillies, Elle McFeast and contemporary TV comedy series.

The most enduring and evocative of Australian class stereotypes, however, is the ocker. Nobody knows for sure where the term comes from. When I was a kid 'ocka' was a sort of slang term for 'mate'; some think the word comes from England, probably from the West Country, where men are sometimes nicknamed 'acker', as with the much-loved trad jazz musician Acker Bilk! But whatever the origins of the word, the stereotype to which it is applied is familiar enough: Paul Hogan, Bazza McKenzie, all those blokes with Broad Aussie accents on the TV commercials, plus all that mob of mates in the beer ads, the larrikins in David Williamson's plays, and the blokes who throw brown-eyes from trains at suburban stations ... what literary critic Max Harris once called 'that ill-educated, dogmatic, incoherent and arrogant psychological phenomenon, the Australian ocker' (Harris, 1975), is your unreconstructed Aussie, crude, philistine, foul-mouthed, a mate to his mate but a yobbo to everyone else, the sort of figure of whom Paul Keating, when he was still Prime Minister, said 'it's time we all left that behind'.

In a way Keating needn't have worried, because the real, undiluted ocker is fading fast already; as I've said, we can only laugh indulgently at cultural stereotypes when they are safely in the past, when they no longer *are* us or a threat to us. As with Andy Capp in England and Dad and Dave in Australia, the ocker has become a figure of fun because he's outdated. John O'Grady did it all years ago with Nino Culotta in *They're a Weird Mob*, which satirised Australia as a nation of rough-as-guts tradesmen. The huge success of a book like that depended upon popular nostalgia for a fading era; it dealt with identification-at-a-distance. O'Grady romanticised an age, and its typical ethos and characters, which everyone suspected was passing. Paul Hogan has done much the same with *Crocodile Dundee*, except here the culture hero is a bushie instead of a city bloke; in both cases we are presented with a kindly, romantic version of a character who we know is disappearing fast from the Australian social landscape.

What many of the satirists and artists who make money from sending up the ocker figure don't admit is that he is essentially a working-class figure. His accent, his style, the way he carries on: that's the old-model Aussie that the middle-class audiences who go to Barry Humphries's shows and David Williamson's plays, and laugh at the TV satire series, know they have left behind forever. He's a prole. Maybe in Hoges's case a prole who's made good and even got married to a Hollywood film star, but still a prole. Max Harris at least got close to admitting this when he talked about 'the Australian reversion to proletarian tribalism' and the 'egalitarian imperative that any ocker can do any job any time with as much expertise as the next ocker' and finally says 'I must confess... that there is an element of class consciousness in this expressed distaste'. An element! It's the essence of the construction of this and other working-class stereotypes, from ocker to yobbo to slob, just as it was in the construction of earlier stereotypes in Australian history.

The most famous of these were probably Dad and Dave and the rest of the bush characters who peopled Steele Rudd's *On Our Selection*. Rudd, whose real name was Arthur Davis, grew up on a Queensland farm and his tales of the bush selectors and the lives they led became fantastically popular, so much so that fifty years later Dad and Dave were still around in radio shows, comic strips, stage jokes and wherever city people gathered together to laugh at their country cousins. Rudd had originally intended his stories to be serious but, as John Barnes says in *The Literature of Australia* (ed. G. Dutton, Pelican, 1976): 'The characters Rudd had created with real affection and pride became eventually caricatures of reality.' And his stories became popular at exactly the time that, in the words of historian Ian Turner, 'the population balance was moving decisively against the bush... In the process, the working class was being transformed into [predominantly] an unskilled proletariat... Much of it was now settled in the cities.'

In other words, at the very time a profound change was occurring in Australian society, a cultural stereotype based upon the way it used to be became immensely popular. People could afford to laugh at Dad and Dave because the satire was no longer directed at them – hell, they were no longer bushies and cow cockies, they'd left all that behind. And yet, because that was their background or that of their families, they could indulge in a sort of nostalgic recollection of their bush past. It was no longer so powerful as to demand loyalty, or something to be ashamed of, it was merely... funny. Paul Hogan's Mick Dundee is an even more exotic version of the Aussie bushman, because everyone knows types like The Man from Snowy River and Dad and Dave hardly exist any longer; these days you have to go to the Northern Territory, and focus on an occupation like crocodile shooter, to discover your real Aussie bush worker...

The only ocker/yobbo/hoon heroes who ever rivalled Steele Rudd's characters in popularity were the Sentimental Bloke and his mate Ginger Mick. Created by C. J. Dennis, these were larrikins from the city pushes who spoke a garbled working-class dialect, had it in for the upper crust, but had hearts of gold underneath their uncouth, up-you-Jack exterior. The contemporary version is the hoon, throwing howlies at the end of suburban streets, cruising around in hot heaps and staging drag races behind the promenade at Bondi, a worry to cops, women and burghers alike. And unmistakably working class.

Published at the time of the First World War, *The Songs of a Sentimental Bloke* sold 60 000 copies in eighteen months; it was even more successful than Banjo Paterson's *The Man from Snowy River*. But both *The Bloke* and *The Man* (whatever happened to female stereotypes? answer: women weren't important enough) were simply romanticised, out-of-date caricatures of the real thing. Paterson was celebrating a pastoral age of squatters, bushrangers and noble horsemen which had all but disappeared by the time he wrote; it's significant that *Clancy of the Overflow*, one of his most popular poems, is written from the point of view of an office worker in the 'dusty, dirty city' remembering how good things used to be in the bush. And C. J. Dennis knew virtually nothing about the push larrikins he was glorifying; as Edgar Waters writes (*The Literature of Australia*, ed. G. Dutton, Pelican, 1976): 'Realistic observation was not open to Dennis who at no time seems to have sought firsthand knowledge of the pushes; he preferred to deal in sentiment.' In fact, while he was writing these verses, C. J. Dennis was living in a shack, and sometimes an old tramcar, some 60 kilometres outside Melbourne. Henry Lawson had a much more realistic view of the pushes. That great bit of Australian folklore, *The Bastard from the Bush*, which is now generally attributed to Lawson, describes the larrikins as 'ghouls . . . slouching around the corners'; it has a nice description of the final fight between them and the Bastard:

> So down in Jones' Alley all the members of the push
> Laid a dark and dirty ambush for the bastard from the bush
> But against the wall of Riley's pub the bastard made a stand
> A nasty grin upon his dial, a bike chain in each hand . . .

Dennis was dealing, like Steele Rudd, in caricatures. The Sentimental Bloke and Ginger Mick were 'lovable larrikins', just like old Hoges up there on the shining screen, knife in belt, chip on shoulder, a string of jokes, quips and homespun philosophies at the ready, the bush Bastard about to conquer the sophisticated purlieus of New York.

In some ways the ocker is a version of a similar phenomenon of the 1960s, the Alf. Nobody knows where the term Alf came from either, just as nobody knows why Aussie expatriates in London are often lampooned as 'Bruce'. But it was common enough for Alan Seymour in *The One Day of the Year* (1963) to call his working-class, booze-and-Anzac liftdriver Alf, and it was taken up as a sort of battlecry by the triumvirate that founded *Oz* magazine: Richard Walsh, Richard Neville and Martin Sharp. Alf represented everything the *Oz* crowd hated; he was the Great Australian Yahoo, the archetypal suburban philistine, dead from the neck up, a talking beergut from the neck down, and he was ruthlessly parodied in everything from Barry Humphries's shows to *Oz*'s attack upon The Great Alf Conspiracy. There was a lot of class antagonism there, of course. Martin Sharp once described Sydney's western suburbs to me hazily as 'where the Alfs live'. The *Oz* trio came from well-to-do, upper-middle-class homes. Walsh and Neville grew up on Sydney's north shore, Sharp at Bellevue Hill. They all went to private schools: Walsh to Barker, Sharp to Cranbrook and Neville to Knox, where he failed to become an officer in the cadet corps because 'I wasn't in the Firsts as well'. They didn't like Alfs and Alfs didn't like them. In those days, perhaps, the working class still seemed to pose some sort of threat to Australian society. They were the enemy. There was talk of socialism and nationalisation and class warfare and, of course, the Red Menace.

Today the true ocker, the dinkum working man, is so much a character from the past for most Australians, especially for middle-class Australians, that he can be turned into a figure of fun. The parallels with Steele Rudd's bush characters are exact. At the very time that most Australians became city people instead of country people, they felt free to poke fun at the bush stereotype they had escaped. At the very time that the majority of Australians feel they have become middle class instead of working class, they feel free to poke fun at the working-class stereotype they have eclipsed. I mean, that's what they *were* like. Maybe that's what Dad and Mum are still like, or Uncle Alf, or others in the family, or some of your mates down the street – but not you. Christ, no, the ocker is always somebody else. You're a class above that.

Right. A class above that.

Whether you like this particular brand of class-consciousness and class hostility depends upon how deeply you feel about the class structure of society. Barry Humphries thinks it's funny. Max Harris revelled in it. Paul Hogan and Jimmy Barnes understand it but don't know what to do about it. The film makers celebrate it, the ad agencies manipulate and exploit it in commercials. Most commentators ignore it. All these responses are inadequate. They are impotent substitutes for action and, perhaps, reveal how helpless most people feel to change the structures of our society.

The ocker, like the Jew, makes you safe in the social hierarchy by giving you someone to sneer at. Some years ago, while driving down the coast of NSW, I stopped at Kempsey golf club to buy some beer. There was a mob of blokes standing in a circle near the bar, drinking from cans, keeping dinner with the wife and kids at bay, hairy arms and short sleeves, talking about Bazza McKenzie. 'Jee-sus, y'should see this bloke, he's so bloody rude!' says one bloke, broad Oz accent, ginger hair. 'Big bloody hat, carries these cans of beer, see, has this airline bag over his shoulder, never takes it orff – that's what they're gonna think all Australians are like!' Cans upended, another swig, everyone agrees it's a bloody disgrace. 'He's a real galah, never takes the bag orff . . . !' says Ginger Meggs. 'Rude! Whose shout?'

To them Bazza McKenzie is an ocker. To Barry Humphries, sneering behind the film credits, they are ockers. Maybe an ocker, or a yobbo, or a hoon is simply somebody you don't like – especially someone from the class below you. And maybe the real problem in Australia is not the ocker but the people who are so ready to despise.

PAUL HOGAN
Class Profile

Paul Hogan noses his maroon Porsche coupé over the rain puddles by the Belongil creek, past the backpacker hostels and the abandoned meatworks and the shabby fibro fishermen's shacks, up the sandy track to his mate John Cornell's beach house and parks under the coral trees and vaulting blue arc of another wintry Byron Bay day. He is wearing clear plastic spectacles which give his familiar Hoges face an unexpectedly studious look. He's smaller and frailer than you'd expect. And quieter. 'G'day.' No smile. Very cool. No charisma, no charm. So unlike the lovable lighthearted larrikin Hoges, or Mick 'Crocodile' Dundee, you think: is this bloke a phoney? Just another actor?

He isn't.

But there are a lot of complicated, unexpected things about Paul Hogan. The full-on Aussie blue-singlet bloke is still there, in everything from broad accent to that dry, laconic humour, but when he talks Hogan sounds more like a homespun intellectual, someone who's thought about life for a long time and examines every idea carefully before he picks it up. He hasn't repudiated his working-class background but he's immensely proud of his achievement as a comedian and film maker and gets hostile at critics who think he's just a Harbour Bridge rigger who got a lucky break.

He's reserved, reflective, a bit shy, full of silences, has 'a bit of the hermit' about him, but he's also very opinionated and argumentative and you get the impression he thinks he's never met his match. He used to be a prizefighter and there's still some cocky aggro about him but he's turned it into something thoughtful and self-controlled. Sometimes he says perceptive, sophisticated things in a language which is pure boorish ocker. It shocks and puzzles people: is he having them on? If class is culture Hogan is still a westie; if class is economic Hogan is one of the elite. It's a paradox which Hogan doesn't find hard to handle but others do.

In fact, he's a type which was quite common at the turn of the century, when Working Men's Institutes were full of self-educated work-with-your-hands thinkers (Henry Lawson's swaggie character Mitchell was one) but which has almost disappeared today, which is why Hogan now seems unique. It's as though the classic Aussie of The Australian Legend, the figure that Hogan celebrated and parodied so affectionately in his TV shows and then in the *Crocodile Dundee* films, were to be suddenly discovered alive and well in Byron Bay but transformed into a movie-making, Porsche-driving international celebrity. Which is sort of how it is – but only sort of.

'There's a bit of confusion between me 'n' Hoges; I mean there's gotta be a little bit of me in Hoges and Crocodile Dundee, obviously as I made 'em up they're gunna have some of my attitudes, like I'm not Sir Laurence Olivier – but I'm not either character,' Hogan explains. 'Hoges was me at seventeen: a sort of know-all, well-meaning, thought of himself as a knight in shinin' armour goin' round doin' wunnerful deeds even when he was makin' a complete galah of himself! I liked Hoges, still do.'

He is sitting on the white leather settee in the living room of Cornell's beach house, gazing out to sea. He is wearing a short-sleeved grey T-shirt, blue jeans, walking boots, as nondescript as anyone else in the Bay. On the third finger of his left hand, a single plain gold wedding ring. Linda Kozlowski is back at the villa in the bush, working on a film script. John Cornell is at the back of the house. And Hogan is trying to explain the difference between him and Hoges.

'He was a product, me and John always talked about what Hoges will do, what Hoges will say,' says Hogan. 'As a kid I had a bit of a Galahad complex, used to take the world full-on a bit, standin' up for the underdog, even the way I got onto television was that thing about bein' a white knight, goin' in there on behalf of all those little people who were bein' humiliated by these bigtime entertainers who half of 'em didn't have as much talent as they did, and on their behalf I was goin' to kick a few heads – I had a noble purpose! I didn't go on to *New Faces* to become a professional entertainer, I went on to take the mickey out of those judges. It was, like, the Christians being fed to the lions, I reckoned the time was right for one of the Christians to jump up and bite a few lions!

'Nah, I don't think I'm that noble, but I do have an instinct to smack people that should be smacked on behalf of those that can't, do y'know what I mean? It's a bit of the old working-class attitude. Yeah, that's my background. Blue singlet. Still have those attitudes? Aw, hard to say, everyone changes, if you don't change you stagnate. Some people try and paint me into that corner, y'know . . .' Hogan adopts his deep meaningful TV/film/celebrity/star persona . . . 'STILL DRIVES A VW, STILL LIVES IN BANKSTOWN! . . . I don't live in Bankstown, I don't drive a VW and I'd be retarded if I did. I don't hate Hollywood. I don't hate the trappings of success. That's ridiculous. Sometimes even well-meaning people manufacture that GOOD OLD HOGES, STILL THE SAME . . . well he's not, he can't be. That was twenty years ago.'

He stops, knocks a cigarette out of a packet in what looks like a compulsively calming habit, blows smoke across a tight upper lip.

'Yeah, I'm sendin' meself up a bit in those characters. I can't take *me* that seriously. I have to live with me! I remember doin' an interview with Phillip Adams, he was tryin' to analyse where I came from comedywise, psychological stuff . . . everyone he knew had some sort of chip on their shoulder, used comedy as a weapon or a shield . . . he decided I was just a regular boring guy who was lucky, I think he resented that. He wanted something deep.' Pause. 'I'm as deep as a teaspoon!'

Now that's straight, typical, unadorned Paul Hogan. He sounds like an ocker and he's still got all the class colouration he was given from being born in Granville (*not* Lightning Ridge, that was Hoges) and going to school at Parramatta Marist Brothers and dropping out at age fourteen and doing forty different labouring jobs before becoming a Harbour Bridge rigger and, astonishingly, breaking into TV: nasal broad Aussie accent, runs his words together, rough uneducated way of speaking, plenty of slang, a lot of true-blue worker beliefs still, and that understated take-the-piss-out-of-anything-includin'-meself sense of humour that Australians like to think is typical of themselves. But you only have to spend a few minutes with him to realise that Paul Hogan is also sharp, super-intelligent, calculating, very competitive, highly articulate, and above all somebody who intellectualises almost everything he does.

You can almost see the two Hogans in his face. Straight on there is the familiar, chiselled, bush bloke look, crooked smile, wispy blond hair, ice blue eyes ('he has the coldest eyes of anyone I've ever seen' says a woman artist); in profile, he's got this long, hooked nose, almost monkish edge to him which makes you wonder, even apprehensive, about what's going on inside that high-domed cranium.

I mean, he's funny, very funny, so much so that you spend a lot of time laughing with him while Hogan hardly cracks a smile. But perhaps because he is so self-contained, so ego-sure, so determined to be himself at all costs, you don't warm to him straight away. It takes time. 'You read one of his scripts and you wonder if it'll work, and then you imagine Paul doing it and you know it'll be brilliant,' says one film maker. Or as Hogan told the hapless Phillip Adams: 'I said to him, "you're humorous and amusing, Phillip, I'm *funny*!" He thought I was a lucky idiot.'

He's no idiot. And though he's long ago left his working-class origins behind he, unlike John Laws and John Hewson, has not turned against the class he comes from. The Hoges legend, from Harbour-Bridge-rigger-to-international-film-star, has become part of entertainment folklore; what isn't so well known is how it all got started. In fact the mayor of Lightning Ridge, in outback NSW, sent Hogan a nice opal belt buckle asking him to put a mark on the map where he was born because so many tourists asked about it – but that was Hoges, not Hogan! The real Paul Hogan is the descendant of a long line of Irish horse thieves from Limerick; his ancestor, John Gilbert, was a forger who came out as a convict in the Second Fleet; Hogan's Dad was in the army, his mother looked after the kids, and he himself grew up as a typical 'working-class westie'. He didn't like school, the formal part and the authoritarianism of it: 'I didn't agree with a lot of it, thought I knew better than they did, argued a lot.' Instead he played Rugby League, joined the diving team, and left as soon as he could, aged fourteen years and ten months, straight after the Intermediate Certificate. Like Paul Keating.

Was he already a bit of a comedian? 'Yeah, I was funny as a kid, sort of,' says Hogan, slowly, 'I thought of silly things to do, I was always a good heckler . . . but I was never one to stand up and entertain at parties, y' know, life-of-the-party people, the minute they see three people together they've got to tell a joke or run out and buy a piano accordion – I was never one of those! I've seen stories, other blokes who knew me in the pub, sayin' YAIRS, HE WAS ALWAYS A FUNNY BASTARD! That's wisdom in hindsight, I wasn't really.'

But he *was* smart: in his early years he was always top of the class: 'My problem was being a know-all, arguin' about what was what, very opinionated.' Then at high school they tested his IQ and found it incredibly high, over 150, even though he'd plummeted down the grades: 'That worried 'em, I was a total larrikin by nature, stuck with this havin' to academically achieve! I was a bit of a guinea pig, there was two kids in the school who had this exceptionally high IQ, the other was Chris Ringstead, he used to be on the Quiz Kids – he was one of the brighter of the Quiz Kids – and that was always reflected in his schoolwork; me, I was runnin' sort of about 11th in the class, gettin' 100 in some subjects and nothin' in others . . . I came under a lot of pressure, some teachers always pickin' on me, naggin' me, I hated it; later on I realised I was makin' the teacher look bad . . .'

So he left and became an apprentice labourer in an iron foundry – something he can laugh about now, but according to Hogan, 'It was just Hades . . . just the worst job in the world . . . filthy and noisy and hard yakka, it used to be 135 every afternoon when they poured, I couldn't have been very bright or I wouldn't have stayed there that long! Studied metallurgy at night. Then the nightmare hit me: I'm studyin' harder than I ever did at school, and I'm workin' all day like, y'know, two horses, and bein' the only kid in the foundry they *worked* me . . . I shovelled and pounded and ironworked all day . . . arrr . . .'n I had nothin' to show for it but eight million blackheads!'

By now this is Hogan at his wry, funny, self-deprecating best; no wonder he became an entertainer! 'I sort of grew up there. By the time I was sixteen I thought WHAT AM I DOIN' HERE? it was such a grotesque job. Pulled out of that and got a job at the Granville swimming pool as a pool attendant, I thought THIS IS MORE LIKE IT! Like I swam all day, swept around the pool, pull some kid out after he was drownin' and got paid for it! Socialised . . . like I had my own swimming pool, in the western suburbs, in the fifties! You'd see a girl you fancied and you'd say, "er, come for a swim after hours, I have me own pool!" Arr, I just drifted around the building industry after that, I had more than forty jobs, fifty, you worked somewhere, saw a mate in the pub, snatched a new job for a few extra quid, if you couldn't find one you went to the railway or the Water Board or the DMR, dug around on the road . . . went through the building industry mainly as rigger, scaffolder, dogman, blue-singlet work, from fifteen to the age of thirty-one, I was probably approaching the stage of gettin' stuck in that; ended up on the Harbour Bridge because that was more stable.'

From there *New Faces*, the *Mike Willesee Show*, his own TV specials ('sixty hours of 'em, I used to think when one was finished, y'know, I'll never write another funny thing in me life'), *Crocodile Dundee 1 & 2, Almost An Angel, Lightning Jack, Flipper* . . . millions of dollars . . . world fame . . . divorce . . . marriage to Hollywood film star Linda Kozlowski . . . media idolatry . . . total transformation.

Or is it?

The amazing thing about Hogan is that, despite all that's happened to him, he still remains fairly close to the working-class background that spawned him. Hell, he likes Jimmy Barnes, barracks for Parramatta. He's changed, of course ('you'd be a cretin if you didn't') but he's held onto a lot of his old attitudes and style and mindset; he was never a stereotype ocker anyhow, nobody is; and you'd expect someone of Hogan's intelligence to realise what an advantage it's given him anyhow, though he remains quite proud of his professionalism as a comedian: 'I was an entertainer, or a comedian, or a social commentator who just happened to be a western suburbs working-class Aussie. No doubt that added to what Hoges was doin' but if that was all he was based on he'd have disappeared like all the other characters that followed him.'

He ponders that, about how Hoges and Andy Capp are both nostalgic figures in a way, icons of dwindling blue-collar identity in a class structure turning whiter by the day: 'the very fact that my background was pure blue singlet gave me a better perspective on what people at home wanted to see,' he says, 'the people that run television stations, they've done that all their life, they're victims of ratings and victims of other people's opinions, but they've never sat at home and watched television as their only means of entertainment. Which I have.

'People say to me, aw, you had the common touch but you'll lose that now because you're not down at the pub hearin' what the guys are talkin' about, but I was never down at the pub hearin' what the guys were talkin' about, I was down the pub talkin'. I was down there expoundin' what I thought. That doesn't change. I could talk underwater with marbles in me mouth.'

In a funny sort of way what Hogan has done is hold on to some of the best of the classic dinkum-Aussie-working-man-true-blue character and abandon the worst of it. He says he's been against the old 'inferiority complex' myth for a long time: 'I don't have any inferiority complex, none whatsoever. A lot of what I'm tryin' to do is on behalf of other people, it's often misinterpreted. I don't idolise the yobbo, I've resented some of the old Australian attitudes . . .' He's not a racist, he says. He might still have 'a bit of the old Aussie chauvinism, but it gets less and less'. He reckons that, if anything, he's still got a Galahad complex ('it comes with a superiority complex!'), he'd like to help other people but isn't sure how. 'It's not a holier-than-thou or a nobility thing . . . I dunno . . . there's gotta be a lot of people out there with a talent for somethin' who never found what it is . . . at thirty I was deep in a rut and thought: what am I gunna do, is this all there is? Part of it is to be a little bit of an inspiration, it sounds egotistical, but enough people know I was a Harbour Bridge rigger at thirty and have achieved some success by just havin' a go, pluggin' away; I think that's an inspiration to people . . .'

The north coast sun has got down under the verandah and is shining into Hogan's face: thin, lightly tanned, familiar. He crinkles his eyes up against it. It doesn't bother him; he sits there, silent, reflective. The sea is starting to turn that milky off-blue it attains before it turns molten pewter. You can just hear the winter swell flopping over onto the beach which swings away towards the Belongil Tyagarah Mullumbimby Possum Creek . . .

When I leave Hogan is strolling down towards the editing shed, a thin-jockey figure dwindling under the melancholy calls of currawongs. John Cornell, Linda and Hollywood await him. As someone said, he's his own man. I have this sudden perception of him as this high-IQ, streetwise, working-class westie who didn't want to be an achiever, wanted to be 'one of the boys' (and still does), and spent half a lifetime mucking around on building sites before he broke through to the sort of career his intelligence had pointed him towards sixteen years beforehand.

That's one vision of him. The other evolved as I walked down Jonson Street, the main street in Byron Bay, a few minutes after leaving the beach house, and suddenly noticed it was full of Hogans: youngish blokes in shorts and suntans with blondey hair and a sort of straight, uncomplicated Aussie look about them. As publican Tom Mooney, ex-footballer, told Hogan when he came to the Bay: 'Look, nearly everyone here reckons they're better than you anyway.'

Well, they mightn't be better than Hoges, but they're much the same. And maybe that's the best thing about Paul Hogan: not that he's bloody smart, which he is, or that he's turned himself into such a bloody success, which he has, but that he's so bloody ordinary. Like the rest of us.

11
Upper Class

Many Australians are reluctant to believe there is an upper class – including some who are members of it. The egalitarian tradition has, in the past, been so strong that many people have been hostile to the idea that there is such a thing as an upper class, and certainly not a 'superior' class; and perhaps out of deference to this sentiment respondents in surveys have often been more willing to call themselves upper-middle class than upper class, even when there was no doubt that they belong to the very top echelon of Australian society. This unwillingness to call yourself upper class has, however, faded somewhat over the years. In 1976 Morgan Gallup polls introduced the category 'upper class' to its class survey in order to take account of this, and found 0.3 per cent were willing to identify themselves as such and another 7.15 per cent identified themselves as upper-middle class. In their social barometer, a more general and less precise survey which checks such things as how many TV sets and washing machines you have in the house, how many husbands, what brand of detergent you use and so on, they divided each class group into 'upper' and 'lower' subsections, with interesting results: this time 1.8 per cent were willing to call themselves 'lower-upper class' and 0.6 per cent 'upper-upper class'.

Returning to the original Morgan Gallup poll, if upper class and upper-middle class are combined the total is 7.4 per cent. The survey by Baxter, Emmison and Western (1991) found 11.1 per cent placed themselves in the upper class or upper-middle class category. R. A. Wild's classic study of class in a NSW country town, *Bradstow* (1974), found that the vast majority of the townspeople in his survey recognised the existence of an upper class and 8.2 per cent believed they belonged to it! It should be added that it is an open secret that Bradstow is really Bowral, a wealthy town outside Sydney which is a favourite retreat for some of Sydney's social elite and is the home of some nationally recognised 'top' families; Wild classified all those who called themselves upper class as belonging to Bradstow's gentry or nouveau riche (the terms are his). On the evidence of his own work and several other research surveys Wild concludes: 'There is some evidence to show that the upper class have a clear idea of the class structure of Australian society, can place themselves within it, and that many perceive a structure of opposing interests, all of which indicates a fairly high degree of class consciousness...' (Wild, *Social Stratification in Australia*, 1978, p. 51).

You'd have to be a mug, anyhow, not to realise there is an upper class in Australia. If anything, because of the social distance between it and the rest of society and the clear recognition that it is very much a minority, the upper class in Australia tends to be very class-conscious and sometimes goes to great lengths to underline how different it is. Whereas in Britain, among the aristocracy, superiority is simply assumed, in Australia it often has to be demonstrated. Not that Australia has a formal, inheritance-based aristocracy in the British sense, but it does have an upper class whose members, compared to other class groups, tend to belong to different families, go to different schools, speak in different accents, live in different suburbs, hold positions of considerable power, and inherit not only wealth but a whole spectrum of class characteristics from their families. Whether Australians like to admit it or not, Wentworth's 'bunyip aristocracy' is now a (virtual) reality. Whenever I come across one of those society matrons with a fruity voice from Toorak or Vaucluse whose life seems to revolve around charity galas/fashion openings/holidays in Europe/operating a trust fund for the school Old Girls, and whose husband is not only a multimillionaire but is an office holder in the Liberal Party and a director of several companies as well, I have to remind myself: there are supposedly no classes in Australia . . .

What is the upper class? Basically it is a class of owners and employers and their families, variously called the Establishment, the power elite, the bourgeoisie or ruling class, who dominate Australian society through the concentration of economic power which is typical of any capitalist society and through the exercise of hegemonic cultural/social power. In this sense it is like dominant class groups in parallel western societies, depending upon the ownership of property and cultural capital to impose its own interests and ideology upon the life of the nation. Through sheer wealth, shareholdings and interlocking structures it certainly dominates Australian business, which is characterised by a high degree of oligopoly, market concentration and large shareholdings in the hands of a comparatively small number of people; a recent analysis of 271 leading companies found that approximately 4 per cent of shareholders owned about 55 per cent of the shares (Trevor Sykes, *Australian Financial Review*) and this concentration of economic power has been confirmed by other detailed surveys. An overview by Encel of analyses of the pattern of ownership and control in Australia led him to conclude 'the legend of free enterprise makes particularly little sense in view of the remarkable high degree of concentration of ownership which has existed since the beginning of the century' (Encel, 1970). The Australian economy is one of the most highly monopolised and oligopolised in the world, and the dominance of a comparatively few corporations, combined with the interlocking networks established by key members of the upper class, makes it easy for them to wield immense power in the financial/business system – a capacity which was intensified by the deregulation of the financial system in the 1980s, after which the then Labor government had to continually watch how the markets would respond to its policy and fiscal initiatives. The Howard coalition government which was elected in 1996 found itself similarly beholden to the response of the markets to its economic initiatives; what Australian politicians of both major political parties have done, whether deliberately or as a by-product of their commitment to economic rationalist ideology, has been to hand over even more power from the public sphere (the government) to the private sphere.

A leading film maker who is experienced in raising money from some of Australia's major financiers, and who has also experienced the internationally expanding power of corporations in the cinema, media and construction industries, concluded recently that Australian society is run by 'the oligarchs'. Adding: 'The democratic system is a sham. The oligarchs, the merchants, the bond traders run the show. It's almost immaterial which government is supposed to be in control in Canberra, the real power resides with the oligarchs. Once I wouldn't have thought that; it's taken a decade for me to realise where the power lies.'

This is a classic formulation, and an oversimplification, but it points to the way in which current economic dogma and the subsequent strengthening of the private sector have combined to overwhelm what was once the countervailing power of the government; both Liberal and Labor governments have set out to withdraw government from key areas of economic activity (banking, transport, media, utilities) or, where they can't do that, to downsize and truncate the services which remain in the public sphere. Hence the daily newspaper headlines about cutbacks, downsizing, rationalising, reductions and public economies. The steady withdrawal of the government and arbitration agencies from workforce arrangements removes another protection for the ordinary citizen. If the government is the prime countervailing force to private exploitation, nearly every withdrawal by government from the public arena reinforces the power of the upper class.

There is some debate as to whether the upper class is a 'ruling class' in the traditional Marxist sense of the term. Some theorists prefer 'governing class', which is a softer term and implies that the governance typically has the support of the governed – which it has, most of the time, in Australia. Research by American sociologists such as C. Wright Mills and G. Domhoff has suggested in the past that the American upper class is in fact a governing class, as anyone who has lived in America for any length of time would attest. More recent research in the 1990s by J. Scott in Thatcher's England came to the conclusion that 'there is in Britain today a ruling class'. Theorists in the cultural studies arena, such as Stuart Hall, Professor of Sociology in Britain's Open University, commonly refer to the controlling group as the 'power bloc', which indicates that the ruling/governing stratum is not a single indivisible class but rather an alliance of powerful groups and class fractions which exercises dominance in advanced capitalist societies such as England, America – and Australia.

What is not contested, however, is that it is a class-based elite which exercises effective control. Thus Scott maintains that British sociological research confirms 'the existence of a power bloc: an alliance of classes rooted in the unifying features of distinct patterns of social background ... within which a capitalist business class holds the dominant position'. He also argues that the state, that is, the government, typically operates in favour of this class, for historic and economic reasons, and that the state's activities generally support the continuance of this class's dominance. There is a complex argument to be worked out here, because in some areas the state can be seen to be, as I have indicated, a countervailing force, in fact one of the few institutions with enough power to modify the exploitative character of the business system. However, the successful push in recent years in Australia to privatise state instrumentalities, cut back the public service, and withdraw the state from as many civic arenas as possible means that private enterprise in the 1990s is succeeding in turning the government into more of a facilitator of the market than a counterweight. 'In other words, the State is historically and structurally biased in ways that favour the continued economic and political dominance of the capitalist class' (Edgell, 1993, p. 60).

The power of the upper class extends right through Australian politics – overtly in the case of the Liberal Party, whose basic constituency is the business section of the community, and less conspicuously through its impact on the Labor Party, the public service, the media and peak business pressure groups and organisations. Labor governments, whether federal or state, have to be careful to keep 'the top end of town' on side and after 1983 the Hawke and Keating governments went out of their way to get support from business and promulgate economic policies which advanced the interests of corporations. Paul Keating as Treasurer floated the dollar, deregulated the financial system, encouraged privatisation, introduced negative gearing and dividend imputation, and reduced income tax levels on high-income earners; as Prime Minister he pursued these policies further as well as beginning to deregulate the labour market through enterprise bargaining and pushing through the sale of further government instrumentalities, including the Commonwealth Bank and Qantas, to private enterprise. The Howard government has continued in this direction, having committed itself at the 1996 election to selling off a third of Telstra and to a radical 'freeing up' of the labour market. Similarly state Labor governments, such as the Carr government in NSW and the ill-fated Goss government in Queensland, have been careful to court the business community and encourage private enterprise investment in their states, sometimes offering crucial economic concessions to obtain investment. The Labor Party is sometimes accused of taking over the Liberal Party's agenda, but the more important fact is that both parties are beholden to the business/financial system and the people who run it. In a capitalist society such as Australia's you could hardly expect anything else.

For 'the people who run it', read upper class. Like any class group, it is not static or utterly closed off. Although many of its members inherit the property and wealth which makes it the most privileged group in the community, it draws its members from anywhere and drops them off just as readily if they fail to 'make it'. There is considerable evidence, however, that the Australian upper class has significant closure and holding power; it tends to be a tight-knit stratum, jealous of its privileges and eminence, imposing a recognisable conformity of 'style' (from back-of-the-throat Cultivated Australian accent to Country Road gear to grammar school intermarriage) upon its young ones and expecting a similar conformity of career success. The younger generation are encouraged to go into the same sort of occupations as their parents, especially business, finance and land management, and sometimes inherit the family business; intermarriage with members of their own class group is strongly approved, as is going to the same school as Mummy or Daddy did. They are encouraged to join the same clubs, play the same sports (Rugby Union, not League plus rowing and yachting), holiday at the same resorts (Thredbo, Aspen or Klosters for skiing, Bermuda or the South Pacific or just possibly Noosa for sun-'n'-sea), get married in the same churches, and then enforce upon their children the same class typology which they swallowed themselves.

> ### Cosy Dens of the Nation's Rich and Powerful
>
> If the Adelaide Club was at all discomforted by the Prime Minister's contemptuous comments about its age-old traditions and its most famous living member, Alexander Downer, there was little sign of it yesterday ...
>
> But it's been a week of rough handling for gentlemen's clubs. John Hewson complained bitterly that moves against him had been spawned in the Melbourne Club and Mr Keating has made great play of Mr Downer's membership of the Adelaide Club.
>
> On Wednesday he told the ABC's *7.30 Report* that Mr Downer should resign "on the basis that in 1994, not 1984 or 1894, no leader of a party that wants to be prime minister of this country should be a member of a club that will not have women as members."
>
> John Huxley & Maryann Stenberg,
Sydney Morning Herald, 27 May 1994

The ruling elites in the more parochial states such as Victoria, South Australia and Queensland have managed to maintain their elite gentlemen's clubs in their original homes – grand old buildings built around the time of colonisation, filled with valuable art and eclectic treasures (the Queensland Club has a stuffed crocodile in its foyer).

In NSW, neither the Australian nor the Union Club held onto their original estates. Instead, they sold the valuable inner-city real estate to rebuild or occupy new premises.

The smaller elites of Melbourne, Brisbane and Adelaide, structured around a few old families, make for a more identifiable ruling class. Anyone in those cities could reel off the names of the old families and point out their clubs to a visitor.

This is just not so in Sydney.

Just as their clubs are virtually unidentifiable to an outsider, so are the ruling elites harder to define.

SALLY LOANE,
Sydney Morning Herald, 27 May 1994

Not all upper-class children conform to this pattern. Indeed, the suffocating conformity and often hypocrisy of upper-class life has produced some outstanding rebels and idealists, many of them women who move into positions of considerable power and influence in the community; there is a grand tradition among some upper-class families, such as the Evatts, the McCaugheys, the Connells, which is both radical and intellectual.

Nor is the upper class a single, monolithic structure. R. W. Connell, in *Ruling Class, Ruling Culture* and elsewhere, has documented the divisions and conflicts which have occurred historically, and continue to occur within what he nominates as 'the ruling class'. These conflicts sometimes take the form of disagreements between the business and rural elites over political policy, especially tariffs, and are reflected in conflicts between the

National and Liberal sections of the coalition; rural interests and the National Party have traditionally supported higher protective tariffs than the Liberals. Others take the form of straight commercial rivalry, or the sort of ideological conflict which surfaced in the struggle between the 'wets' and the 'dries' in the Liberal Party – won by the dries and John Hewson's New Right philosophies, with disastrous results in the 1993 election; a subsequent consensual regrouping under John Howard's leadership brought electoral victory in 1996. Nevertheless, there is enough common interest among members of the class to form a recognisable, interlocking class group in which social and kinship ties can be almost as important as financial ones. Encel (1970) describes the economic elite as: 'A complex network of small groups interlocked by a high degree of cross-membership; kinships, the private school, the club, the philanthropic institution and the activities featured on the social pages of the newspapers all contribute to the essential fabric provided by the interlocking directorates of companies.'

The takeovers and mergers of the eighties and nineties not only intensified the integration of large corporations, of which the Coles Myer group is an example, but also reinforced the importance of the power bloc in the Australian social and economic structure.

Owners

Who belongs to the upper class? The key group, as I have indicated, are the owners, which includes both the landed gentry and the business/finance/merchant families who dominate Australian corporate life. Australia has long had a landed 'aristocracy' of old grazing families and millionaire landowners who are sometimes regarded (and regard themselves) as at the absolute top of the social pecking order: they include the Macarthur-Onslows, the Downers, the Katers, the Duracks, the Falkiners – not forgetting the landed families of the western districts of Victoria, such as the Armytages and the Frasers. (John Pringle spent a long section of his book *Australian Accent* on these grazing dynasties and lamented that they did not involve themselves in politics; not long after Malcolm Fraser arrived on the scene.) With their grand old country mansions, their wealth, their first-class education, their network of intermarriages and above all their social cachet they represent an undeniable upper caste in the local hierarchy.

Then there are the wealthy business and merchant and finance families, the Knoxes and Baillieus, the Darlings and Myers and Horderns, the Bonythons and Rymills, which crop up in each of the capital cities. In the eighties their power was challenged by the brash new breed of entrepreneurs, the Bonds and Skases and Holmes à Courts and Connells, who made immense amounts of money during the boom years and used that to consolidate their position in the corporate structure, but by the nineties many of these had fallen by the wayside (or into jail) and the old entrenched dynasties still controlled much of Australian business. The formidable power and interlocking connections of this business elite have been exhaustively documented by Encel, Wheelwright, Karmel and others. And the concentration of sheer wealth at the top is even more remarkable.

FALL OF A BANKING HIGH ROLLER

Timothy Marcus Clark, a member of the famous retailing family and godfather of the Adelaide Grand Prix, was yesterday ordered to pay $81.2 million plus costs for presiding over the State Bank of South Australia's financial disaster.

> It is the largest personal damages order yet made in the wake of the financial excesses of the 1980s.
>
> Other large personal damages claims from the 1980s include Fosters Ltd's $66.5 million damages claim against John Elliott and three other former executives of Elders IXL, which is still to be heard, and liquidator Richard England's $300 million claim against Alan Bond on behalf of a former Bond Corporation subsidiary. This claim was dropped when Bond allowed England to become a creditor for the purposes of his bankruptcy settlement, in which creditors were paid less than one half a cent in the dollar...
>
> A dapper man with a very proper accent, Marcus Clark had an enviable family pedigree, membership of the right clubs, such as the Melbourne Club and the Victorian Racing Club, and an education from the right schools, Scots College in Sydney and Harvard Business School.
>
> This background gave Marcus Clark the self-confidence that would allow him, after an unexceptional career with the family retailing business and then later with financier General Credits, to try and turn the equivalent of a small building society into a Morgan Guaranty overnight... The results, of course, were horrendous.
>
> COLLEEN RYAN,
> in the *Sydney Morning Herald*, 30 March 1996

A study by Philip Raskall in 1978 of estate duty statistics revealed that 1 per cent of the population owned 22 per cent of personal wealth; the top 5 per cent owned 46 per cent of personal wealth; and the top 10 per cent owned almost 60 per cent of the wealth of all Australians. The top 5 per cent owned more than the bottom 90 per cent put together. This general pattern was confirmed by a later 1989 study which reported that 1 per cent of the population controlled 20 to 25 per cent of private wealth, 5 per cent controlled 40 to 50 per cent, and 10 per cent controlled 50 to 60 per cent. This class group not only inherits much wealth but its members are often in occupations which generate wealth fairly easily: stockbroker, business consultant, developer, financier, business proprietor and so on. The power which inherited wealth and inherited ownership can bestow is demonstrated by the way in which Gina Hancock (Rinehart), in Western Australia, has taken over the mining empire of her father, Lang Hancock, and by the sudden ascension of James Packer and Lachlan Murdoch, both still young men in their twenties, to key management positions in the media empires run by their respective fathers, Kerry Packer and Rupert Murdoch. But it should be remembered, as well, that both Kerry and Rupert inherited enormous wealth and privilege from *their* families, who had already established major media corporations. The persuasive power and political influence of such class dynasties can hardly be overestimated.

The 1980s and 1990s have been great years for wealth generation by the upper class. In 1990–91 a total of 306 taxpayers reported taxable incomes of over $1 million a year, compared to only 62 five years earlier. And their tax rate was significantly lower, largely due to the Labor government's lowering of marginal tax rates on high-income earners and the introduction of dividend imputation. According to one analysis of tax statistics, the average tax rate of Australian millionaires had fallen from 55 cents in the dollar in 1987 to just 26 cents in the dollar in 1991. Some tried to pay virtually no tax at all. At the height of the 1996 federal election campaign the government revealed that it intended to claw back $800 million a year from just 100 wealthy Australians who were using complex trust funds and other arrangements to avoid tax; the Tax Office revealed that in 1993 some eighty rich people, each with a net worth of more than $30 million, had reduced their taxable incomes to less than $20,000 a year and had thereby qualified for low-income rebates, Medicare exemptions and so on. The then Treasurer, Ralph Willis, described it as 'probably the biggest tax avoidance scheme that has come to light since bottom-of-the-harbour', a reference to the notorious tax-dodging schemes of the 1970s. The timing of the announcement was no doubt designed to help Labor's election campaign, but it forced the subsequent Liberal/National coalition Treasurer, Peter Costello, to confirm that the new government would crack down on such schemes and would attempt to recover some of the money – sums big enough to substantially affect the Budget deficit!

An analysis by *Business Review Weekly* in 1995 of the 200 richest individuals in Australia gave some interesting results. Under the grand title of 'How the wealth has percolated up', *BRW* announced that 'the Rich 200 had a great year: their total wealth rose by more than $3 billion'. To even get into the list you had to possess a personal fortune of at least $42 million, as opposed to $37 million the year before. The combined wealth of these top 200 was estimated at $37.2 billion. Kerry Packer, as expected, headed the list with $3 billion. Next came Richard Pratt, the Melbourne paper and packaging magnate, with $1.4 billion. Then came thirty-three individuals and families who were worth over $200 million each. John Laws, the Right-wing radio broadcaster, came in at $123 million. The Smorgon family reached $770 million, the Baillieu family $90 million, the Murdoch family $6 billion. Down the bottom were a few hapless individuals who were worth only $42 million each – including John Singleton, the advertising/media man famous for his class-based ocker ads which took the mickey out of true-blue Aussies ... and took a lot of money out of their pockets as well.

It isn't just the super-rich who have benefited; so have those in senior executive and management positions. The growth of senior executive salaries outstripped that of average weekly earnings quite significantly between 1980 and 1992, according to data compiled by remuneration consultants Cullen Egan Dell (*Sydney Morning Herald*, 12 October 1992); senior executive salaries grew at a rate 75 per cent faster than average weekly earnings. In recent years there has also been a spectacular rise in salaries and benefits paid to the chief executive officers and other senior managers of Australia's major corporations. In 1995 Westfield Holding's Frank Lowy earned $3.7 million, BHP's chief John Prescott received a package of $1.9 million and James Strong at Qantas got a package worth $1.3 million. Others: CRA-RTZ's Leon Davis got $1 012 000; National Australia Bank's Don Argus got $1 320 000; News Corporation's Ken Cowley got $1 730 000; and Western Mining Corporation's Hugh Morgan got $790 000. Richard Walsh, then head of Australian Consolidated Press, Kerry Packer's magazine empire, had to make do with $750 000 a year. But Coca-Cola Amatil's Norb Cole got $2 210 000, which meant he was being paid more money in one week than the average Australian earns in a year, and in 1996 Coles Myer chief Peter Bartels set off a brief media uproar when it was revealed he was being paid $2.8 million. He kept the money ... and retired early.

Research by Professor Bob Gregory at the Australian National University has revealed that among non-managerial adult employees in the private sector, real earnings for the top 10 per cent increased by six percentage points from 1976 to 1992 whereas real wages for the bottom group fell by 10 per cent. This means the real wage gap opened by 16 per cent. It is the richest and most prestigious suburbs, those which are most obviously identified with the upper class, which have seemed to benefit most from growing income inequality. A study of the average taxable incomes of taxpayers in 235 NSW postal districts in the 1989–90 and 1979–80 tax years produced some amazing results. For instance, the average taxpayer in Double Bay, a wealthy harbourside suburb in Sydney's east, saw her/his income grow two-and-a-half times as fast as the average taxpayer in Broken Hill and more than twice as fast as the average taxpayer in Cabramatta, Wollongong, Campsie, Bega and Port Kembla. In Lindfield, on the wealthy north shore, the average taxpayer saw his/her income grow by 160 per cent, which was one-and-a-half times the rate of growth of income of taxpayers in Fairfield, in Sydney's mid-west. In other words, not only do Sydney suburbs display extremes of wealth, but the richest suburbs are fast becoming richer still.

Professionals

Who else belongs to the upper class?

The 'owners' are probably the most easily identified, because of their assets and key positions in the financial/business/landholding echelon. Then there are the high-status achievers who are sometimes regarded as upper class and sometimes as upper-middle class: professionals such as doctors, barristers, solicitors, academics, architects and judges; plus those at the top of public career structures, such as Cabinet ministers and department heads; plus those in key managerial positions in the corporate world, such as managing directors and chief executive officers. These positions, especially those in medicine and law, rate very highly in studies of occupational prestige in Australia. Ann Daniel's classic study *Power, Privilege and Prestige* (1983) follows

Athol Congalton's pioneering work in this domain (Congalton, 1963) and confirms that doctors and lawyers are perceived as prestigious and highly influential. In a scale of 162 occupations by workforce sectors, in which occupations were ranked from one (at the top) to seven (at the bottom) by a wide variety of people, *judge* came out at the very top with a prestige ranking of 1.2, but *medical specialist* came third at 1.5, followed by *barrister* at 1.7, with *general practitioner* seventh on 1.8. (It's often said that tribal societies put the witchdoctor at the top of the pole; is Australia tribal?) At the bottom of the prestige scale is *prostitute* (6.9), with *road sweeper* and *garbage collector* (both 6.7) not much better off.

As Daniel points out, prestige in a society such as Australia is a prime expression and recognition of power, which is itself closely related to occupation. The high degree of consensus among the people surveyed, despite their disparate backgrounds, shows that there is a great deal of agreement among Australians as to who has power and who has not; it is interesting, too, that those most familiar with power and how it works, namely those towards the top of the class ladder, had a somewhat clearer idea of the exact prestige of various occupations than did those towards the bottom of the class scale, though there was nevertheless no significant disagreement. Says Daniel: 'Occupational prestige remains the most powerful single indicator of the power and privilege any individual or group may command ... The status of occupations reflects the class structure; from the upper class are drawn those persons whose interests and activities constitute the dominant or governing elite in society.' Her scale of the prestige of occupations by workforce sectors, reproduced here with her permission, is a simplified version of a much more exhaustive scale which lists over 1100 different occupations (Daniel, p. 64):

Rating order of occupations by workforce sectors

Judge	1.2	Draftsman	3.4
Cabinet minister	1.5	Systems analyst	3.4
Medical specialist	1.5	Social worker	3.5
Barrister	1.7	Chiropractor	3.5
Church leader	1.7	Health inspector	3.5
Professor	1.8	Playwright	3.5
General practitioner	1.8	Speech therapist	3.5
Managing director	1.8	Dietitian	3.5
General, army	1.9	Secondary school teacher	3.5
International pilot	2.0	Media news reader	3.6
Dept. head, govt.	2.2	Kindergarten directress	3.6
Architect	2.2	Electrician, business	3.6
Dentist	2.3	Restaurateur	3.6
Mayor	2.3	TV actor	3.6
Solicitor, male	2.3	Private secretary	3.7
Parliamentarian	2.4	Personnel officer	3.7
Engineer, prof.	2.4	Professional fisherman	3.7
Research scientist	2.4	Librarian	3.8
Solicitor, female	2.5	Reg. nurse, female	3.8
Veterinary surgeon	2.5	Asst. minister religion	3.8
University lecturer	2.5	Primary school teacher	3.8
Bank manager	2.5	Bank officer	3.9
Govt. medical officer	2.6	Owner, small business	3.9
School principal	2.6	Professional model	3.9
Chartered accountant	2.6	Research officer	4.0
Economist	2.6	Laboratory technician	4.0
Colonel	2.7	Air hostess	4.0
Owner large business	2.7	Chef	4.0
Psychologist	2.7	Publican	4.0
Govt. legal officer	2.7	Reg. nurse, male	4.0
Geologist	2.7	Ambulanceman	4.0
Orchestra conductor	2.8	Professional footballer	4.1
Director, nursing	2.8	Acupuncturist	4.1
Newspaper editor	2.8	Farm manager	4.1
Accountant	2.9	Professional golfer	4.2
Minister religion, own parish	2.9	Small landowner	4.2
Producer, TV program	3.0	Advertising agent	4.2
Lecturer, tech. college	3.1	Foreman	4.2
Surveyor	3.1	Trade union secretary	4.2
Large farm owner	3.1	Real estate agent	4.2
Second division officer	3.2	Policeman	4.2
Physiotherapist	3.2	Photographer	4.3
Grazier	3.2	Carpenter	4.3
Stockbroker	3.2	Contract cleaner	4.3
Works manager	3.3	Senior clerk	4.4
Superior, religious	3.3	Policewoman	4.4
Master builder	3.3	Disc jockey	4.4
Journalist	3.4	Airline steward	4.4
Computer programmer	3.4	Fireman	4.4

Upper Class

TV technician	4.4	Taxi driver	5.5
Jockey	4.5	Nurse aide	5.5
Trainer, racehorses	4.5	Sailor	5.6
Electrician, wages	4.5	Professional punter	5.6
Stenographer	4.5	Clerk, junior	5.6
Insurance agent	4.6	Shearer	5.6
Bank teller	4.6	Bus driver	5.6
Beauty consultant	4.6	Housekeeper	5.6
Housewife	4.6	Waiter	5.6
Sergeant, army, male	4.7	Waitress	5.7
Bar manager	4.7	Sales assistant	5.7
Motor mechanic	4.7	Barman	5.8
Hairdresser	4.8	Truck driver	5.8
Sergeant, army, female	4.8	Storeman	5.9
Undertaker	4.8	Jackeroo	5.9
Fitter and turner	4.8	Machinist	6.0
Telephone technician	4.8	Barmaid	6.0
Toolmaker	4.8	Domestic worker	6.0
Printer	4.9	Debt collector	6.2
Sales representative	4.9	Car assembly worker	6.2
Potter	5.0	Farm labourer	6.3
Typist	5.0	Service station att.	6.3
Bookie	5.0	Process worker	6.4
Punchcard operator	5.1	Builder's labourer	6.4
Butcher, wages	5.2	Ticket collector	6.4
Bricklayer	5.2	Wharfie	6.5
Telephonist	5.2	Seasonal labourer	6.6
Milkman	5.2	Cleaner	6.6
Plasterer	5.3	Massage parlour op.	6.6
Nightwatchman	5.4	Garbage collector	6.7
Car salesman	5.4	Road sweeper	6.7
Postman	5.5	Prostitute	6.9

This does not mean, of course, that the work of those at the bottom of the scale is less important than the work of those at the top; nor does it mean that the people who work in these occupations necessarily subscribe to the status hierarchy which has been formulated; but it does mean that there is a fair amount of consensus among the people surveyed about the prestige which they believe attaches to particular occupations. Australians, it would seem, have a very fine nose indeed for occupational status distinctions.

Finally, there are those whose main qualification for membership of the upper class is sheer wealth. Although someone who has made enough money can usually break into the most exclusive social groups in the country (indeed, the self-styled leaders of Melbourne and Sydney society are largely nouveau riche or their immediate descendants) there is still a certain social stigma attached to having made your money as a pubkeeper, bookie or the owner of a crematorium instead of having inherited it or gained it from shares and land. The socially minded wife of a leading master butcher had to give a considerable number of grandiose parties and had to join (with a donation) some of the very best charities before her daughter was regarded as eligible for the social round.

Academic research confirms that the upper- to middle-class group, understandably, thinks family background and upbringing, and what you inherit or are born into, are more important in placing you in the class hierarchy than anything else. Indeed, a higher proportion of this group nominates these factors than do middle-class or working-class groups (Baxter, Emmison & Western, 1991, p. 273). Next, in these people's minds, is money and income. After all, that's what enables you to live in the 'right' suburb: Ascot, North Adelaide, Peppermint Grove, Toorak, Vaucluse. It leads to the right sort of car: Rolls Royce, BMW, Mercedes, Jaguar or a top-of-the-line 4WD. And the right sort of house: an old mansion in huge grounds, or an architect-designed piece of postmodern bravura, or one of those darling restored terraces in Woollahra or Paddington. It enables those who desire it to keep up with the social round of balls and cocktail parties and charity dinners, to furnish the house to a proper height of luxury, and to invest in contemporary or colonial Australian paintings. It means a regular trip overseas; a year in England and the Continent with a flying trip home through the United States is standard for many young upper-class people – a sort of local version of the nineteenth-century Grand Tour – with perhaps, for young women, a finishing school thrown in.

Above all, wealth means being able to send one's children to the 'right' school. There are few social doors which a suitably refined education will not open, and this usually means attending one of the influential private schools which are the counterpart of English public schools. At these schools pupils will meet the right people, learn the right manners, and when applying for a job after leaving school they will probably have an advantage over anyone who merely went to a state or Catholic school. As the adage has it, 'It's not *what* you know, it's *who* you know that counts.' Like their English counterparts, these schools are citadels of snobbery, caste and privilege, and are one of the most important means by which the upper class perpetuates its own existence.

Boys Told: Play Safe, Hide Your Uniforms

A top Anglican school has relaxed its policy on the wearing of uniforms as a response to parents' concerns following the murder of a Sydney schoolboy.

St Andrew's Cathedral School has told students they can take off their ties and blazers and put them in their bags if they are travelling alone after 4.30 p.m. during terms two and three when it gets dark early.

Trinity Grammar student Peter Savage, sixteen, was stabbed to death on his way home from football practice on August 24, and his death may have been linked to his wearing a uniform...

A St Andrew's Cathedral School parent, Mr Stephen Nowicki, said: "The boys do get harassed by other boys and it is a concern for us." His son, Mark, fourteen, has been teased when travelling to choir on a Sunday wearing his uniform.

Sydney Morning Herald, 7 September 1995

> ## THE CASE FOR SCHOOL UNIFORMS
>
> The shocking stabbing to death of sixteen-year-old Trinity Grammar student Peter Savage has once again raised the question of school uniforms and what they tell us about our society.
>
> Are they badges of snobbery, advertisements for the school, or an integral part of educating young people about the mutual responsibilities of living in a close-knit social group? . . .
>
> It is inescapable that (uniforms) are often a badge of relative affluence and therefore raise very primitive emotions of class distinction . . .
>
> Fifty years ago there were parts of Sydney where no kid from a private school would venture wearing his uniform. In those days snobbishness was clearly defined geographically.
>
> It is a wry mark of progress that these days school kids can do each other damage just as well on the stations of the North Shore as on the streets of Redfern . . .
>
> PETER ROBINSON,
Sun-Herald, 10 September 1995

The rural and business elites which form a large proportion of the upper class have been studied by Encel (1970, p. 301ff) in great detail and his research confirms the importance in their education of such schools as St Peter's College in Adelaide, Melbourne Grammar and Scotch College in Melbourne, The King's School and Sydney Grammar in Sydney, and Geelong Grammar in Victoria. In a sample of 214 male members of the rural elite, 142 had gone to private schools. In the total sample there was a similarly close social patterning: more than 95 per cent were Protestants; they belonged to exclusive clubs like the Melbourne Club, the Australian Club, the Union Club and the Royal Sydney Golf Club; and 55 held directorships in 108 companies.

As might be expected, members of this class tend to spring from the British Protestant strain in Australian society rather than from the Irish Catholic strain or from European ethnic groups. Anglicans tend to have a higher proportion of upper- and upper-middle class members than other religions, just as Catholics embrace a larger proportion of working-class people than other religions do. A Cultivated accent is found more often here than in other class groups and can take the form of an extraordinary fake Oxford accent; considerable emphasis is placed in upper-class families upon the importance of speaking correctly, dressing correctly, creating the right impression, conforming to the class style. For many years the ABC used only announcers with upper-class or Cultivated accents; certainly a Broad Aussie accent is rare among upper-class members, except occasionally among those class jumpers who have made it from the working class and hold on to their Broad accent as an emblem of their 'common' origins – hence the phenomenon of the professional ocker.

The upper class is certainly the best educated, the most refined and most sophisticated of the class groups: as American Express constantly reminds us, membership has its privileges – largely bestowed by education and wealth. Encel found that a high proportion of members of the business and rural elites had gone on from school to tertiary education; many of the private schools make it their business to prepare their pupils specifically for a university education. A certain refinement of taste and manners can also be discovered. Upper-class Australians can afford to frequent the best restaurants and shops, and sometimes patronise the arts as well. By virtue of their education and overseas experience they are often among the most civilised and urbane of people; they typically despise the vulgar taste and manners of the nouveau riche and represent the closest Australia comes to an aristocracy of style; they include among their numbers some leading intellectuals, artists and genuine philanthropists. The men, especially if they are professional people, are often hard-working and unpretentious, while their wives involve themselves in charity work, climb hard up the social ladder, or seek careers for themselves. A dominant conservatism, political and social, characterises the class ethos. And its characteristic style is perhaps most perfectly expressed by the former Prime Minister, Malcolm Fraser, whose hauteur, arrogance and supreme confidence in his right to govern (until his defeat by Bob Hawke in 1983) had an almost nineteenth-century quality to it. Fraser is more typical of the rural stratum of the upper class than the business stratum, and it should be said at once that he displays a certain idealism which is also not uncharacteristic of his group. Yet, when it came to the point of using the authority of his class and its political arm in 1975, he wielded its power with absolute ruthlessness to have the Whitlam government dismissed and the 'born-to-rule' elite installed in its place.

At the core of the upper class, therefore, is power. It is a power which is exercised directly, through sheer financial and economic force, and indirectly through politics and hegemonic control. It is a power which is jealously guarded and preserved; despite its willingness to accept talented outsiders the upper class strives to safeguard its position through education, intermarriage and family inheritance of wealth and position – hence the well-known dynasties of all the capital cities, such as the upper-crust Baillieus in Melbourne and the more recently arrived Packers in Sydney, a three-generation dynasty which has made Kerry Packer one of the most powerful men in the nation (and one of the most feared). When the former editor of the *Bulletin*, David Dale, once tried to explain to Packer, its owner, and property developer Warren Anderson that 'you have to realise...' Packer cut him brutally short: 'We don't HAVE to do anything,' he informed Dale. Packer obviously regards himself as above the politicians, the media (much of which he owns) and the rules; he's probably right.

Broom and Jones (1976), in their study of generational mobility and attainment, found that there was less mobility *out* of high-status groups than other groups; 'high status occupations show lower rates of out-mobility because better-off parents can promote the careers of their children,' they say bluntly. It is simply a fact of everyday observation that upper-class groups do their damnedest to give their children every possible advantage of wealth, education and career advancement and so keep them within the class into which they were born. There are various ways of measuring the closure of any class group, but it is clear from academic research that the upper class in Australia has a substantial degree of closure. R. A. Wild (1978, p. 52) summarises:

> It is possible to conclude tentatively that the upper class has a low rate of out-mobility and medium to high rates of intermarriage and internal property arrangements, leading to a degree of closure greater than that at other levels.' The upper class, he says, has a common basis in 'the ownership of private property, a firm class consciousness emphasising their propertied interests against the labour interests of others, and a medium level of closure through low rates of mobility and periodic intermarriage.

The upper class, therefore, is a formidable reality in the Australian class structure. Although it is the smallest of the class groups it is the one which wields the most institutional and organisational power. Although there is argument, at a theoretical level, as to whether it constitutes a ruling class or a governing class, and precisely who its constituents are, to those who are ruled and/or governed the brute power of the class is obvious enough. These are the bosses. They control much of the life of those who work for them. They can sack their employees, manipulate them, use the political system to regulate their options and freedoms. The division between employer and employee, between boss and worker, is one of the crucial divisions in Australian society. You'd have to be a boss not to think so.

In terms of sheer numbers, of course, the middle class has more impact upon the Australian way of life. In this sense it is possible to argue that the middle class is more powerful culturally than the upper class, because the middle-class lifestyle (or lifestyles) is more typical. Similarly one could argue that the working class has exerted more mythic power upon the Australian consciousness than any other, because so many Aussie icons/stereotypes/images are derived from the working class. The cultural impact of these groups should not be underestimated; indeed, Australian popular culture is largely the creation of the working and middle classes. Some of this culture offers a powerful resistance to and critique of the hegemony of the upper class. But in terms of sheer financial and economic power, and the ability to create a social order which serves their own interests, it is the upper class which dominates. The ruling ideas of any society at any time, argues Marx, are those of the ruling class. In Australia, as in any other western country, a comparatively small elite controls much of the nation's life and consciously sets out to impose its world-view upon the rest of society. In that way it manages, very effectively, to reproduce the privileged position which it has attained.

KYLIE v. SNOBS.

Class is not just a matter of snobbery, which is merely stupid; it is a matter of 'the right to rule'. And who has it.

LEONIE KRAMER
Class Profile

Leonie Kramer and Patrick White are wrestling in Desolation Row, the *Titanic* sails at dawn, there are masks on the onlookers with the heart attack machine; as the contestants separate, each recognises his/her own face in the other. Sceptics. Refugees from the death of God. Class conformists. Critics entrammelled by the society they berate. At such times the distance between them is illusory.

Patrick White is dead, but Leonie Kramer is alive and formidable in Vaucluse. The quarrel between them is one of the most famous in Australian letters. Patrick White habitually referred to Kramer as Killer Kramer, and wrote in his autobiography *Flaws in the Glass* about 'those who are unequivocally male or female – and Professor Leonie Kramer'; Kramer, for her part, has been one of White's most stringent critics and wrote about his novel *Memories of Many in One*, 'it raises real doubts about White's seriousness as a novelist'. And yet there are remarkable similarities between them: their spirituality, their detestation of the mundane and the suburban, their sense of estrangement from their own society – and their ineffable upper classness.

In many ways Leonie Kramer represents the best qualities of the class into which she was born, and which she has conformed to ever since: she is intelligent, highly cultivated, moral, concerned for the good of the whole culture rather than her own fortune. And yet she also displays some of its worst traits: its conservatism, its narrowness, its willingness to accept the privilege which has been handed to it as though it were a right instead of an accident of birth.

She has spent much of her life defending what she regards as traditional values against the barbarians at the gates. 'The need I feel to *do something* is a consequence of the moral training I got from the church,' she explains. Do something? She's been doing things all her life: Professor of Australian Literature at Sydney University, former chairperson of the ABC, on the boards of Western Mining, ANZ Bank and the NRMA, an influential conservative voice in everything from the Institute of Public Affairs to *Quadrant* magazine to dozens of groups, movements and advisory bodies, and now Chancellor of Sydney University, where she has gathered unprecedented power to the position and to herself; if you give someone like Leonie Kramer (or John Kerr, for that matter) power you should fully anticipate them exercising it untrammelled by any silly notion of convention.

Kramer, needless to say, doesn't see it like that and repudiates her reputation as an arch conservative as well. She's never belonged to any political party, she says; she votes Liberal quite often but not always; no, she won't say who else she has voted for. 'I was asked to go on the Liberal Senate ticket in 1983 and I was very flattered by that' – but she turned it down. 'I'm a terrible dumbhead about this; I can't stand labels or slogans, all those things that try to make it simple for you not to think. I believe in private enterprise but I'm not an absolute free market forces person; I don't believe in the Moral Majority. I'm not an extremist. I don't like the exercise of power. I found that when you are at the top of the hierarchy what you acquire is enormous responsibility, but your capacity to exercise power is absolutely limited. Australians are obsessed with power. Yes, I do express firm views but there's no way I'm going to try to force that on anyone.'

Which is all very surprising, and perhaps a bit disingenuous. Critic John Docker has analysed her at length as a baleful and authoritarian influence on Australian literature; at the ABC she was regarded as the Maggie Thatcher of the airwaves. Part of the problem is the distance between her personal manner, which is witty and quite beguiling, and what she actually says, which can be hair-raisingly Right-wing. And when her secretary politely refuses to bring her a cup of tea Dame Leonie remarks, without malice: 'Every now and then she asserts her authority and I get the tea. This is the way the world is. This is egalitarianism.'

That's the last thing she is: egalitarian. She feels she's worked 'damned hard' and been 'very tenacious' and was 'lucky enough to have a good family, a good education, a lot of luck and a lot of accidents' and no, she doesn't feel any guilt, 'I am not privileged, I'm sorry for people who don't make it, but I don't think people should have equality of reward – I'm concerned with quality, not equality'. She's saying this in a three-storey house in Vaucluse Road, Vaucluse, with a swimming pool foregrounding the harbour view, in an old-fashioned, rather gloomy drawing room of Chippendale furniture, gilt-framed watercolours, china plates, floral carpet, a lace tablecloth loaded with Scotch, a book on Slessor and a copy of the *Institute of Public Affairs Review* ('Australia's journal of free enterprise opinion') and mementos of the housekeeper who 'was a member of the family'. In this hushed ambience the loudest sound is the ticking of the grandfather clock.

Her personal style is a mixture of upper class and idiosyncratic. I remember her, when I was an English undergraduate at Sydney University, as a young woman with her hair pulled back in a tight bun, a brusque manner, enthusing about Les Murray and scorning the vernacular satire of Bruce Dawe; now she seems almost a dowager, hair cut back to a mannish shortness, spectacles dangling around her neck, a Victorian cloak over her shoulders as she sips from a teacup, little finger of her left hand sticking out, a slow teardrop forming in the corner of her eye as she talks briskly and purposefully about public policy, the galloping consumption of progressive education, the unresponsiveness to large ideas in Australian life – conventional stuff. But after a while you realise she is not as straight as she appears. She has a lighthearted, playful way of talking which she uses dextrously to poke fun at others and herself; that, and her sardonic sense of humour, make her a lot of fun to be with.

Upstairs, which is also stereotypically *Upstairs*, is a portrait by Harley Griffiths, a minor Melbourne impressionist, of Dame Leonie as a child of three: a tubby, doleful girl in a blue dress, pants drooping below the hem, one leg up, one leg down. Six decades later she can still remember posing for it: 'I felt very bored.' A few years ago she annoyed feminists by saying she found a lot of Australian women 'boring', and then that they didn't get into management positions because they tended to 'go limp' in crisis situations. Some feminists responded by arguing that Dame Leonie had acquired her considerable success at the cost of turning herself into a man-in-drag. The male sex gains its revenge by giving women balls.

She thinks that's silly. If anything she is a truer representative of her class than her gender. Father in the bank, a lay Church of Christ preacher; mother wanted to do medicine but was channelled into music. A cultivated household in Kew, Melbourne. She had a happy childhood; encouraged to read books, educated at the Presbyterian Ladies College. Which one? 'There is only one,' she says, smiling. Strong training in moral obligation and responsibilities; 'It was taken for granted that we would go out to university, take leadership roles'. In a way she has conformed to that moral imperative ever since, though she went through a rebellious period at school and was threatened with expulsion. 'I got myself into trouble because I got very cross with a couple of girls, prefects, who were frightful snobs. They were fiddling around with the duty roster and I got stuck into them. I had a burning sense of injustice. That rebelliousness is still there, I think. As an undercurrent. The reason I won't wear the dour conservative label is because I'm constantly dissatisfied with the status quo.'

Dame Leonie is herself unfailingly polite, and she is proud of the fact that PLC was 'very firm in its inculcation of proper social attitudes; snobbery, of course, you can never completely eliminate, but it was dealt with.' And adds, with some passion, 'I really cannot bear people treating other people as inferior human beings. Education should bring out someone's abilities, whether it be dressmaking or Ancient Greek.' And later, leaning up against the wall near her girl-in-blue portrait: 'Equality has to do with style, how you treat people.'

And there, of course, is the trouble. Behind Dame Leonie Kramer's lack of snobbery and personal commitment to civility lies an absolutely patrician acceptance of the inequality which surrounds her and the society which produces it. She argues for scholarships – but accepts the profound educational inequalities which make scholarships necessary. She espouses equal opportunity – but for grossly unequal rewards. The notion that equality has to do with 'personal style', not real social justice, befits an eighteenth-century philanthropist or a Mississippi plantation owner. No wonder that in a public lecture (in honour, ironically, of socialist Dr Nugget Coombs) she delivered a blast at 'education policy which panders to our sacred cow, egalitarianism'. Explaining: 'I'm antisocialist. I'm opposed to the idea that planners can bring about some social utopia. Equal opportunity legislation is planning gone mad!'

Such narrowness in someone as intelligent as Leonie Kramer is genuinely surprising. It's as though, all her life, she has accepted the attitudes and traditions of her class and has never been forced to question them. The straightness of her trajectory she confirms herself. 'Yes, I've gone straight ahead from my family, my school.' She moved remorselessly up the academic ladder: student, tutor, lecturer, professor, chair, Dame. Never any need to rethink the direction in which she had been pointed since, at the age of six, she was delivered to the PLC kindergarten, Melbourne. 'I don't think I've changed much. I do believe in order.' She looks around her islanded drawing room. Images of comfort and stability. 'I accept it, I don't question it, because it works.'

She could be talking about our entire society. It works . . . for her. As she talks another slow bead forms in the corner of her eye; she removes her spectacles, wipes it away. In the corridor the girl-in-blue, aged three. One up, one down. Pleasant. Responsible. Doleful. Like Kylie, a victim of her class. Sixty-five years later she is manifest, unchanged, in a drawing room in Vaucluse, overlooking the harbour, as the future slouches towards her . . . and us all.

12
Underclass

The concept of an underclass is one taken from American sociology which has become increasingly used in Australia – largely because Australian society has begun to show some of the features of American society which so appal visitors to cities like New York and Los Angeles and which everyone thought could never happen here. It refers to the development of a permanently and chronically disadvantaged group of people who seem to be outside the traditional class structure and 'under' even the working class: a terribly distressed stratum of the unemployed, the sick, the homeless, the mentally disturbed and the poverty-stricken who reproduce these characteristics from generation to generation and become locked into a state of permanent disenfranchisement.

In America they are typically black, Hispanic or poor white; in Australia they are typically Aboriginal, ethnic or poor white. In America they are typically ghetto-dwellers in big cities; in Australia they are typically inner-city or outer-suburban dwellers in big cities. Sometimes they are people who slip or fall into the underclass for a period of time, because they lose their jobs or become sick or suffer some disastrous trauma, and then claw their way out again and join conventional society (usually at working-class level); more worrying is the fact that many in this group are born into it and spend their lives permanently disenfranchised, with little hope or expectation of ever leaving it. Levels of drug abuse, alcoholism, crime and prostitution are high; so is the existence of violence, self-mutilation and suicide. As the term 'underclass' implies, these are people at the very bottom of the social hierarchy, a virtually dispossessed group of outcasts who not only seem to have been discarded by society but who, in turn, sometimes discard that society (and its values) and wreak a violent revenge upon it. Thus, in America, the familiar spectacle of entire city precincts racked by crime, crack, gangs and sexual violence, erupting in riots like those in Los Angeles in 1992.

In Australia the social distress suffered by the underclass, and others, has not so far reached that point of despair, though there is a real fear that if the Howard government pushes ahead with repressive economic and social policies which polarise the community and worsen the tension between social groups a similarly explosive situation could be created here. No matter what government is in power in Canberra, the social conditions which have created a clear Australian underclass run the risk of a parallel result. According to the former Victorian Commissioner of Police, Kel Glare, 'we run the risk of the development of an underclass, a group of young disadvantaged people without jobs and without hope, a class of unemployed at risk of becoming unemployable . . . The high levels of unemployment which will continue will almost certainly lead to the development of a disadvantaged underclass who will not embrace the norms and values of the society which has failed them . . .' (address to Liberal Party's Job Forum, July 1992).

Mr Glare got it right except for one thing: the underclass is already here.

Despite theoretical argument about whether the underclass is a class in its own right, or should be regarded as an underemployed or unemployed fraction of the working class, most people know what it means – and the social deprivation which it infers. Thus Stephen Edgell in *Class* (1993, p. 78):

> The ideologically loaded term the "underclass" is often used to describe those at the bottom of the class structure who are persistently poor due to permanent or irregular economic inactivity, which in turn is often attributed to a culture of poverty and/or a cycle of deprivation rather than economic change. Studies of class which focus on the economically active, by definition exclude the underclass from class analysis and imply that this "class" is outside of "society".
>
> Yet for both Marx and Weber, the underclass was an integral part of the class system. Marx referred to the underclass as a "relative surplus population" or "industrial reserve army" and argued that capital accumulation at one end of the class structure depended on the growth of a disposable labour force at the other. In other words, wealth and poverty are two sides of the same coin; the underclass is a permanent feature of capitalism and not a temporary feature of the business cycle. For Weber the underclass was a negatively privileged class which included "outcasts", "debtor classes" and the "poor", some of whom may experience segregation on the basis of ethnic status . . . Moreover, the growth of the underclass in America and Britain, due to economic recession, cuts in expenditure on social welfare, and deindustrialisation, suggests that it is a regular feature of the class structure of advanced capitalist societies.

Such as Australia.

Professor Paul Krugman, at the Massachusetts Institute of Technology (MIT), believes the underclass began growing in the United States in the 1960s and has possibly accelerated since then. In Australia a similar phenomenon has occurred, with the generalised affluence of the sixties and the early seventies, and the boom years of the late eighties, disguising the development of structural (as opposed to cyclical) unemployment and a pool of largely unskilled, inexperienced workers who remain permanently outside the workforce and depend upon welfare and charity handouts to survive at all. It is a situation which many Aborigines, especially those in bush towns and inner-city ghettos like Redfern, and recently arrived migrants have been familiar with for years.

Family background is probably the single greatest factor in determining whether someone is condemned to the underclass or not; poverty-stricken, out-of-work families are likely to bring up their children in an environment which the children themselves reproduce in later life – partly because of the sheer power of cultural conditioning, and partly because the opportunities to escape such an environment are so limited. But unemployment is also a major factor, especially long-term unemployment, which can lead to someone eventually giving up all hope of finding a job and relying on social security to keep alive. Petty crime, prostitution and drugs can soon follow. The growth of a discernible underclass in Australia is clearly linked to the growth of unemployment over the last three decades. By 1993 the number of officially unemployed workers had topped one million, or over 11 per cent of the workforce, for the first time in the nation's history. By 1996 the unemployment level had dropped to 8.6 per cent, but this was still historically high. Nor was this level of unemployment simply due to the recession which began in 1990; much of it is structural rather than cyclical unemployment, due to structural changes in the Australian economy, the replacement of workers by computer technology, the increasing productivity of those workers who have jobs, and the predilection of corporations for job-shedding in harsh economic times. In the 1996 federal election both major parties, Labor and the Liberal/National coalition, promised to reduce unemployment; John Howard targeted youth unemployment in particular and made its reduction a key election policy. However, it is forecast by government and private-sector economists alike that unemployment is likely to stay high for the rest of this decade. Professor Bob Gregory (ANU) says that the loss of full-time jobs in the last two decades is unprecedented. 'After adjusting for population growth, one in four male full-time jobs has disappeared. A job loss of this magnitude has never occurred before in our history,' he said in his Copland Oration to the Conference of Economists, July 1992. Professor Gregory estimates that for Australia to return to 'full' employment its economic growth would have to outstrip its performance in the boom years of the 1980s – which is unlikely.

Many of these unemployed people are long-term unemployed, namely those who have been out of work for a year or more; and it is from this group that the underclass draws many of its recruits. By mid-1993 the number of long-term unemployed had jumped to 370 000, or nearly 40 per cent of the total unemployed. Nor does a return to strong economic growth necessarily produce a dramatic fall in these long-term unemployed because the new jobs which are created tend to go to young people entering the workforce for the first time, or married women re-entering the workforce, or others who squeeze out the long-term unemployed. Labour market and training programs help some people, but the federal government estimates that less than half the long-term unemployed have access to these programs. Many will never work again, because they don't have the necessary skills, or are regarded as too old, or suffer disabilities, or just give up. What the system seems incapable of doing, as it turns more and more to computer technology, restructuring and job-wastage, is finding enough work to go around.

The people who run the greatest risk of falling into long-term unemployment are often those who are disadvantaged in other ways. An ANU study by Dr Bruce Chapman and Mr Peter Smith found that the key characteristics of the at-risk group were having left school early, being young, living in a rural area, being born in a non-English-speaking country, being unwilling in the early stages of unemployment to accept a poorly-paid job, and being male. Children are sometimes the starkest victims of this situation. In Australia in 1992 more than one million children, or 29 per cent of children under fourteen years old, were in families which had some sort of government income support, though this included middle-class families getting family allowance. Almost 700 000 children were living in homes where nobody was earning an income.

The impact of unemployment on these children, and on people who continually fail to get a job, is well-known. It can have disastrous psychic and physical effects, ranging from depression to debilitating illness to, at worst, suicide. The federal Department of Health has confirmed that there is a clear link between 'socio-economic status' (class) and health: strokes, heart disease, skin diseases, lung cancer, hypertension and infectious diseases are all more prevalent in lower income areas. The National Heart Foundation has found that male blue-collar workers and unemployed are at far greater risk from cigarette smoking and insufficient exercise than professional and administrative workers. A Community Health Studies research program found that the incidence of death from respiratory and digestive diseases increases dramatically the lower down the socio-economic scale you go. The poor health of many Aboriginal communities is notorious; what isn't commonly recognised is that poor white communities often suffer a similar syndrome.

The social cost of this class-skewed situation is enormous: in the loss of productive labour, in the cost of unemployment benefits and other social services, in the impairment of so many citizens, and in the by-products of crime and violence. A study for the

NSW Bureau of Crime Statistics and Research of city and rural local government areas showed that areas with high rates of criminal offenders tend to be those with high proportions of unemployment, poor families, single-parent families, public housing tenants and Aborigines. It is precisely these social groups, of course, which form a sort of catchment area for the underclass. The study was based upon an examination of where offenders lived, not necessarily where the crimes took place; crimes against property (for example, burglary, car theft) often take place in wealthier suburbs where people have more to lose. If society is prepared to tolerate the development of such an underclass, it has to put up with the consequences.

Inequality

One of the great characteristics of the 1980s and 1990s has been the growing inequality of incomes: the gap between the haves and have-nots has been growing, despite the partly successful efforts of the federal Labor government of 1983–96 to provide more support for low-income and single-parent families. Unemployment and low incomes threaten more and more people with the spectre of falling into the underclass.

The figures outlining this have been well disseminated but they are worth repeating. In 1981–82, according to the Australian Bureau of Statistics, the total income of all families was $102.5 billion. The top 20 per cent of these received 9.5 times as much money ($45.2 billion) as the bottom 20 per cent. By the 1990s total family income had risen to $228 billion but the top 20 per cent had dramatically increased their advantage over the bottom 20 per cent – they now received eleven times as much ($106.9 billion). Welfare and income support payments improved the living standards of some people right down the bottom of the income scale, but these did not prevent the gap widening. Indeed, the United Nations Human Development Report for 1992 reported that the income share of the bottom 40 per cent of Australian households between 1980 and 1988 was just 15.5 per cent – the lowest of twenty-one countries. In the United States, for instance, the parallel income share for this lower segment of income earners was 15.7 per cent, in Britain it was 17.3 per cent and in Japan 21.9 per cent. Australia also revealed greater inequality when the top 20 per cent were compared to the bottom 20 per cent; according to the UN calculations, the top group earned 9.6 times more than the bottom group, compared to 8.9 times in the United States, 6.8 times in Britain and 4.3 times in Japan.

It's a grim truth: there is more income inequality in Australia than any other developed nation. So much for the egalitarian myth.

Real wages were held down by government policy throughout the 1980s, allegedly to increase the profit share of corporations (which it did) and encourage investment and incentive. But many companies simply indulged in property and asset speculation and gave huge pay rises to their executives; it was the age of paper entrepreneurs like Bond, Skase, Holmes à Court and others whom the business media, to their eternal disgrace, turned into folk heroes. Well, they were heroes to the financial writers, at least. A study by Bradbury, Doyle and Whiteford for the Social Policy Research Centre in 1990 found that the average income of the top 5 per cent of (married) men had climbed by a half in the four years to 1989–90, while the average income of the bottom 5 per cent increased by only a quarter. Professor Bob Gregory has estimated that in today's dollars it would take a wage increase of about $4000 a year for the bottom 10 per cent of male, full-time, non-managerial adult employees to regain the position they held relative to the top 10 per cent in 1976.

No chance.

Some of the class effects of this maldistribution are truly appalling. In 1995 an official report to the NSW government showed that students living on Sydney's north shore and in the eastern suburbs, which are the two richest areas of the city, gained a tertiary entrance rank (TER) in the Higher School Certificate exams on average twice as high as students living in Sydney's less privileged south-west. The students in the most affluent suburbs got an average TER score between 70 and 84, which granted them access to a wide range of courses in all the state's universities; those in large areas of the south-western suburbs, however, received an average TER score of between 30 and 40, which would not win them a place in any Sydney-based university which used only the TER score to select students. The statistics confirmed what many educators already knew, and have known for years: that students from wealthy backgrounds receive a remarkable advantage in the education system. Commenting on the details of the report, the president of the Parents & Teachers Federation, Mrs Ros Brennan, said she was 'ashamed' of what it revealed. 'We should be ashamed that a person's geographical location, that their class and their economic circumstances should be allowed, by the HSC system, to engage in social replication.'

Income inequality isn't the only inequality which has worsened; so has the inequality between different urban neighbourhoods. In a 1995 paper on 'The Macro Economy and the Growth of Ghettos and Urban Poverty in Australia', Dr Bob Gregory and B. Hunter pointed out that in census districts of low socio-economic status ghettos of unemployment and urban poverty have grown up which highlight appalling spatial and geographic inequality between Australians living in different suburbs. They conclude:

> The data show that the economic distance between Australians from different parts of the city has widened to an extraordinary degree . . . We were surprised and alarmed at the extent of the changes for the

worse that have occurred since the mid 1970s . . . It is evident that income inequality has increased across neighbourhoods for both genders and by substantial amounts . . . The income gap between the top and bottom 5 per cent of census districts has almost doubled and has widened by $20 144 (92 per cent) . . . For males, Australia has returned to neighbourhood employment patterns of the 1930s where there are substantial ghettos of non-employment . . . The census data suggest that those from low income neighbourhoods are increasingly losing contact with the world of employment. The pattern of the high rates of joblessness in census districts of low socio-economic status is very disturbing . . . It seems likely that the greater the economic polarisation within our cities the less equal are the opportunities for young people and the more likely that bad neighbourhood pathologies will emerge.

This is gentle language. By 'socio-economic status' Gregory and Hunter basically mean class. There are now class ghettos in Australia which are not so different from their American counterparts; not unexpectedly, equivalent patterns of social distress and violence have begun to emerge.

Some families have tried to combat their situation by taking on extra part-time work, or by turning themselves into two-income families. Between January 1983 and January 1990 the total number of jobs in the workforce grew by more than 1.5 million, but half of this increase was due to part-time jobs; full-time jobs grew by far less. Many of the new jobs went to families where one person was already working; in fact during the decade of the 1980s more than a third of employment growth went to households which already had an income earner. Peter Saunders at the Social Policy Research Centre at the University of NSW estimates that the number of families with two or more members working increased by just over half a million, or 30 per cent, from 1983 to 1989; those with just one breadwinner fell by 11.5 per cent; families where no-one had a job rose by 3.6 per cent. In other words, employment growth tends to privilege those families which already have work, rather than going to the unemployed. As two-income and one-and-a-half income families move closer to being the norm, so the gap between 'average' families and the unemployed becomes larger.

Unemployment is the chief cause of poverty in Australia. In the 1990s the nation faces not only a long period of sustained high unemployment but an intractably large proportion of long-term unemployed. The reality, therefore, of a dispossessed and growing underclass is now something which Australians have to face up to – together with the concomitants which nations like the United States and Britain have been experiencing: beggars in the street, cardboard cities, poverty-stricken ghettos, violence, the revenge of the hopeless. A redistribution of work and income, financed in part by higher taxes on those (especially the well-off) who have jobs, would help combat this, but so far the Australian political superstructure has shown no willingness to tackle such radical solutions. The situation is worsened by the reluctance of so many Australians to come to grips with the way in which Australia is a class society, much less admit that we have an underclass. In 1967 Sir Robert Askin, Premier of NSW, said: 'We have no poor people in NSW. Nor any very rich people. Ours is a classless society.' But then Askin was corrupt, and a crook. Most Australians are neither. In a way the theoretical discussion as to whether there is an identifiable underclass in western societies such as Australia, or whether it is a fraction of the traditional working class – a sort of non-working working class, as it is sometimes denigrated, or marginalised *lumpen proletariat* – is less important than the fact that such a desparately disenfranchised and underprivileged social group exists, whatever it is called. And that it has been created by a class system which, incontrovertibly, destroys people's lives.

BOBBI SYKES
Class Profile

'I was the oldest of three black children. All-white town. A very weird situation happened. I lived in this white area. My sisters and I used to walk home from the school and the white kids used to throw stones at us, they used to stone us every afternoon. So I used to walk backwards and send my two sisters running on ahead of me, and I used to stay there till they were safe, and then I used to exchange stones with all these white kids who thought it was great sport to stone us. These kids split my head open so many times. One time I was layin' on the ground and my mother raced up, she's picked me up and ran all the way to the hospital with me with blood pourin' out of my head. I still don't understand those sorts of people . . .'

It's Bobbi Sykes. In the seventies she became a national figure as a militant black activist, and today she looks much the same: the same tough, cool gaze, the same finely moulded, quite beautiful face, the same passionate commitment to the Aboriginal movement she showed when she was arrested at the Aboriginal tent embassy confrontation. But these days she is Dr Roberta Sykes, Harvard graduate in education, poet, writer. She is older, probably in her fifties, frailer, warier.

She comes from the underclass, or so it would seem (she doesn't like talking about her background). She was born in Townsville, in north Queensland, a few kilometres from the Aboriginal encampment of Black River. Her father was black, but she hardly knew him; her mother, who is still living 'up the coast', is white and raised Bobbi and her two younger sisters. When quite young, Bobbi went to St Joseph's orphanage in Rockhampton. She went through primary school and then briefly to high school, studied fourteen subjects, including Latin and all the prerequisites for a science or medicine degree. 'But they didn't have blacks at school after your fourteenth birthday,' she says. 'The teachers told me there was no way I could do medicine, that I had to go into domestic science. So I thought: I'm not going to do that either, so I did typing, bookkeeping and shorthand, just to have all the bases covered.'

She laughs, a harsh, ironic laugh. 'In a lot of ways I'm pretty bright, in other ways I'm not. I know now that many teachers speak two languages at the same time so the whites get one message and the blacks get another. The whites would be encouraged to proceed and the blacks would be discouraged . . .'

She'd have liked to be a surgeon, maybe doing heart or lung transplants by now – 'I don't doubt I had the brains.' But she was up against three insuperable barriers: class, racism and sexism. For much of her life Bobbi Sykes has been struggling to overcome those barriers and working to make sure that other black Australians don't have to fight the way she did. It took a long time. Instead of studying medicine she became a trainee nurse at Charters Towers hospital, didn't finish the course, and worked in factories in Townsville and Brisbane. 'I regret that options weren't open,' she says. 'No, I don't feel sour. Or cynical. What's the point in nurturing all those useless emotions?'

Sykes worked her way down to NSW and soon got involved in the activist movement. She read and read, educated herself, started writing for newspapers and magazines and became the first secretary of the tent embassy set up on the lawns outside Parliament House. The embassy, of course, was a symbolic act, a deliberate defiance of those at the top by those at the bottom. She was fierce and articulate and there was a personal edge to her anger; in her first book of poetry she thanks Mum Shirl Smith, the Aboriginal elder who could neither read nor write, for 'pushing' her.

In 1978 a visiting black academic from Harvard, Professor Chester Pierce, Professor of Education and Psychiatry, saw some of her writing on social issues and asked her to send more to him; the following year she got a cable inviting her to be a postgraduate student at Harvard. She wrote her thesis on Aboriginal education issues, got her doctorate, returned to Australia in 1983, began lecturing at the School of Medicine at the University of NSW and wrote discussion papers and reports for government authorities such as the Commonwealth Office for the Aged. She also got involved in Black Women's Action, an unfunded organisation which has begun sending other Aboriginal women to the United States for higher education. She got married, had two children, Russell and Naomi, and then when her marriage broke up moved to a quiet cottage near bushland in North Sydney to work and write, and involve herself in Aboriginal issues.

It's an extraordinary and heartening story, but it also reveals how difficult it is for anyone in the Australian underclass – especially a black Australian – to break free of the barriers and restrictions which imprison them. Only some Aborigines are unmistakably members of the underclass, but enough are to make it clear that it isn't just racism which Aboriginal Australians confront, though that is bad enough, but a class and economic system which institutionalises their inferior life chances. Unemployed, poorly educated Aboriginal parents are likely to raise unemployed, poorly educated children, who not only tend to take their parents as life models but also come up against the forces which condemned their parents to a disadvantaged position in society in the first place. In a sense these Aborigines are repeating the experience of rural blacks in the southern states of America earlier this century: they grow up and perpetuate a black underclass which even the 'white trash' can despise.

At the centre of her consciousness, her experience, is her blackness. She says she isn't anti-white, meaning individuals; she has white friends. 'Sure. Stacks of 'em. Some of my best friends,' she says, straightfaced. But she talks bitterly about 'white folks', white society, Mr White Man, the reality of racism in contemporary Australia. And just as her class position is inflected by her race, it is also inflected by her gender. 'Y'know, white males don't have to have any of this consciousness of themselves, they float around saying things like "we're all people" . . . that's a load of bullshit, because women are always aware and conscious of the fact that they're a woman . . . well, with the black, you're always conscious of the fact that you're a black. You get attacked far more for being a black than for being a woman, though they attack black women in a different way . . . they're more likely to rape a woman than a man. I don't think I understood that until I was in the embassy and I saw the police. I saw them come over and start punching out the black women. I mean, the police force at that time was all male, they walked over to this predominantly female group, and they started sockin' our people, hittin' 'em with truncheons, punching 'em on the jaw and everything, and I thought, I just can't believe this. The people they attacked turned into being *blacks*, not *women*.'

She stops, lights a cigarette. Long fingernails. Gold wedding rings. She is thin, graceful, in dark blue sweater, dark blue pants, sneakers. There is about her this constant sense of disjunction, of dissonance, of surprising and jarring contradiction between the Townsville black and the Harvard sophisticate, between the escapee from the underclass and the academic.

Is she a revolutionary?

'I don't think of myself as a revolutionary. I don't think you can be a revolutionary unless there's a revolution; otherwise it's fairly sad. But I have revolutionary ideas – about race, about women's issues, about the whole political system.' For Bobbi Sykes, these are all interlinked. 'I believe the environment is designed to make people feel impotent, make them feel they should limit the areas they hope to change. Stuff like that. Now I feel: why shouldn't I change the system if I don't like it? Why shouldn't I change the political process, or the relationship between blacks and whites, or men and women, if I don't like it? We should all be working for that.'

13
Class and Culture

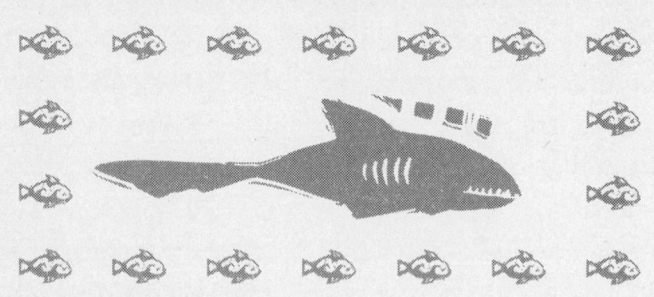

Culture is a smoking gun: it can be used against an entire people as readily as it can be turned against the individual. It is the great equaliser or the great unequaliser, according to who holds the gun – and who it's pointed at. It can be a brick hurled through the shop window, a credit card scissored in the street, a 100 000-strong protest march through the streets of Melbourne, or it can be a multi-million-dollar advertising campaign to persuade people to smoke/vote Liberal/shut up and watch TV and let those who really *know* get on with the business of running the country. If power flows from the barrel of a gun, in places like Australia the gun is more likely to be a satellite TV transmitter or a think tank or a political jingle than an AK-47 automatic weapon. If your weapon is cultural dominance you don't need the real thing. Example: 'equality' has been given such a bad name in Australia that the media virtually never mention it and even the Labor Party resorts to words like 'equity' so no-one will be scared off. It's a tribute to the power of the upper class, or the ruling elite, in Australian society that the challenge to its position implied by the word should have been so effectively ruled off from mainstream political discourse.

Culture, in its inclusive sense of the rituals, activities, icons, relationships and ways of thinking which go to make up the Australian way of life, is obviously crucial to the pattern of class relationships and the distribution of power in society. It is, for instance, the generalised culture of a community which delineates what is politically acceptable and what is not, what is 'extreme' and what is mainstream, what you can do to change the system and what you can't (most Australians, it would seem, are prepared to tolerate changing the system through the ballot box, are divided about strikes and demonstrations, and are opposed to violent protest and action), what the limits to radicalism are, indeed what is thought to be utopian or impractical or unrealistic (like socialism) and what is commonsense.

The concept of 'commonsense' is crucial to the theory of Antonio Gramsci, the unconventional Italian Marxist who developed the theory of hegemony to explain the continued dominance of ruling groups or a ruling class in modern industrial societies and the apparent failure of the revolutions which Marx had predicted would occur. What Gramsci set out to explain was the phenomenon, which is very apparent in Australia, of the rule of the governors with the consent of the governed, so that most people come to accept a system which exploits them and not only tolerate but actively endorse the continued dominance of a small, extremely powerful group in politics, finance, industry, civic affairs and the society at large. Hegemony strictly means the indirect rule of one group or country over another; Gramsci expanded it to describe the way in which the ruling class in modern capitalist societies exercises power not through direct political coercion, at gunpoint (though this occurred in Nazi Germany and in Mussolini's Italy, where Gramsci was jailed), but through *ideological* and *cultural* control – so that the great mass of people comes to accept the way society is organised as natural and 'commonsense'. People begin to think that *how things are* is *how things should be.* Those who think otherwise are dismissed as freaks, crazies, subversives or at best misguided idealists. Or else people are persuaded that, even if they know things are wrong, there's nothing much they can do about it.

By hegemony Gramsci meant

> the permeation through civil society – including a whole range of structures and activities like trade unions, schools, the churches, and the family – of an entire system of values, attitudes, beliefs, morality, etc. that is in one way or another supportive of the established order and the class interests that dominate it. Hegemony in this sense might be defined as an "organising principle", or world-view (or combination of such world-views), that is diffused by agencies of ideological control and socialisation into every area of daily life.
>
> To the extent that this prevailing consciousness is internalised by the broad masses, it becomes part of "commonsense"; as all ruling elites seek to perpetuate their power, wealth and status, they necessarily attempt to popularise their own philosophy, culture, morality, etc., and render them unchallengeable, part of the natural order of things ... From Gramsci's perspective, what [was needed] was an understanding of the subtle but pervasive forms of ideological control and manipulation that served to perpetuate *all* repressive structures ... Ideological domination rather than direct political coercion had become the primary instrument of bourgeois rule ... (Boggs, 1980, p. 39).

This seems to me an apt description of the situation in Australia today. It is commonplace these days for Australia to be described as 'conservative'; that is certainly the view of ALP leader Kim Beazley and a great many others in the Labor Party, which is used as a justification for the party's adoption of essentially conservative, non-reformist policies. But it is not true that the society, or the electorate, is 'innately' conservative, any more than it would be true to say it is 'innately' radical; such phrases merely describe the current balance of forces within the society, and that balance can be changed by a number of things, from political action to economic circumstance; conservative, in this sense, merely means that conservative interests have managed to achieve a dominant position in the nation's life through exactly the means which Gramsci describes.

Consensus politics, of course, plays directly into the hands of these interests because the consensus which emerges must accommodate them. On the social/political scales it is the side which has the most weight which moves the fulcrum, the point of balance, closest to its side. Bob Hawke made consensus such a dirty word that few politicians use it any longer, but this does not mean it has disappeared from the political process; it is one of the major means by which governing structures seek to gain consent to the status quo. This means, in practice, the formalising of the dominance of the most powerful groups and interests in society; in Australia it means the dominance of an extremely small, powerful class of owners, managers and their allies – the power bloc – over other groups. This dominance is not conspiratorial or covert; there is no need for a conspiracy theory; it is quite open. So are the forms of cultural persuasion and manipulation which are used.

Sometimes, as I have argued, it comes down to the way in which single words – and concepts – are coloured and disarmed. For instance, 'socialism' is a political philosophy which is opposed to any class structure and in particular to the class system as it has evolved in western capitalist countries, including Australia. It is inevitable, therefore, that it should be vehemently opposed by the capitalist 'owning' class which it threatens, and which in our society has mobilised an armoury of propaganda, persuasion and political action against it. In innumerable election campaigns, in business forums, in the newspapers and television and radio, for generation after generation, socialism has been presented as evil, authoritarian, Communistic, old-fashioned, or at best impractical – 'it would be all right if people were perfect, but they aren't' was the cliché I was fed at the private school I went to. The Cold War was used to associate socialism with the excesses of Soviet Stalinism, with spying and betrayal, with the McCarthyist scare about 'traitors in our midst', with everything from the Petrov affair to traditional xenophobia about Red China; in the year 1984 George Orwell, a socialist to his dying day, was resuscitated yet again to conjure up terrible images of Big Brother. The result was to turn socialism into a dirty word, so that the Labor Party now fears it is an electoral liability and deliberately avoids the word in its electoral propaganda. The Socialist Left is daily pilloried in the media as extremist and its policies as those of the 'lunatic fringe'; even the most neutral of journalists and commentators habitually colour the word 'Left' to indicate ideological rigidity and excess. If you asked Kim Beazley if he was a socialist, he'd say no. Game, set and match to the conservatives.

The cultural conditioning which reinforces the dominance of the upper class begins early. The family, which is the chief socialising unit in the individual's early years, typically reproduces in the child the dominant attitudes and ethos of capitalist society: individualism, competitiveness, and of course the different sex roles assigned to women and men. There is some resistance to this, especially in families which try to bring their children up to act in cooperative rather than competitive ways, but a family which is struggling with the daily grind of work, house mortgage (or rent), credit cards and, sometimes, the effort of a career for the husband and the wife as well, is much more likely to reproduce the system's emphasis upon security and possessions and competitive success than challenge it. The segregation of the social classes and the imposition of the existing class structure upon the next generation has already begun, with the different social groups living in different suburbs, moving among different people, adopting different lifestyles, working at different jobs and inculcating different attitudes, including attitudes of superiority and deference, in their children. The gross inequality of the system, and society's acceptance of it, is already apparent to most children by the time they go to school.

The Schools

At school the socialisation into the system is carried still further. The segregation which began at home is now formalised by the different school systems. There have been so many studies made of what actually happens to the children of different social groups when they go to school that it is hardly necessary to stress that the schools, either consciously or unconsciously, reinforce the existing class structure. Private schools, for instance, set out quite openly to provide a 'different' education for upper-class pupils and to emphasise the distance between them and students at other schools (boaters, hats, blazers, uniforms, school songs, speech days and so on are emblems of this); they stress leadership, academic success, discipline, and the importance of a career for both girls and boys; considerable attention is paid to good manners and style. There is no doubt in anyone's mind, pupils, teachers and parents alike, that they are providing a 'superior' education for 'superior' people.

At the opposite end of the scale, working-class kids usually go to a local school in a working-class suburb; sometimes the schools are old, poorly equipped and overcrowded. The difference between these schools and wealthy, lavishly equipped private schools which are heavily subsidised by the government is stark; they often have a high proportion of non-English-speaking migrant children, which complicates teaching and places even more strain on the overburdened state school system; many of the pupils expect to leave school as soon as they can, and the school curriculum often steers them, in ways which may be quite specific or subtle and unconscious, towards working-class jobs, apprenticeships, the lower end of the workforce. No-one doubts that this is an inferior education for – well, let's say 'less privileged' people.

In the newer comprehensive schools a deliberate attempt is made to avoid this class typing, but the process of streaming pupils according to their apparent academic ability, whatever its educational advantages, quickly establishes a hierarchy among the pupils. The selective high school system, which lingers on in various states, establishes a hierarchy between schools in the government system which apes the differentiation between private and government schools. It also leads to some bizarre social results, as recounted by Kessler and others in *Ockers and Discomaniacs* (1982, p. 12):

> The system of academic competition constructs a group of losers, and helps shape sexual identity for them . . . A reminiscence by a friend of ours sharpens the point. She went to MacRobertson Girls' High, a very well-known selective school in Melbourne. There were four streams at the time, A, B, C and D, sorted on the usual basis of supposed 'ability'. Girls in the C and D stream gradually got excluded from positions of leadership in the school, and came to be regarded as stupid and sexually precocious. The point was that all of them had been academically selected, and would have been in the A stream of a local comprehensive, where they would have looked down on others as stupid and precocious.

By the time young Australians leave school, then, their class typing has been strongly reinforced. In a minority of cases the school enables pupils to move from one social class to another. In private schools the sons and daughters of ambitious or upwardly mobile parents may be socialised into the style and career patterns of the upper-middle or upper class; in state schools academic achievement can provide working-class and lower-middle-class kids with the chance of going on to university and professional-level careers. There is also a certain amount of downward social mobility, though this is less publicised. The majority of young people, however, stay within the social class they come from and their schooling in general reinforces rather than challenges this social pattern.

The invidious nature of this process is disguised by the myth of 'equality of opportunity', a delusory catchcry which has been taken up by the major political parties of all persuasions. As I have pointed out in *Soundtrack for the 'Eighties* (1983), equality of opportunity is a fraud; not only does it manifestly not exist, it can be (and is) used to justify offensively unequal rewards on the grounds that everyone had the same chance; on that argument you could justify a slave state . . . one in which a tiny minority of winners rules over a great mass of losers. Come to think of it, that is not so far from what happens right now.

The 'equality of opportunity' argument also presupposes that what we want is a society characterised by competition rather than cooperation, one in which everyone is out to do the others down, climb on their shoulders, stab them in the back, achieve enormous privilege and wealth and power at the expense of damning others to terrible underprivilege, poverty and powerlessness (Aborigines, single mothers, the chronically sick and out of work, to take a few home examples, or the millions who die each year in the Third World) . . . whereas what Australian society needs is not equality of opportunity to be unequal, but genuine equality of reward. The meritocratic argument, with its stale equation of merit plus effort equals reward, has long been exposed as a camouflage for gross inequality and privilege, but even on its own grounds it is hardly applicable to a class society like Australia. M. J. Berry, in his study of inequality in *Australian Society* (Davies, Encel & Berry, 1977, p. 43), concludes:

> Economic inequality could only be fully justified in merit terms in a society with perfect social mobility, in a society where, regardless of accidents of birth, those individuals possessing the appropriate merit characteristics rise to the top . . . A meritocracy is like a fairly contested race in which all competitors start together and run over the same track, with victory and the spoils going to the swiftest. The Australian situation, in contrast, more closely resembles the case where a few competitors start one metre from the finishing line, a few more fifty metres back up the track, a larger group are further back hammering in their starting blocks, others are still changing in a crowded dressing-room, while the remainder are at home under the impression that the race starts tomorrow.

The inequalities of class are obvious enough. What the dominant culture does is make people accept them. The family and the school, as two key modes of the transmission of culture, begin this process. The education system is under continual pressure to make schools more oriented towards the workforce; despite the efforts of curriculum devisers to resist this pressure and to create courses (social studies, general studies and so on) which at least begin to question the dominant system and to examine how it works, most young people leave school without having been consciously taught about their own society, its conflicts, and the critiques which can be made of it. Politics, that is, the formal study of politics or civics, is not taught in most schools, which reinforces the dominant system by withholding examination of it; if you do not question, or are given no chance to question, the status quo the balance of power remains with the conservatives. By the time young people leave school most of them have come to accept the system as it is.

This acceptance is reinforced, of course, by many other conservative institutions which purvey the ideology of the system or legitimise it in one way or another: the churches, which characteristically support the established order; the monarchy, which in the rump form of the Governor-General has been particularly powerful in Australia, as the dismissal of the Labor government in 1975 proved, but is now likely to disappear as Australia moves towards being a republic; the armed forces and police, both of which have been and are used by governments to suppress strikes, protests and demonstrations; the judicial system, which has a key function in upholding and enforcing the existing order *as it is*; business organisations such as chambers of commerce and chambers of manufactures; the honours system; even such familiar symbols and rituals as the flag, the national anthem ... the list goes on.

There are, of course, diversity and dissent within these institutions. There are attempts at reform, reconstitution, democratisation, but the overall effect remains one of reinforcing the conservative hegemony. Faced with such a barrage of indoctrination it is hardly any wonder that most Australians grow up to accept the class system which exists and the entire panoply of divisions, rewards, limits, baits, contests, snakes and ladders, penalties, channels, failures, manipulations and outright repressions which go with it. The surprise is that there is as much resistance as there is.

The Media

Before leaving school, and certainly afterwards, Australians are also subject to indoctrination by one of the most potent propaganda forces of all: the media. This includes the advertising industry, which each year spends $11.6 billion ($6 billion in media advertising and $5.6 billion in direct marketing) promoting goods and services and the system which produces them. It has become popular to use the Australian media as a sort of Aunt Sally which can be blamed for all sorts of social evils, so it's probably necessary to point out that in its overall character Australian TV, radio, newspapers and advertising are very similar to other western countries, with the same extremes of refinement and vulgarity, exploitation and information, responsibility and trivialisation as, indeed, one might expect from a media system which imports a great deal of its material, such as TV programs and advertising, from the United States and Britain. There is more conflict and diversity than is commonly allowed, via regionalised media spread out over a large continent. There is also at times a significant difference in stance and political approach between newspapers within the one chain, as the publications of the Fairfax group demonstrate.

Nevertheless, the media in Australia are one of the most heavily monopolised and conservative in the western world, and a major force in constructing the culture and ideology which sustain the class system. Just three media chains dominate the nation's television, press and radio: the John Fairfax group, Rupert Murdoch's News Ltd, and Kerry Packer's Publishing and Broadcasting Ltd. Under changes to the media laws considered by the Howard government this may dwindle to two. These media chains are among the biggest and certainly most powerful corporations in Australia and so entrenched that the Labor Party is unable to tackle them when it is out of office and scared to tackle them when it is in office. These corporations usually, though not invariably, support the conservative Liberal and National parties in elections and usually propagate an anti-Labor, anti-union, anti-radical stance; every major Australian media corporation supported the Vietnam War, supported conscription, and supported Fraser after the dismissal of the Labor government – though the *Age* had hesitations about the legality of the dismissal. During the 1983 election campaign, which brought Bob Hawke to the prime ministership, Malcolm Fraser and the then leader of the National Party, Doug Anthony, complained about the media coverage of the campaign, but the *Sydney Morning Herald* published a survey which showed every major newspaper, including itself, had decided to support the conservative government – yet again. In 1993, when John Hewson and Paul Keating led their respective parties to the polls, every major newspaper except one supported Hewson; virtually all the political commentators prophesied a Hewson victory; the backtracking and self-exculpations after Keating won were an ugly thing to see. In 1996 many of the same commentators turned in a fine feeding frenzy upon Keating, who despised them. This time they, and most of the papers they worked for, backed the right side: Howard won. As Keith Windshuttle writes (1984):

> Compared with most western democracies, the one-sided political bias of Australia's press is unusual. Most comparable countries have major daily newspapers that support a range of political opinion... The Fairfax organisation has endorsed Labor for a federal election only once this century... No publications of the Herald & Weekly Times nor of the Packer family's Consolidated Press have ever supported Labor in a federal election. On the historic record, then, the best that Labor can hope for from the press is a lack of pro-Liberal bias once or twice every hundred years.

This open political bias is not only significant in itself, it is a pointer to the way in which the media consistently present Australians with a one-sided view of the world and manipulate their consent to the existing system. The great weight of the media and advertising industries is daily thrown behind this system, in ways which are both deliberate and unconscious. It is well-known, for instance, that newspapers purvey a particular slant or world-view not just through their editorials but through their choice of news stories, headlines, quotes, captions, columnists, cartoons and so on. Media news and views are in general opposed to the Labor Party, unions, strikes, socialism, protests, demonstrations, Left-wingers, radicals, activists and pacifists (a neat trick, this), 'dole bludgers', Big Government, militants, or any groups which want to make dramatic changes to the power structure; they are generally in favour of free enterprise, big companies, entrepreneurs, profits, development, employers, monopolies, oligopolies, commercialism, the Liberal Party, the National Party, the private sector, private schools, private banks, private health funds, private property, the private instead of community ownership of the means of production, distribution and exchange. As nearly all the media organisations are business companies, one could hardly expect them to take any other approach. The ABC is supposed to act as some sort of balance to this, but when it does display an attempt at 'even-handedness' or a countervailing stance it is often heavily criticised or, as happened under the Howard government, has its funds drastically cut. It can also show itself to be particularly responsive to the government of the day.

Over a period of time particular words, such as *strike* or *Left-wing* or *radical*, acquire a clear political (and very critical) 'spin' because of the way they are used in the media. The concepts associated with the words acquire the same colouration. The weight of media disapproval of strikes and trade unions over the years has reached the point where many Australians think the unions have too much power and that 'illegal' strikes, whatever they are, should be suppressed – even though a third of the workforce belongs to unions. The media also tend to avoid any discussion of class or class conflict; I know one newspaper editor who regards himself as a sort of *rebel terrible* but who refuses to publish anything serious on class because he doesn't believe in it.

Victims.

At the same time the world presented by the media is very much class-based. Not only are the dominant stances and views those of the upper class, but much of the news and reportage is about such people: business people, politicians, heads of corporations, academics, professionals, those who are clearly successes or have considerable power. It is their views and opinions which take up a great deal of newspaper space and, apparently, are listened to by government. In *Ruling Class, Ruling Culture* (1977, p. 198) Connell quotes a survey of the occupations of people who appeared in the then two Adelaide papers, the *News* and the *Advertiser*, in a single week and comments:

> It is obvious how overwhelmingly middle-class is the world as seen by the press . . . 87 per cent of people in the *Advertiser* are from white-collar occupations. The predominance of these groups would be even greater if we counted numbers of mentions rather than numbers of people, for some politicians, businessmen and senior civil servants reappear in successive stories and issues. It is hardly going too far to say that there are only three ways for a working class man to get into the paper; to become a jockey or horse trainer; to suffer a catastrophe, preferably bizarre; or to commit a rape. A working class woman has only the second way.

Since then women have become jockeys and horse trainers; hopefully they don't commit rapes; but to suffer a catastrophe, or become a sporting hero(ine), is still one of the few ways working-class women can get into the media. It's a bit like the options which used to face poor blacks in the United States who tried to escape the ghetto: you become a boxer, or a cop, or a crim.

Resistance

For all the overwhelming influence of the media and the other institutions of cultural control which exist in Australia, there is nevertheless a great tradition of resistance to the power of class division. As Gramsci argues, hegemony is a 'moving equilibrium' which has to be constantly argued for and reinforced by the ruling group; similarly it is always open to challenge, dispute, resistance. The political and industrial history of the nation throughout the twentieth century has largely been one of conflict between rulers and ruled, capital and labour (to use the traditional terms), the 'haves' and 'have nots'. In recent years a spectrum of new movements has challenged the status quo: the women's movement, the sexual liberation movements, Aboriginal land rights, the greens. They have been, in objective terms, extraordinarily successful, though the struggle to obtain their original objectives continues. Their members and supporters suffer burnout and become disheartened; 'I sometimes feel we'll never get anywhere,' a community worker told me once; but to take two test cases, relations between men and women in Australia have been transformed by the women's movement, and the Sydney Mardi Gras has become the largest gay festival in the world (a symbol, only, of a wider and historically unpredictable acceptance of gay culture).

More specifically, there is considerable resistance to the sort of class typology which is taken as a given in countries like the United

Kingdom. This can take two somewhat contradictory forms: one is to simply ignore or refuse to be affected by class distinction, a kind of negative resistance which withholds from class its power to intimidate; the other is to intensify class-consciousness and create class solidarity within, for instance, the working class as a conscious means of combating class power. The first is very common in Australia and lies behind, I think, a great deal of the vernacular refusal to accept class labels or to regard class as important; this general attitude extends from manual labourers right through to powerful Labor politicians. It also explains, as I have argued, some of the confusion about class self-identification which opinion polls regularly uncover, because someone who thinks that class is unimportant, or that class does not basically define a person, is more likely than others to give confused or contradictory or deliberately challenging answers; hence, in part, the vagaries of unskilled workers who call themselves upper class and of business entrepreneurs who call themselves working class. There is also an element in the population which readily responds to populist demagogues who proclaim that only *they* are the real workers, and that all others are drones. Manipulation piled upon confusion.

Despite this, the resistance to class typing by large numbers of working people, and the reluctance of many middle-class or 'successful' Australians to adopt distinctive class attitudes and styles, helps create the freer and more flexible class ambience which so many visitors comment upon. Australians themselves can (quite misleadingly) reinforce this. In a pamphlet published after the Second World War called 'Facts About the Woman's Angle on Australia', the Department of Immigration told intending migrants: 'The expressions "upper class, middle class and working class" don't convey much to Australians ... the concept of class as a distinct category and pre-determined way of life is quite alien to Australians.' (It's interesting that the pamphlet used, nevertheless, precisely the class model of upper class/middle class/working class which is the one most commonly used in everyday Australian life.) All this points to the continuing influence, albeit diluted, of the egalitarian tradition in Australian society. Whenever I begin to doubt that some of that attitude persists I am put right by friends who return home after a couple of years overseas, or by English migrants who have stepped off the plane a little while ago and tell me how comparatively free from snobbery and class distinction Australia is. I know a leading craftswoman who still retains an English accent and language and many English attitudes who swears she will never go back to her home in Cheam because of how 'stuffy' (equals class-conscious) it is there, and another cultivated woman who was educated at Roedean, one of England's most exclusive private schools, went back to England not long ago, and returned to Australia saying how traditional and enclosed by class British society was still, and how pleased she was to be 'home' again.

They exaggerate, these ladies, I am sure; after all, the evidence of class inequality here stares you in the face every day; but there must be some recognisable difference in class relations in Australia or people simply wouldn't keep saying it 'feels' different.

One can argue about the political effects of this covert resistance to class distinction. It can lead to a significant decrease in class-consciousness and class solidarity, and therefore in class action to challenge or change the existing class structure. A. F. Davies, in the 1960s, compared his own class surveys with the earlier surveys of Oeser and Hammond and concluded that there had been 'evaporating proletarian consciousness' and a loosening of definitions of class. Evaporating class-consciousness can mean evaporating commitment to activist class institutions such as the union movement and the Labor Party. On the other hand this indirect class resistance can express itself in cultural ways – for example, mateship, cooperatives, grassroots movements, communalism – which are crucially supportive of ordinary people living in a class society. I knew a bloke once who always ended his sentence with 'mate'; he was a frail, dependent sort of man, a worker, who slept in the back of his brother's workshop . . . with the greyhounds. I came to realise after a while that calling everyone mate was a sort of defence against the system: it was both a covert plea for friendship and an affirmation of the solidarity of ordinary working people, their communality, in the face of a society which had reduced him to nothing. Mates. You won't let me down, will you? In the everyday words we use, the rituals of class defence.

So mateship, sisterhood, the sexual liberation groups and the burgeoning subcultures of our time can be seen as popular enactments of a cooperative ethic which is more formally expressed in political institutions. These institutions cover an enormous range: from Workers Educational Associations and Friendly Societies to the trade unions, trades and labour councils, and the Labor Party itself. The situation is complicated by the way they can bend or adapt to the conservative hegemony, for example, the ALP by retreating from socialism and the unions by retreating from political concerns to mere labourism, but they remain crucial points of resistance. The single-issue movements which have arisen in recent decades, such as the green movement, are similarly important. They have often been based in the middle class, but in a predominantly middle-class society middle-class radicalism assumes a major role. As Encel argues, after the 1950s, 'the political ground for social democratic party activity . . . shifted into territory where the influence of middle class rather than proletarian radicalism became increasingly important . . . Changes in the class equilibrium are also reflected in the increased salience of political issues which are predominantly middle class in character. They include education, the environment movement, the women's movement, racial discrimination, sexual permissiveness, drug laws, and public support for the arts.' (Encel in eds E. Wheelwright and K. Buckley, 1978, Vol 2).

Subcultures

Australia's thriving subcultures can be seen, in part, as vernacular responses to class. Sometimes this response takes the form of *intensifying* class characteristics, sometimes it takes the form of *escaping* them. The bikies' subculture is an example of the first, the alternative lifestyle subculture is an example of the second. Most motorcycle groups, certainly those that hold to the traditional 'outlaw' bikie style, are working-class groups and are part of a separate, continuing rebel subculture which has existed in Australia since the first half of the century. In Melbourne and Sydney their focus is typically the outer western suburbs, where bikes can be both an essential way of getting around and a symbol of independence; bikies are typically mechanics, factory hands, labourers, often from deprived working-class homes, Orwell's 'proles' in a technocratic age. Their symbolism, from long hair and beards and helmets to swastika emblems and highly decorated leather gear, is defiantly anti-social and yet class-conscious in all sorts of subtle ways: the heavily worn jackets and boots, the unkempt appearance, the contempt for straights and authority, yet the authoritarian sexism of their treatment of women ... In a sense these are the powerless, the workers at the bottom of the industrial scrapheap, who wreak an often violent revenge upon industrial society by creating their own alternative power groups, status ranks and rituals. The bike itself is the central symbol of this: it is an icon, a defiant paradigm, and a deliverer of real hands-on power in a technological society which had done its best to strip these people of any other sort of power; there is something absolutely incontrovertible about the brute, hulking, cyclotronic energy of a 1000 cc four-cylinder water-cooled race-derived street machine, or a made-over Vincent, or a classic long-stroke Harley Davidson. By intensifying the culture of their class to an extreme bikies are able to distance themselves from it. The style becomes a parody.

The alternative lifestyle groups which, contrary to predictions, still flourish in north Queensland, on the NSW north and south coasts and elsewhere in Australia, signify a different response to class. The most recent and to some extent the most extreme of these groups are the self-styled 'ferals' of the NSW north coast, groups of young people who have taken to living in the bush in a quite deliberate attempt to emulate Aboriginal modes of life and to care for the land in the same way. The ferals have rejected white middle-class life, as have other alternative groups. These groups are determinedly *classless*: many of their members are young people who have decided to drop out of the 'system', including the class system, and are attempting to create an alternative way of life free from any capitalist concept of hierarchy. The communes are self-consciously non-hierarchical, cooperative, democratic. Because the class background of their members is quickly subsumed to other demands it is impossible to classify the communes as 'working class' or 'middle class'; the retreat from class often goes hand in hand with a deliberate rejection of the nuclear family, traditional sex roles, and the symbols and artefacts, such as clothes, which go with them. There is nothing more classless than a sarong – except, perhaps, for the naked body.

Many alternates/ferals/hippies are refugees from factories and the workforce. Others are students, high school drop-outs, runaways from affluent middle-class backgrounds. A few are graduates and ex-professionals. The longer they spend in the counter culture, as it was called in the seventies, the less these differences count and the more they merge into a sort of classless lifestyle in which other differences (cosmic/non-cosmic) count for much more. Nor is this movement away from class an accidental one, because many of those in alternative lifestyle groups carry within them a deep consciousness of what they have left behind and what they do not wish to re-create in their current lives; indeed much of their rhetoric about the exploitation, competition, and lack of caring which characterises the mainstream culture is really a disguised or confused attack upon the class structure of capitalist society. Certainly in their practice the communards try to act out a non-authoritarian, classless alternative.

A parallel analysis can be made of other Australian subcultures. This is not to say they are entirely or exclusively a response to class, but class is an element and sometimes a dominant element. Punk began as an authentic British working-class movement, quickly became a cross-class music, evolved in Australia into a middle-class style, and later became the subject of upper-class exploitation in clothes, fashions and hairstyles but punk as an attitude, a stance, a resistance, remains alive and well in Australian rock/media culture. The conflict which broke out between surfies and rockers years ago, and which still surfaces in hostility between middle-class beachside surfers and working-class westies, is partly a conflict of class styles. Radical women's groups (separatists, lesbians, radical feminists) circumvent class through sisterhood; it's significant that they are often 'classless' and have constructed an alternative ethic based upon a quite different world-concept in much the way the bush communes have.

Even the urban demi-monde, that fashionable, hi-style, cosmopolitan subculture which seems to grace the arts and the glossy magazines in equal doses is, in part, an attempt to escape class. There are quite a number of refugees from the upper class who have rebelled against the traditional codes of their class, that is, against the concepts of 'responsibility', 'leadership' and the rather stuffy roles imposed by their families, and have used the demi-monde as an escape route. The *enfants terribles* who originally launched *Oz* magazine – Richard Walsh, Richard Neville, Martin Sharp – all came from privileged private school backgrounds. Richard Neville's book *Play Power*, as the title indicates, emphasised *play* not *work* or *responsibility*; the *Oz* push represented a clear retreat by a young generation of upper-class Australians from the traditional Protestant work ethic. The current demi-monde has abandoned that code even more thoroughly.

The field where much of the struggle for cultural control is carried out is popular culture. This is where people in the past have been able to create their own rituals, activities and lifestyles without too much interference from the dominant culture; most bosses didn't care too much what went on at the annual butchers' picnic, or at the gala night at the local town hall, or at the sports grounds where new Aussie versions of old games like football were being evolved. Of course the myth of a golden age in which people created an absolutely independent folk culture of their own is just that, a myth, but there have been enough studies and descriptions of Australian working-class institutions and working-class culture to show that it did provide a broadly based focus for resistance to class domination.

In the last half-century this culture has been diluted and commercialised, a process seen very clearly in the invasion of sports like Australian Football, Rugby League and motor racing by commercial and advertising interests, so that a game like Aussie Rules, which for most of its history has been a genuinely popular sport thriving on powerful class and local loyalties, has now been commercialised to the point where the teams scarcely represent such constituencies any longer and are in the hands of business people.

Footie Class Codes

Aussie Rules is essentially classless. Football is the social glue of the city. Industrial Collingwood counts among its supporters some of the city's bluebloods, including former chairman and David Syme descendant, Ranald McDonald...

Rugby League in Sydney is class-based, mainly because loyalty is suburb-based. As with (Tom) Keneally, a change of suburb often means a change of team. The average St George supporter is aged 45 with children growing up as Cronulla supporters. Cronulla is the suburb to the south whose support comes largely from young home-buyers in the cheaper land of Sutherland Shire...

Another factor that makes rugby league a code based on class is the support in the city for its gentlemanly amateur cousin, rugby union... Rugby union eventually became the secondary code, but it survives in the northern and eastern suburbs of Sydney. Because these are principally wealthy suburbs and the home of the private schools, the top strata of Sydney society follows rugby union... Most of the rugby clubs – Manly, Gordon, Eastwood, Northern Suburbs and Warringah – are in the north with the almost unbeatable Randwick in the east.

Most of the Sydney rugby league teams are in the middle to working-class suburbs of the south and west. The game became entrenched in these suburbs largely through the Catholic school system. Even the Christian, Marist, De La Salle and Patrician Brothers who came across from Ireland embraced the new code, perhaps identifying with its grim, painful, sacrificial, stoic endeavour and its egalitarian ways... Because rugby league was concentrated in the parish and inner city technical high schools, it entrenched its cloth cap image as a proud working-class sport.

Booker prize winner Keneally, Manly's No. 1 supporter, worships the game. He says he sees much of the working class culture that he loves writing about in rugby league. He says:

"The conventional view from high culture is that you meet only working-class thuggery in rugby league. Overwhelmingly, the adjective I apply to rugby league players is a kind of innocence, a kind of alacrity . . . The virtues of the Australian bush and the working class are demonstrated in the accessibility of players to the public . . ."

Fans of the Sea Eagles and the Bears, the only two rugby league clubs in the salubrious suburbs, go to great length to diminish their "silvertail" reputation. In the late 1970s, when I coached Lidcombe-based Wests, we deliberately cultivated the image of ourselves as "the Fibros". Although most of our fans lived in weatherboard or brick houses, they embraced the idea, dressing down to go to the football. Chemists rushed home to change into boiler suits. Standing on the Lidcombe hill, holding narrow slats of fibro joined by a nail to form a V for Victory, they would chant the mantra of the working class.

ROY MASTERS,
Meanjin, Vol. 54, No. 3, 1995

The struggle for control of Rugby League, after Rupert Murdoch's raid on the leading clubs and his attempt to set up a world-wide Super League, represents a further stage in the commercialisation of sport in order to provide Pay-TV entertainment fodder.

This process of cooption is a very common one; it was displayed in all its infamy in the Tooheys beer TV commercials, which very successfully latched on to the emotion generated by hard-fought sporting victories and directed it towards the 'I feel like a Tooheys' theme. But it doesn't do to overstate the process. The success of the Tooheys ads depended very much upon the unique, virtually indestructible qualities of the sports themselves, and though the theme song encapsulated the emotion which is generated it simply formalised something which most of us feel at such times: elation, relief, confirmation. Beaudy! The cooption doesn't destroy the emotion, it is utterly dependent upon it, a parasite. In a funny sort of way the ad becomes part of our popular culture, instead of the other way around; it is absorbed, made over, like Aeroplane Jelly generations before. The paradox is that the advertisement reinforces the popular virtues which it attempts to coopt.

A great deal of popular culture displays a similar resistance. From sport to rock music to subcultural styles like punk there is a genuine grassroots process at work in which people, especially young people, try to create their own culture for themselves. Most of the developments in the popular arts (rap, funk, graffiti, vernacular design, rock'n'roll itself) come from this mulch of activity; the commercialisers seize upon it as quickly as they can, but they usually find the original culture has moved on or broken out somewhere else. Despite the theories of Adorno and the Frankfurt school, it is this energetic process of popular creativity which prevents one class from dominating our culture *completely*, and which guarantees some sort of perpetual resistance to the dominant order. In Australia the forms of opposition are sometimes indigenous (the Aboriginal land rights movement, folk/union songs), sometimes imported (the women's movement, alternative medicine), and sometimes a mix of both (the anti-Vietnam and later the various conservation movements). As Connell points out (1977):

There are also ways in which a weakening of repressions has led in an anti-capitalist, counter-hegemonic direction; most significantly in the sexual liberation movements that took shape in the early 1970s. The women's movement, to the extent that it has not been simply anti-male but has sought the sources of the oppression of women in the specific history of this society, has been very much concerned with the way a social order hooks private motivation up to the maintenance of a social structure.

If the conservative hegemony of the power bloc were as triumphant and irresistible as some pessimistic critics believe, it would be hard to explain the process of change, reform and even transformation which occurs in Australian society; on pluralist theory the class structure is never a static 'given', an immovable hierarchy, but rather a constantly changing and flexible series of class relations which respond to the critical new forces which have evolved in the twentieth century; post-industrialism, Third World development, postmodernity, the globalisation of not just the Australian economy but Australian culture. The recognition that cultural and ideological control are the contemporary weapons used to sustain a manifestly unfair class system is itself a weapon to challenge the system. Thus, if elite culture is often an instrument of social control, which it is, then popular culture (including popular movements) is often an instrument of social opposition. The resistance to the conservative hegemony can take more organised and highly structured forms – political parties, unions, radical groups – which are essential to the countering of class domination. But such forms depend finally upon a generalised culture of opposition in which people recognise there is something wrong with the system and do something about it.

Class rules, OK?

Only if we let it . . .

MARG BARRY
Class Profile

She is gut-strong, mind-quick, moral-certain. Therefore formidable. But also light-of-heart, vivacious, funny, and a self-put-down merchant. She is single, single-minded, singular. She is a young woman who has grown old (almost) trying to make things fairer and has, therefore, grown fair. She is irreplaceable, therefore has to be. She is what every community needs. If this society, Australia, hasn't got a frontline of young Marg Barry's coming on, we're in trouble.

Officially she is the coordinator of the Inner Sydney Regional Council for Social Development. Unofficially she is a networker, a provocateur, a community activist, an organiser, more a barbed-wire fence than a thorn in the way of bureaucrats. She is sometimes regarded as a character, as happens to those who do not conform. She is not – though she looks occasionally like Bea Miles. She is the survivor of an era in which the working class of Sydney, and especially South Sydney, where she lives and works, was a *community*. Now she is trying to make that idea of the 'hood a reality in a contemporary context. Meanwhile her turf is being gentrified, fractured, subdivided, developed and pushed into the New (post-industrial) Order. She is, in fact, in the heart of the maelstrom. South Sydney is a symbol of what is going on throughout Australian society. And Marg Barry is a symbol, not of the past, but of what has to be worked out now.

'It looks like the cult of personality in here!' says Marg. She strides past the portrait-in-oils of her which adorns her shabby office in the back of Waterloo Town Hall. As other community workers say, it's bad enough having the real Marg staring at you demandingly without the double whammy of the portrait as well. 'The big issue now? It's the big division that's growing between the wealthy and the poor. Here, in this neighbourhood, public housing is becoming housing-of-last-resort. Yet we're getting gentrified at the same time. People are being forced out. God knows, mate, where they go to! The Olympics will make it worse. We need more affordable housing. We need a mix. Not extremes . . . we need a *mix*.'

It could be a statement about Australian society.

She gets paid for doing three days' work but in fact works all week and weekends too. She is on boards, regional forums, Labor committees, was on Sydney City Council, is now secretary of the Waterloo branch of the ALP; she networks, gossips, publishes, gets angry, tells governments what to do; she loses, she says, most of the time, but she has some wins too. Powerful, symbolic wins. Like the green bans. And the end of slum clearance and those monstrous high-rises ('stack-a-proles', the Russians are said to call them) which rear above the flatlands of Redfern and Waterloo.

She got into all that years ago when, living peacefully in Raglan Street, Waterloo she got a notice under the door saying her terrace house, which she shared with her mother, was scheduled for demolition to make way for Housing Commission high-rises. Marg and her mates went into action, organised protests, teamed up with Jack Mundey at the Builders Labourers' Federation, helped turn the black bans into green bans – and saved Raglan Street. The high-rises went up elsewhere in Waterloo, but the counter-movement had started. Fourteen-and-a-half years later the Housing Commission admitted: we were wrong. No more high-rises. Ever. You are safe.

But is the superstructure safe? From Marg, gnawing away at the foundations in South Sydney?

Today she lives in the same house she always did, alone, with a cat called Dylan (after Bob). No, she says, she's not lonely. She could have got married, but didn't. She could have had children, but didn't. The crusade – for people, for some bloody justice – took her over. It swallowed her up. Remembering: her father was a Water Board clerk, her mother a schoolteacher. Irish Catholic. She was born Margaret Mary, learnt to wear her hair in a braid, still does. Went to school at Our Lady of the Sacred Heart in Kensington with Deirdre Grusovin (whom she gets on well with) and her brother Laurie Brereton (whom she doesn't). Left in fourth year to go to business college, worked in an accountant's office, got bored, took a job helping the Student Council at Sydney University. From that to community work.

Not long ago she had her sixtieth birthday. Tom Uren, Michael Kirby, Lionel Bowen, Peter Baldwin – many of whom she had known from her work at university – and hundreds of other politicians, locals, community workers and activists paid her homage. Including her niece Martine, who puts out *Inner Voice*, the journal of the Inner Sydney Regional Council. The tradition lives on.

In repose, her face is Churchillian: all jowls and determination. When she laughs, she is transfigured: she becomes provocative, tempting, simpatico. She starts swearing, joking, parodying the politicos, acting out their over-the-top boys' games. She would have liked to have been a theatre director. Instead she is up to her neck in this daily theatre of crisis, aggro, retreat, compromise, try to make it fair, try to make it right. The whole world, that is.

She is rotund, track-suited, slow on her feet, fast in her head. 'I'm voluble,' she admits. Also: elliptical, intelligent, discursive, anecdotal, sceptical, passionate, idealistic, unique, therefore formidable. Hopefully repeatable.

14
Not Classless but Class-less

One of these days people are going to do something about class. We're never going to achieve the old socialist ideal of the classless society: it was never attainable anyhow. But utopias are important not because they are achievable but because they provide an ideal, a model, a map to help us work out which way we want to go. Because class is the chief distributor of inequality, of privilege and underprivilege, of gross power and terrible deprivation in our society, the task of reducing the effects of class is one of the crucial endeavours in our society.

Sometimes I think nothing short of a revolution will achieve that. But Australia is one of the least revolutionary of contemporary societies, and twentieth-century experience has shown that revolutions may end up substituting a new class formation for the one which has been destroyed. Given the hierarchical nature of most societies, and the inevitability of a conflict of interests and ideas in pluralist democracies such as Australia, it is probably pissing in the wind to imagine that class groupings and class distinction can disappear altogether; if class is thought of purely in terms of cultural difference rather than in terms of inequality then the existence, for instance, of a clear and energetic working-class culture in Australia has immensely enriched all of our lives. As I have argued, a great deal of the iconography and mythology which are perceived as 'typically Australian' are in fact working-class. Nor is this to sentimentalise working-class culture; middle Australia, for instance, has worked out its own equally significant rituals, ceremonies and ways of living. It is not *difference* that critics of class wish to abolish, it is the innate *unfairness* of a class-based system.

At the corrupt heart of class is an acceptance of the terrible inequalities which exist in our society and the appalling constraints which are placed upon most people's lives – constraints which are based upon the sheer accident of where you happen to be born, or what your family background is, or what school you go to, or what job you happen to be steered towards, or how much wealth and power and material possessions your parents manage to pass on to you. Politicians talk about equal opportunity but it's a laugh, a cruel joke; in Australia it's your class which mainly determines what opportunities you have and there's absolutely no equality in the process. Of course with a lot of luck, talent and energy you may be able to force your way up through the class hierarchy and grab some of the glittering prizes at the top – you may even make yourself into a John Laws or an Alan Bond or a John Elliott if that's your idea of success or the sort of person you want to become! – but it's at the expense of everyone else, and it leaves the society exactly as it was: corrupt, unfair, disfigured by extraordinary inequalities in life chances and life outcomes. Even if there were equality of opportunity, which there isn't, it would not justify the ugly extremes which exist in contemporary Australia.

What we need is not just equality of opportunity but equality of outcomes. Real equality. So people are different but not unequal. This may not be pragmatically attainable but it is something towards which people can strive and which can act as a criterion for judging the actions of governments, parties and political movements alike. The great mass of people in contemporary societies such as Australia are clearly not prepared to support revolution but they will support reform; it seems to me that social democratic parties such as the ALP always underestimate the amount of popular backing which exists for social reform, or which would exist given a determined and radical political leadership. Thus the idea that Australia is innately conservative, or that the electorate is, becomes a comfortable self-fulfilling prophecy for leaders who are themselves conservative and simply do not wish to tackle, or do not even understand, the way in which the hegemonic power of a ruling elite continually reinforces the status quo and tries to make everything in the current system acceptable. Even class. That's why counter-hegemonic movements are so important, even when they do not seem to be aimed directly at class; they challenge, crucially, the idea that *the way it is* is *the way it should be*.

Sometimes politicians on the Right talk about the need for a compassionate society. *Compassionate?* Compassion is the demeaning emotion of those who are well-off for those who don't happen to be as supersmart, wealthy, successful or self-satisfied as themselves; it's the twentieth-century equivalent of the nineteenth-century concept of 'charity', another ugly word. What people want and deserve is not compassion but justice. If the immense wealth and social capital of Australian society, which after all are created by the work and striving of millions of ordinary Australians, were shared around more fairly there would be no need for compassion. In a truly just society, there would be virtually no-one to feel compassionate for – certainly not because they were poor or underprivileged. I wouldn't blame those who are the subject of such well-meaning patronage if, in their bluff Aussie way, they told the charity-mongers to stick their compassion up their arse.

Given class is probably inevitable, what do you do about it?

To get rid of the destructive effects generated by class would require nothing less than a radical restructuring of society. This is possible in the long run and is certainly worth working for. In the meantime, more limited, pragmatic actions are worth taking. First, recognise that class exists and that Australia is a class society. Second, recognise the damage done by class to the lives of virtually all people. Third, work to lessen and change its impact.

This may seem ameliorist, and unacceptable to those who demand a more thoroughgoing transformation of society, but in fact if Australia (or any other nation) were able to abolish the destructive inequalities created by class it would have transformed itself as radically as any revolution. The exact nature of these changes is the stuff of politics and immediately brings up profound questions of social and political policy, to which there are no easy answers and solutions. It might mean that everyone received much the same level of income after tax transfers down and across the salary scale; after all, the progressive income tax system which already exists in Australia is aimed (in theory) at precisely that sort of levelling out. It may mean abolishing private schools and giving all pupils, no matter what their class/ethnic/gender background, an absolutely equal education. It would mean severe restrictions upon inherited wealth. It would certainly mean the extension of industrial democracy throughout all Australian workplaces and the redistribution of power from corporate heads to the people (including managers, white-collar workers and blue-collar workers) who carry out most of the work. It would mean systematically dismantling the rigidities and inequalities of the current class system and creating an alternative society which, while not absolutely classless, is as close to being free of the destructive impacts of class as it is possible for human society to be.

This may seem unduly idealistic, but the great reforming movements of the twentieth century would have seemed impossible to nineteenth-century politicians and reformers; societies can transform themselves with amazing rapidity, and even when they don't the hard, grinding process of reform eventually produces far-reaching changes in the social landscape. It is easy to be cynical about such a process but this, after all, is the arena where those who are involved in public life and in the creation of a civic culture operate for much of their lives; whether they recognise it or not, the immense effort which so many good-hearted Australians make to 'improve' our public systems – the education system, the health system, the welfare system and the immense spectrum of social services which stretches from local community centres to national medical campaigns – is really a disguised effort to even out the cruel effects of class. The sustained effort, for instance, over many years to get more working-class children into universities and tertiary education may sometimes be justified on strictly utilitarian grounds, in that Australia needs to nurture and develop whatever talent it possesses, but behind that has been a clear recognition by educators and political groups that a system which excludes most working-class children and is so heavily biased in favour of upper-class students is simply unacceptable. So far this attempt has been grievously flawed and has been handicapped by such reactionary moves as the former Labor government's reintroduction of tertiary fees and the corporatisation of universities, but the effort to make education in Australia less responsive to the vagaries of class continues.

The same can be said of the continuing effort to extend an adequate national health system to all Australians, irrespective of class background – an effort which sometimes runs into self-interested attack and outright political opposition, but which has survived a number of widely different governments in Canberra and the state capitals. At present in Australia working-class people suffer a higher incidence of disease, suicide and disability than any other class group; this is both shameful and avoidable. The lack of adequate health standards among Australian Aborigines has become, rightly, a focus for international criticism, yet this is almost as much a factor of class as of Aboriginality; most Aborigines belong to the working class or underclass, and suffer the deprivations of their class group (the concern for Aboriginal health is not usually directed at affluent middle-class Aborigines). This is not to deny the unique disadvantage and racism suffered by Aborigines; it is to point out that, for example, underclass Australians suffer shocking underprivilege whether they be black or white, Anglo or ethnic, female or male.

Education is not only the best way out of the class trap, it should be the best way of ensuring that the trap does not exist. As mentioned before, a truly egalitarian education system would be one in which all children, from all class backgrounds, got educated to the best of their ability – a not unattainable goal, and one which is given lip-service by educators and politicians alike. But the implementation of such a policy is where the serious discussion and divisiveness begin. It would probably entail, for a start, a massive redistribution of education expenditure towards positive discrimination in favour of schools in working-class and lower-middle-class suburbs and in favour of working-class and lower-middle-class pupils. It would mean the abolition of tertiary fees and the institution of really wide-ranging special entry systems for class-disadvantaged students instead of the token schemes which exist at present. It would mean the abolition or the opening up of private schools, so that the much-touted educational 'advantages' of such schools became available to all. It would mean transforming the secondary school curricula to change the work and educational expectations of pupils in the most vulnerable strata of the class system and bringing in programs to help them achieve the further education and jobs they have the ability for. It would mean instituting programs to combat the destructive effects of class wherever they were apparent in the educational system, in much the same way as so much effort has been expended in the past to combat the destructive effects of gender bias. In other words, it would mean a radical transformation of the educational system to provide the equal opportunity which people profess to believe in. Now, this is an abbreviated overview of a complex topic; nor would these sorts of changes eradicate the effects of class completely. But it does point out that it is possible, through specific programs in specific policy areas, to reform the educational system to make it less class-biased. This would in itself be an enormous step forward.

The redistribution of opportunity is only part of the massive redistribution which would be required to make Australia, not a classless society, but a less-class society. This would mean a radical transfer of wealth, income, power and privilege down through the class hierarchy via techniques which are already well-known and heavily debated in social democratic parties: a much more highly progressive taxation system, expanded social services, a high social wage, a steep redistribution of personal and corporate wealth, changes in work conditions, a democratisation of power in the workplace, and an unprecedented increase in transfer payments to the unemployed, the needy, the underprivileged, the victims. An analysis by economic commentator Maximilian Walsh in late 1995 of transfer payments in OECD countries came to the conclusion that Australia had the lowest level of transfer payments of any OECD nation. We are also one of the lowest-taxed peoples in the OECD, with tax levels only just slightly higher than Turkey. On some indices, such as the United Nations Human Development Report for 1992, Australia is also the most inegalitarian nation in the OECD, with levels of inequality which make nonsense of Australia's self-image as a place where everyone has a 'fair go'. This is a nation where very few people have a fair go. It is a nation in which, to repeat, just 1 per cent of the population own almost a quarter of the country's wealth, and the top 5 per cent own more than the bottom 90 per cent put together. It is a nation where the richest man, Kerry Packer, has amassed a personal fortune of over $3 billion and is reputed to have lost $17 million in a single night's gambling playing blackjack at the London Ritz, while at the other end Aborigines in the NSW country settlement of Toomelah are living in such squalor that it brought tears to the eyes of Justice Marcus Einfeld when he visited it. Somewhere in between are 700 000 Australian children living in homes where nobody is earning an income.

Such extremes are not only shameful, they are unnecessary. Kerry Packer doesn't need personal wealth of $3 billion to operate as a successful businessman, any more than the other billionaires and millionaires in *Business Review Weekly*'s Rich 200 need such enormous personal fortunes; a society which redistributed a major part of not just that wealth but the wealth and income of the upper class and upper-middle class would be able to eliminate poverty altogether. There is no reason why a society as richly endowed as Australia, which the Australian Bureau of Statistics has estimated has a net worth of $1700 billion, should tolerate the extremes it has.

Nor, of course, is it just wealth that needs to be redistributed; it is power, privilege, educational and cultural opportunity, access to everything which is at present dominated by a class elite. This means taking on some very powerful institutions which characterise the power bloc, not least of which is the media; the freeing up of the media in Australia and the purposeful distribution of media access right across the social spectrum would be a critically important counter-hegemonic act. The democratisation of the media is, in a sense, a symbol of the sort of democratisation of society which a remaking of the class system would entail.

All this is not a criticism of the egalitarian tradition in Australia, which has created a social ambience and ease of social relations which other peoples sometimes envy, and the very persistence of Australians' belief in a 'fair go' is a heartening base on which to build a fairer nation. But egalitarianism, if it is to be more than a popular myth, has to be worked for. It results from the hard grind of social and political policy over decades of idealism, effort and disappointment. It means confronting those with power, privilege and special interests to defend. It means substituting the public good for private greed and disseminating the cultural and social capital of elite groups throughout the entire society. The means to do this are familiar. The Labor Party, for much of its history, has been involved in precisely that effort; in the last two decades Labor governments have betrayed some of those ambitions – for reasons in which class plays a major role, as analysed in Chapter 4, 'Class and Politics' – but the social idealism of the broad labour movement remains intact. So does the idealism of the community groups and movements which work endlessly to make the current system bearable, and to replace it with something better; being involved in these, I sometimes think, is like being involved in some perpetual frontline. Crucial resistance movements of the last three decades include everything from the women's movement and sexual liberation movements to the Aboriginal/land rights movement, the environmental movement and the proliferating subcultural and alternative groups of our time. They have all been involved, one way or another, in a continuing effort to make over the system and its values. In fact, that radical/reformist tradition holds out our best hope for a liberating and transforming future.

Surprisingly enough, that hard sustained effort to make class matter less has had some success. The Australia of today is, I think, less bitterly divided on class lines than the Australia I grew up in. The education system has made higher education more available across class boundaries; more kids stay at school longer. Social services are more widespread and supportive than they used to be, and of more benefit to those at the bottom of the class scale. The welfare state, despite repeated attacks, has survived. Class matters less in the media, in the public service and even in the boardrooms of the major corporations than it used to. Australians, according to the academic evidence, are less class-conscious than they used to be, perhaps because of increasing affluence since the Second World War and a general feeling that class shouldn't matter, even if it does. The effects of class are so stupid and unnecessary that I sometimes think Australians are right to (in the words of an old mate) 'treat them with ignore'. But in the unbrave new world of post-industrial capitalism, class divisions and inequalities are likely to deepen, class hostility and social distress are likely to increase, and the damaging consequences of class on our working lives likely to become more pervasive. Australian politicians, like their counterparts overseas, seem powerless to control the vast social changes generated by the global economy, the move to computer-based tertiary and quaternary industries, and a ruthless new stage in the evolution of private enterprise practice and ideology. The simultaneous attack upon Australia's traditional civic culture, and its replacement by a much more competitive, individualist culture dominated by the free market and large corporations, is likely to worsen the divisions in our society. And at the core of these divisions is class. Class is ugly. I'm not concerned about the snobs, I'm concerned about the victims. There shouldn't be any.

KYLIE v. SNOBS.

Kylie, where are you?

Appendix

The Department of the Parliamentary Library, Canberra has published an analysis of all Australian federal electorates, ranking them according to their 'socio-economic status'.

The ranking is based on such factors as the unemployment rate, proportion of single-parent families, proportion of people aged 65 and over, proportion of children aged between 0 and 4 requiring daycare, proportion of people with professional occupations, proportion of families with annual income below $16 000, proportion of people with tertiary education, proportion of owner/purchaser dwellings, plus the proportion of dwellings with two or more cars and with four or more bedrooms.

The higher the index number, the higher the socio-economic status; the lower the figure, the lower the socio-economic status.

The figures are based on the 1991 census.

Ranked By Index Of Socio-Economic Status

Rank	Electoral Division	Index	Rank	Electoral Division	Index
1	Gellibrand (Vic)	73.4	24	Moncrieff (Qld)	89.3
2	Reid (NSW)	75.8	25	Page (NSW)	89.3
3	Fowler (NSW)	76.4	26	Wide Bay (Qld)	89.3
4	Port Adelaide (SA)	77.3	27	Corio (Vic)	89.4
5	Batman (Vic)	78.3	28	Hotham (Vic)	89.5
6	Blaxland (NSW)	81.3	29	Throsby (NSW)	90.5
7	Newcastle (NSW)	82.8	30	Fairfax (Qld)	90.5
8	Watson (NSW)	84.0	31	Lilley (Qld)	90.8
9	McPherson (Qld)	84.4	32	Sydney (NSW)	91.1
10	Kingsford-Smith (NSW)	84.5	33	Leichhardt (Qld)	91.1
11	Bonython (SA)	84.6	34	Dobell (NSW)	91.3
12	Lyne (NSW)	85.1	35	Chifley (NSW)	91.5
13	Hindmarsh (SA)	86.4	36	Parkes (NSW)	92.0
14	Grayndler (NSW)	86.5	37	Robertson (NSW)	92.1
15	Richmond (NSW)	86.5	38	Gilmore (NSW)	92.5
16	Cowper (NSW)	86.5	39	Adelaide (SA)	92.7
17	Fisher (Qld)	86.9	40	Gwydir (NSW)	93.6
18	Perth (WA)	87.9	41	Barker (SA)	93.6
19	Melbourne (Vic)	87.9	42	Barton (NSW)	93.7
20	Swan (WA)	88.0	43	Melbourne Ports (Vic)	93.8
21	Grey (SA)	88.2	44	Bendigo (Vic)	94.0
22	Shortland (NSW)	89.1	45	Holt (Vic)	94.8
23	Wills (Vic)	89.1	46	Kennedy (Qld)	94.9

Rank	Electoral Division	Index	Rank	Electoral Division	Index
47	Cunningham (NSW)	94.9	98	Rankin (Qld)	104.6
48	Paterson (NSW)	95.1	99	Bowman (Qld)	105.2
49	Braddon (Tas)	95.1	100	Maranoa (Qld)	105.6
50	Bass (Tas)	95.5	101	Wentworth (NSW)	106.2
51	Griffith (Qld)	95.9	102	Kalgoorlie (WA)	106.6
52	Hinkler (Qld)	96.1	103	Goldstein (Vic)	106.8
53	Wakefield (SA)	96.6	104	Isaacs (Vic)	107.4
54	Hunter (NSW)	96.9	105	Parramatta (NSW)	108.2
55	Sturt (SA)	97.2	106	Corangamite (Vic)	109.4
56	Maribyrnong (Vic)	97.3	107	Lalor (Vic)	109.8
57	Charlton (NSW)	97.7	108	McEwen (Vic)	110.1
58	Oxley (Qld)	97.7	109	O'Connor (WA)	110.3
59	Farrer (NSW)	97.7	110	Boothby (SA)	110.8
60	Herbert (Qld)	97.8	111	Burke (Vic)	111.7
61	Brisbane (Qld)	98.0	112	Deakin (Vic)	111.7
62	Prospect (NSW)	98.1	113	Macarthur (NSW)	112.7
63	Flinders (Vic)	98.1	114	Macquarie (NSW)	113.0
64	Banks (NSW)	98.2	115	Jagajaga (Vic)	113.3
65	Ballarat (Vic)	98.3	116	Fadden (Qld)	113.8
66	Stirling (WA)	98.5	117	Lindsay (NSW)	115.3
67	Dunkley (Vic)	98.7	118	Higgins (Vic)	115.4
68	Calare (NSW)	98.8	119	Makin (SA)	115.4
69	Eden-Monaro (NSW)	99.0	120	Canning (WA)	116.9
70	Denison (Tas)	99.1	121	Chisholm (Vic)	117.3
71	Dawson (Qld)	99.2	122	Curtin (WA)	117.5
72	Northern Territory (NT)	99.7	123	Bennelong (NSW)	118.1
73	Murray (Vic)	99.8	124	Cook (NSW)	120.1
74	Werriwa (NSW)	100.0	125	Scullin (Vic)	122.0
75	Hume (NSW)	100.0	126	La Trobe (Vic)	124.5
76	Riverina (NSW)	100.1	127	Fraser (ACT)	126.5
77	Petrie (Qld)	100.1	128	Casey (Vic)	127.5
78	New England (NSW)	100.3	129	Warringah (NSW)	127.8
79	Fremantle (WA)	100.4	130	Dickson (Qld)	127.9
80	McMillan (Vic)	100.6	131	North Sydney (NSW)	128.5
81	Brand (WA)	100.7	132	Mackellar (NSW)	128.5
82	Lyons (Tas)	100.7	133	Pearce (WA)	129.6
83	Corinella (Vic)	100.9	134	Mayo (SA)	129.8
84	Mallee (Vic)	101.0	135	Kooyong (Vic)	130.7
85	Capricornia (Qld)	101.0	136	Cowan (WA)	130.9
86	Groom (Qld)	101.3	137	Bruce (Vic)	136.3
87	Wannon (Vic)	101.6	138	Aston (Vic)	136.7
88	Forde (Qld)	101.7	139	Moore (WA)	138.4
89	Moreton (Qld)	102.0	140	Tangney (WA)	141.0
90	Gippsland (Vic)	102.1	141	Ryan (Qld)	142.5
91	Kingston (SA)	102.9	142	Menzies (Vic)	143.4
92	Greenway (NSW)	103.0	143	Hughes (NSW)	148.6
93	Lowe (NSW)	103.5	144	Canberra (ACT)	152.1
94	Indi (Vic)	103.5	145	Berowra (NSW)	156.7
95	Forrest (WA)	104.2	146	Mitchell (NSW)	173.0
96	Calwell (Vic)	104.2	147	Bradfield (NSW)	178.0
97	Franklin (Tas)	104.5			

Bibliography

Aitkin, Don (1982): *Stability and Change in Australian Politics*, ANU Press, Canberra.

Baxter, Janeen, Emmison, Michael & Western, John (1991): *Class Analysis and Contemporary Australia*, Macmillan, Melbourne.

Boggs, Carl (1980): *Gramsci's Marxism*, Pluto Press, London.

Broom, Leonard & Jones, F. Lancaster (1976): *Opportunity and Attainment in Australia*, ANU Press, Canberra.

Chamberlain, C. (1983): *Class Consciousness in Australia*, Allen & Unwin, Sydney.

Congalton, Athol A. (1963): *Occupational Status in Australia*, School of Sociology, University of NSW.

Connell, R. W. (1977): *Ruling Class, Ruling Culture*, Cambridge University Press, Melbourne.

Connell, R. W. (1995): *Masculinities*, Allen & Unwin, Sydney.

Connell, R. W., Ashenden, D. J., Kessler, S. & Dowsett, G. W. (1982): *Making the Difference: Schools, Families and Social Division*, Allen & Unwin, Sydney.

Connell, R. W. & Irving T. H. (1980): *Class Structure in Australian History*, Longman Cheshire, Melbourne.

Dahrendorf, R. (1959): *Class and Conflict in an Industrial Society*, Routledge, London.

Daniel, Ann (1983): *Power, Privilege and Prestige: Occupations of Australia*, Longman Cheshire, Melbourne. Also article 1988.

Davies, A. F. & Encel, S. (1965): *Australian Society*, Cheshire, Melbourne (also 1977 edition with M. J. Berry).

Docker, John (1974): *Australia's Cultural Elites*, Penguin, Ringwood, Victoria.

Dutton, Geoffrey (ed.) (1976): *The Literature of Australia*, Penguin, Ringwood, Victoria.

Edgar, Don (1974): *Social Change in Australia*, Cheshire, Melbourne.

Edgell, Stephen (1993): *Class*, Routledge, London.

Encel, Sol (1970): *Equality and Authority: a study of class, power and status in Australia*, Cheshire, Melbourne.

Fiske, J. (1993): *Power Plays Power Works*, Verso, London.

Game, A. & Pringle, R. (1983): *Gender at Work*, Allen & Unwin, Sydney.

Goldthorpe, J. H. (1969): *The Affluent Worker in the Class Structure*, Cambridge University Press, Cambridge.

Harris, Max (1975): *Ockers*, Maximus Books, Adelaide.
Hiller, Peter (ed.) (1981): *Class and Inequality in Australia*, Harcourt Brace Jovanovich, Sydney.
Hoggart, Richard (1958): *The Uses of Literacy*, Penguin, London.
Horne, Donald (1964): *The Lucky Country*, Angus & Robertson, Sydney.
Horvath, Ron (1989): *Sydney – A Social Atlas*, Sydney University Press, Sydney.
Hughes, Robert (1993): *The Culture of Complaint*, Oxford University Press, New York.
Jackson, J. A. (1968): *Social Stratification*, Cambridge University Press, London.
Jamrozik, A. (1991): *Class, Inequality and the State*, Macmillan, Melbourne.
Kelly, Paul (1984): *The Hawke Ascendancy*, Angus & Robertson, Sydney.
Kemp, David (1978): *Society and Electoral Behaviour in Australia*, UQP, St Lucia, Queensland.
Kessler, S., Ashenden, D., Connell, R., & Dowsett, G. (1982): *Ockers and Discomaniacs*, Inner City Education Centre, Stanmore, NSW.
Kress, G. (ed.) (1988): *Communication and Culture*, University of NSW Press, Sydney.
Lette, Kathy & Carey, Gabrielle (1979): *Puberty Blues*, McPhee Gribble, Melbourne.
McGregor, Craig (1980): *The Australian People*, Hodder & Stoughton, Sydney.
Mackay, Hugh (1993): *Reinventing Australia*, Angus & Robertson, Sydney.
Mayer, H. & Nelson, H. (1976): *Australian Politics, a fourth reader*, Cheshire, Melbourne.
Mitchell, A. G. & Delbridge, A. (1965): *The Pronunciation of English in Australia*, Angus & Robertson, Sydney.
Morley, D. & Chen, K. H. (1996): *Stuart Hall: critical dialogues in cultural studies*, Routledge, London.
Najman, J. M. & Western J. S. (eds) (1988): *A Sociology of Australian Society*, Macmillan, Melbourne.
Neville, Richard (1970): *Play Power*, Cape, London.
Oeser, O. A. & Hammond, S. B. (1954): *Social Structure and Personality in a City*, London.

O'Grady, John (Nino Culotta) (1957): *They're a Weird Mob*, Ure Smith, Sydney.
Pringle, John M. D. (1958): *Australian Accent*, Chatto & Windus, London.
Pusey, Michael (1991): *Economic Rationalism in Canberra*, Cambridge University Press, Melbourne.
Rees, S., Rodley, G. and Stilwell, F. (eds) (1993): *Beyond the Market*, Pluto Press, Sydney.
Reeves, James (1961): *The Idiom of the People*, Mercury Books, London.
Scott, J. (1991): *Who Rules Britain?* Polity, Cambridge.
Seymour, Alan (1963): *The One Day of the Year*, Penguin, Harmondsworth, England.
Stretton, Hugh (1987): *Political Essays*, Georgian House, Melbourne.
Thompson, Elaine (1994): *Fair Enough: egalitarianism in Australia*, University of NSW Press, 1994.
Thompson, E. P. (1966): *The Making of the English Working Class*, Random House, London.
Wallace, Christine (1993): *Hewson: a portrait*, Pan Macmillan, Sydney.
Walsh, Maximilian (1979): *Poor Little Rich Country*, Penguin, Ringwood, Victoria.
Western, John S. (1983): *Social Inequality in Australian Society*, Macmillan, Melbourne.
Wheelwright, E. L. & Buckley, K. (eds) (1978): *Essays in the Political Economy of Australian Capitalism*, Vols 2 & 3, Australia and New Zealand Book Company, Sydney.
Wild, R. A. (1974): *Bradstow: a study of status, class and power in a small Australian town*, Angus & Robertson, Sydney.
Wild, R. A. (1978): *Social Stratification in Australia*, Allen & Unwin, Sydney.
Williams, Raymond (1985): *Keywords*, Fontana, London.
Windshuttle, Keith (1984): *The Media*, Penguin, Ringwood, Victoria.

Index

Aboriginal tent embassy, 273
Aboriginality, 47
Aborigines, 91, 182, 264, 274–5, 312
   health, 266, 310
accent, 150, 191–3, 252
Accord agreements, 197, 199
ACER (Australian Council for Educational Research), 56, 148
advertising industry, 286
Aitkin, Don
   Stability and Change in Australian Politics, 77
Alf, 219–20
alienation, politics of, 108–9
ALP (Australian Labor Party), 2, 11, 76, 77–81, 85, 196, 235–6, 278, 313
   leadership, 57, 78, 89–90, 91, 199
   loss of support, 104–5
alternative lifestyle subculture, 294, 295–6
America *see* USA
aristocracy, 231
   see also landed aristocracy
Ashenden, D., 184, 282
Askin, Sir Robert, 271
associations and trade unions, 127
Australian Council for Educational Research, 56, 148
Australian Labor Party *see* ALP
Australian national image, 201–2, 205–6
Australian National University, 16, 182
Australian Rules football, 207–8, 297–8
Australian Values Study (1983), 190, 193
authority, workplace, 33

Baillieu family, 243, 253
Bannon, John, 78
Barnes, Jimmy, 208–13
Barnes, John, 217
Barry, Marg, 302–4
Barwick, Sir Garfield, 62–6
battlers, 106–7

Baxter, J., Emmison, M. and Western, J.
   Class Analysis and Contemporary Australia, 15, 27, 39, 61, 87–8, 162, 174, 182, 193, 231, 249
Beazley, Kim, 113–17, 278
Benjamin, Colin, 173
Berry, M. J., 195, 284
bikies' subculture, 294–5
billionaires, 168–70
   see also richest 200 list
Birmingham Centre for Contemporary Cultural Studies, 42
blue-collar workers, 181–2
   see also workers, blue-collar and white-collar
Boggs, Carl, 278
Bondi Junction, Sydney, 154–7
bosses and workers, 31
   factory, 26
   newspaper office, 126–7
   rural, 119–20
Bradbury, Doyle and Whiteford, 268
Brennan, Ros, 269
Broom, L. and Jones, F. L., 25, 58, 59, 134, 140, 182, 198, 254
   with Zubrzychi, J., 147
Buckley, K., 139, 294
bureaucratisation, 36
Burke, Brian, 78
business, Australian, dominated by upper class, 232–3
Business Review Weekly, 169–70, 243

Cadzow, Jane, 67
Cain, John, 78, 102
Carey, Gabrielle and Lette, Kathy
   Puberty Blues, 187–8
Carr, Bob, 78, 88, 103, 105, 110–11
Cass, Bettina, 133
centre political parties, 83
chain of command, workplace, 33, 126–7
   see also workforce hierarchy
Chapman, Bruce, 265–6

civic culture, 112–13
Clark, Manning, 133
Clark, Timothy Marcus, 240–1
class
    affecting political involvement, 92
    in Australia, 1–7, 19
    effect on education, 149–50
    holding power, 57, 58–60, 69, 130, 236–7
    and politics, 76–99
    reducing effects of, 305–14
    shaping of individuals by, 132
class conflict, 31–2, 198–201, 290
class-consciousness, 12–19, 131, 137
class determinants, 23–47
class distinction, 124
class division, resistance to, 290–4
class identification, 9, 15–16, 140, 145–6, 147, 162, 182–3, 230, 291
class imagery, 6
class jumpers, 54–75
class mobility, 3–4, 5, 54–75, 136, 147–8, 164–5, 254
class profiles, 48–53, 70–5, 94–9, 113–17, 154–7, 176–9, 208–13, 222–9, 256–60, 272–5, 302–4
class rigidity, 54–5, 61, 129
class schemes, based on occupation, 27–9
class stereotypes, 214–21
class struggle *see* class conflict
class theory, 23, 27, 30
classless society myth, 124–5, 305
    see also egalitarian myth; equality of opportunity; inequality
clubs, gentlemen's, 237–8, 252
collectivism, 153
Collins, Bob, 67
communitarianism, 107–8
Comparative Project on Class Structure and Class Consciousness, 27, 61, 87, 162, 174, 182
Congalton, Athol, 144, 246
Connaghan, Terry, 207
Connell, R. W., 133
    with Kessler, S., Ashenden, D. and Dowsett, G., 184, 282
    Ruling Class, Ruling Culture, 197, 238, 289, 300–1
Connell, R. W. and Irving, T. H.
    A Working Paper Towards a Historical Theory of Class, 24
    Class Structure in Australian History, 13
consensus politics, 279
    see also Accord agreements
conservation and environment, 110–11
conservative institutions, 285
consumerism, 68
Coombes, H. C. 'Nugget,' 51
Country Party *see* National Party
Court, Richard, 31
Cranbrook School, 121–3
crime rate, 266–7
Cullen Egan Dell, 244
cultural conditioning, 280–1
culture
    and class, 276–304
    and lifestyle, 42–4
    see also popular culture
'culture of complaint', 101

Dad and Dave, 217, 218
Dahrendorf, R., 35
Dale, David, 253–4
Daniel, Ann, 185
    Power, Privilege and Prestige, 245–6
Davies, A. F., 133, 292
Davies, A. F. and Encel, S., 36, 137
Davies, A. F., Encel, S. and Berry, M. J.
    Australian Society, 195, 284
Davis, J. R. and Spearritt, Peter, 144
Delbridge, A., 191, 192
demi-monde, 296–7
Democrats, 77, 83, 101, 111
Dennis, C. J.
    The Songs of a Sentimental Bloke, 218, 219
deregulation and globalisation, effect on workers, 106–7, 132, 158, 314
determinants of class, 23–47
Disney, Julian, 160

Dobie, Don, 82
Docker, John, 133, 257
Domhoff, G., 234
Downer, Alexander, 6, 237
downward mobility, 56
Dowsett, G., 184, 282
Ducker, John, 200
Dutton, G.
    The Literature of Australia, 217, 219

economic rationalism, 175, 233
Edgell, Stephen
    Class, 29–30, 235, 263
education, 39–40, 281–5
    inequality, 269
    middle class, 148–50, 172
    scholarship system, 63, 65
    school curricula, 284–5
    tertiary, 40, 56–7, 189, 269
    working class, 189–91
    see also government schools; private schools
education system, 309, 310–11
egalitarian myth, 170
    see also classless society myth; equality of opportunity; inequality
egalitarian tradition, 13, 291–2, 313
Einfeld, Marcus, 312
elite, Australian, 57
embourgeoisement, 66–70, 81, 148
Emmison, M., 15, 27, 39, 61, 87–8, 162, 174, 182, 193, 231, 249
employment inequality, 270–1
Encel, Sol, 133, 240
    in Wheelwright, E. and Buckley, K., 139, 293
    with Davies, A. F., 36, 137
    with Davies, A. F. and Berry, M. J., 195, 284
    Equality and Authority, 30, 66, 91, 145, 151, 152, 232, 239, 251, 252
entrepreneurs, 168–70, 240
environment and conservation, 110–11
equality of opportunity myth, 61, 283–4
    see also classless society myth; egalitarian myth; inequality

Establishment, Australian, 62, 232
ethnicity, 17, 45–6
    see also migrants
Evatt, Clive Snr, 71
Evatt, Elizabeth, 70–5
Evatt, H. V., 71
Evatt family, 71–5

Facey, Albert
    A Fortunate Life, 44
factory workers, 26, 183–4
Fairfax, John, 286
false consciousness, 23–4, 137
family background, 40–2, 249, 264
family, nuclear, 176–9
Farrell, Denis, 161
Fitzgerald, Tom, 138
Ford factory, 26
Fraser, Bernie, 38, 48–53
Fraser, Malcolm, 3, 61, 65, 240, 253

gender, 44–5
Gini scale, 166
Glare, Kel, 262
globalisation and deregulation, effect on workers, 22–3, 106–7, 132, 158, 314
Goldthorpe, John, 27, 29, 35, 44, 69, 87, 88, 193
Gorz, Andre, 107
Goss, Wayne, 101, 102–4
governing class, 234, 254
government effect on class power, 235
government schools, 281–2
Gramsci, Antonio, vi, 130, 277–8, 290
Gray, Gary, 67, 100, 106–7, 111, 113
Greens, 77, 83, 101, 110
Gregory, Bob, 162–3, 164, 244, 265, 268, 269–70
Greiner, Nick, 46, 82, 102

Hall, Stuart, 133, 234
Hammond, S. B., 14, 15, 16, 39, 56, 182, 292
Hancock, Lang, 242
Harris, Max, 216, 217

Hawke, Bob, 2, 80, 197–8, 199–200, 279
Hayden, Bill, 146–7
health, 266
　working class, 185
health system, 309–10
hegemonic consciousness, 130
hegemony, 277–8, 290
Henderson report on poverty in Australia, 194
Hewson, John, 6, 82, 84
Higley, Deacon and Smart, 57
Hiller, Peter
　Class and Inequality in Australia, 14, 60
Hogan, Paul, 216, 222–9
Hoggart, Richard
　The Uses of Literacy, 202
home ownership, 38, 141, 143–4, 159, 164
　see also housing, working class
Hone, B. W., 122
Horne, Donald
　The Lucky Country, 12, 202
Horvath, Ron
　Sydney – A Social Atlas, 164–5
housing, working class, 185–6, 195–6
　see also home ownership
Howard, John, 7, 85–6, 94–9
Howe, Brian, 97
Hughes, Robert
　Culture of Complaint, 101
Humphries, Barry, 142, 215, 221
Hunter, B., 269–70
Hutton, Drew, 110
Huxley, John, 237

iconography, 201–8
income, 160–1, 171
　inequality, 167, 244–5, 267–8
　upper class, 244
　working class, 193–4
　see also wealth distribution
income groups, 144–5
individualism, 153–4
industrialisation, 139

inequality, 17, 166–8, 170–1, 186, 267–71, 284, 306–7
　abolishing, 308
　class as source of, 128, 131, 133
　John Howard on, 96
　of salaries and wages, 244–5
　see also income; wealth distribution
Irving, T. H., 13, 24

Jackson, J. A.
　Social Statification, 147–8
Jaensch, Dean, 111
job loss, 162–3
jobs *see* occupation
Jones, F. L., 25, 58, 59, 134, 140, 147, 182, 198, 254

Karmel, 240
Keating, Paul, 3, 6, 51, 80, 206, 216, 235
Kelty, Bill, 200
Kemp, David
　in Najman, J. M. and Western, J. S., 88–9
　in Western, J. S., 145
　Society and Electoral Behaviour in Australia, 77
Keneally, Thomas, 298, 299
Kennett, Jeff, 31, 103
Kernot, Cheryl, 105, 111–12
Kerr, Sir John, 62–6
Kessler, S., Ashenden, D., Connell, R. and Dowsett, G.
　Ockers and Discomaniacs, 184, 282
Kirner, Joan, 78
Kramer, Leonie, 256–60
Krugman, Paul, 263

Labor Party *see* ALP
'labour aristocracy', 147
landed aristocracy, 239–40
　see also aristocracy
Latham, Mark, 79
Lawrence, Carmen, 78, 110
Lawrence, D. H., 13
Laws, John, 55, 243

Lawson, Henry
   The Bastard from the Bush, 219
   The Union Buries Its Dead, 199
legal profession as path to upper class, 63, 90
Lette, Kathy and Carey, Gabrielle
   Puberty Blues, 187–8
Liberal Party, 2, 22, 76, 81, 82–4, 85–6, 89–90, 235–6
lifestyle
   and culture, 42–4
   differences in, 69
   middle class, 144–8
Loane, Sally, 238
Lockwood, D.
   The Blackcoated Worker, 136, 137
Lombard, 166
Lovett, Graham, 207
lower class, 86
   see also working class
lower-middle class, 151–2, 165–6, 171
   battlers, 106–8

Macdonald, Alexander, 12–13
McGregor, Adrian, 153
McGregor, Craig
   The Australian People, 132, 144, 198
   Don't Talk to Me About Love, 130
   Headliners, 132
   People, Politics and Pop, 130
   personal experience of class, 118–33
   Profile of Australia, 81, 129, 201–2
   Soundtrack For the 'Eighties, 283
Mackay, Hugh
   Reinventing Australia, 16, 159–60, 171
managerial government, 102–4
managers, 33, 34–6
Martin, Jean, 60
Martin Committee report, 56
Marx, Karl, 23, 27, 30, 263, 277
masculinity, working class, 184–5
Masters, Roy, 206, 207, 299
Mayer, H. and Nelson, H., 93
media, 286–90
   democratisation, 312

Menzies, Robert Gordon, 81
meritocracy, 54, 284
middle class, 9, 125–6, 134–57
   characteristics, 60, 141–3, 172–4
   in crisis, 158–76
   diversity, 136
   divisions, 29–30, 35, 151–2, 154, 165–72
   education, 40
   expansion, 68–9
   occupation, 27
   proletarianisation of, 107
   satire of, 142, 215, 217
   supply of Labor politicians, 90–1
   voting patterns, 81, 85, 87–8
middle-class radicalism, 110, 128, 153, 293
middle classing of Australian society, 132
migrants, 182, 264
   see also ethnicity
Mills, C. Wright, 234
minority groups, 61, 109–10
Mitchell, A. G. and Delbridge, A.
   The Pronunciation of English in Australia, 191, 192
money *see* wealth
Morgan Gallup polls, 16, 230–1
Morgan Research, 173
Murdoch, Rupert, 242
   News Ltd, 286
Murdoch family, 243

Najman, J. M. and Western, J. S., 89, 172
National Party (formerly Country Party), 22, 76, 89
Neill, Rosemary
   What Does Working Class Mean Now?, 32
Nelson, H., 93
Neville, Richard, 220
   Play Power, 297
New Class, 34, 35, 36
new constituencies, 109–13
new middle class, 137

new politics, 101, 107, 112, 113
Norman, Greg, 55
nuclear family, 176-9

occupation, 26-30, 58-60
   changes in, 161-2
   as determinant of class, 25-6, 27-9, 151-2
   working class, 181-2
occupational prestige, 245-8
ockers, 215-21
Oeser, O. A. and Hammond, S. B., 14, 15, 16, 39, 56, 182, 292
O'Grady, John
   They're a Weird Mob, 192-3, 216
Orr, Sydney Sparkes, 64
Orwell, George
   Down and Out in London and Paris, 43
O'Shea, Clarrie, 64
owners and ownership, 24, 25, 30, 239-45
   see also bosses and workers
Oz magazine, 220, 297

Packer, Kerry, 168-9, 242, 243, 253-4, 312
   Publishing and Broadcasting Ltd, 286
Parsler, R.
   Sociology, 69
Paterson, A. B. 'Banjo,' 218-19
Petty, Bruce, vi, 133
petty bourgeoisie, 137
political bias of press, 287-8
political breakout groups, 111
political involvement, 92-3
political movements, 153-4, 290, 293, 313
political participation, 92, 143
politicians, 89-91
politics and class, 76-99, 174, 176
popular culture, 130, 203-4, 255, 297-301
   see also culture and class
post-industrial workforce, 32-3

see also globalisation and deregulation
Poverty and Education in Australia report, 190
power, 30-7, 246
   middle class, 143
   ruling class, 277
   upper class, 131, 232-4, 253, 255
   working class, 33-4, 196-201
   workplace, 127
power bloc, 234, 239, 279
Pratt, Richard, 243
Pringle, John
   Australian Accent, 12, 129, 240
private schools, 121-3, 249-51, 281
privatisation, 233-4, 235-6
professionals, 245-9
public housing, 195-6
punishment vote, 112
punk, 296
Pusey, Michael, 133
   Economic Rationalism in Canberra, 112, 174-5

Radford and Wilkes, 148
Raskall, Philip, 166, 167, 175, 195, 241
Reeves, James, 8
religion, 252
Reserve Bank charter, 48
resistance to class division, 290-4
richest 200 list, 169-70, 243-4
   see also billionaires
Roy Morgan Research Centre, 173
Rudd, Steele
   On Our Selection, 217
rugby league, 207-8, 297-9
rugby union, 298
ruling class, 234, 254, 277
rural class distinction, 118-20
Ryan, Colleen, 241

salaries, executive, 244
Saunders, Peter, 160, 166-7, 270
Savage, Peter, 250-1
school uniforms, 250
schools *see* education; government

schools; private schools
Scott, J., 234
Seymour, Alan
  The One Day of the Year, 219–20
Sharkey, Lance, 200
Sharp, Martin, 220, 297
Singleton, John, 11, 243–4
skilled workers, 147
Smith, Peter, 265–6
Smorgon family, 243
snobbery, 124, 214–15
social cost of underclass, 266–7
social mobility *see* class mobility
social organisation and control, 18–19
social reform, 307–8, 311
social wage *see* transfer payments
socialism, 279–80
socio-economic character, 144
socio-economic ranking of electorates, 315–16
socio-economic status, 266, 315–16
Spearritt, Peter, 144
St Andrew's Cathedral School, 250
Steketee, Mike, 82
Stenberg, Maryann, 237
stratification theory, 8
strike action, 197–8
subcultures, 294–301
suburban lifestyle, 68
suburbia, 123, 143–4, 154–7, 185–8
  inequality, 244–5, 269–71
surfing culture, 187–8, 204, 296
Sutton, John, 31–2
Sydney Morning Herald, 126–7
Sykes, Bobbi, 272–5
Sykes, Trevor, 232

Tabakoff, Jenny, 140–1
tax avoidance, 242–3
taxation of wealth, 37–8
terminology, 7–10, 43, 86
tertiary industry, 139, 161, 314
Thompson, Elaine, 110, 111
Thompson, E. P.
  The Making of the English Working Class, 154

Toohey, Brian, 147
trade unions, 196–201
  and associations, 127
  membership, 104, 196–7
transfer payments (social wage), 113, 311
Tritton, Duke
  Time Means Tucker, 44
Turner, Ian, 133, 217
two-income families, 160, 163, 270–1

underclass, 261–75
unemployment, 141, 168, 264–5
  long-term, 265–6, 271
unions *see* trade unions
United Nations Human Development Report, 268, 311
university fees, abolition of, 41, 57, 189
upper class, 11–12, 86, 230–60
  characteristics, 61, 231–2, 252–3
  education, 40
  holding power, 236–7
  occupation, 26–7
  voting patterns, 87, 88
  see also elite; Establishment
upper-class families, 41
upper-middle class, 151–2, 165–6, 171–2
USA (United States of America)
  class exploitation in, 131, 133
  underclass, 261–2

van Sommers, Peter, 42
violence, working class, 34, 185
voter disillusionment, 100–1
voting patterns, 82–3, 86–9

Walsh, Maximilian, 311
  Poor Little Rich Country, 12
Walsh, Richard, 220, 297
Ward, Russell, 201
Waters, Edgar, 219
wealth, 36–9, 55
  distribution, 167–71, 194–6, 241–5, 268, 312
Weber, Max, 27, 30, 263
Western, J. S.
  and Wilson, P. R., 92–3

with Baxter, J. and Emmison, M., 15, 27, 39, 61, 87–8, 162, 174, 182, 193, 231, 249
with Najman, J. M., 89, 172
Social Inequality in Australian Society, 57, 59–60, 93, 143, 144, 145, 148, 149, 150, 189, 190, 195, 196, 198, 199, 200
Wheelwright, E. L., 240
and Buckley, K., 139, 294
White, Patrick, 256
white-collar workers, 68, 138–43
see also workers, blue-collar and white-collar
Whitelock, Tony, 124
Whitlam, Gough, dismissal of, 64, 65–6, 131–2
Wild, R. A.
Bradstow, 231
Social Stratification in Australia, 14, 25–6, 33, 134–5, 136, 198, 231, 254
Williams, Raymond, 8, 10
Williamson, David, 142
Don's Party, 3, 205–6
Willis, Ralph, 243
Wilson, P. R., 92–3
Windshuttle, K., 287
women, 17, 44–5, 110
income, 194

radical groups, 296
in the workforce, 163, 184
workers
blue-collar and white-collar, 23–5, 135–6, 137, 138, 161, 182
factory, 183–4
workers and bosses, 31
factory, 26
newspaper office, 126–7
rural, 119–20
workforce hierarchy, 32–3, 135–6
see also chain of command, workplace
working class, 41–2, 180–213
affluence of, 68
characteristics, 60, 203–5
culture, 42
education, 39–40, 148–50
lack of representation, 90–1, 93, 199
occupation, 27
satire, 217–20
voting patterns, 78, 80, 82, 87–8, 104–6
Wran, Neville, 4–6, 62
Wright, Erik Olin, 27, 29, 35, 87, 194

yahoos and yobbos, 215
yuppies and dumpies, 164–5

Zubrzychi, J., 147